THE
CHURCH HYMNARY

Third Edition

THE
CHURCH HYMNARY

Third Edition

WORDS ONLY

OXFORD UNIVERSITY PRESS

*Oxford University Press, Ely House, London W.*1

GLASGOW   NEW YORK   TORONTO   MELBOURNE   WELLINGTON
CAPE TOWN   IBADAN   NAIROBI   DAR ES SALAAM   LUSAKA   ADDIS ABABA
DELHI   BOMBAY   CALCUTTA   MADRAS   KARACHI   LAHORE   DACCA
KUALA LUMPUR   SINGAPORE   HONG KONG   TOKYO

Set by the Oxford University Press, Oxford
Printed by Robert MacLehose and Co. Ltd·
Printers to the University of Glasgow

PREFACE

IN 1963 the General Assemblies of the Church of Scotland, the Presbyterian Church of England, the Presbyterian Church in Ireland and the Presbyterian Church of Wales authorized the preparation of a new edition of *The Church Hymnary*, the previous editions having appeared in 1898 and 1927. The Joint Committee appointed to undertake this task invited the United Free Church of Scotland to be represented on the Church Hymnary Revision Committee.

In the selection and preparation of the contents of *The Church Hymnary: Third Edition* the Committee has been helped by discussion in successive General Assemblies of the participating Churches, and also by the careful scrutiny of its work by the Presbyteries of these Churches, leading to many useful alterations and improvements. Moreover, much specialized knowledge, biblical, theological, liturgical, hymnological and literary, generously shared with the Committee, is gratefully acknowledged.

The General Assembly of the Church of Scotland gave general approval to the draft of *The Church Hymnary: Third Edition* in 1968, and similar authorization was received from the General Assemblies of the Presbyterian Church in Ireland, the Presbyterian Church of Wales, the United Free Church of Scotland, and also the Presbyterian Church of England, which, on 5 October 1972, was united with the Congregational Church in England and Wales to become the United Reformed Church.

The Committee had corporate responsibility for the selection and preparation of the music, but acknowledges its debt to those appointed as Music Consultants, Dr. Kenneth Leighton, Mr. Herrick Bunney, Mr. John Currie and Mr. David Murray; also the late Mr. Guthrie Foote who, in addition to professional competence, had wide experience in the publication of music. Mr. Ian Barrie also assisted.

Grateful acknowledgement is also made of the professional help so unsparingly given by the staff of Oxford University Press in the whole preparation of this hymnary.

The Church Hymnary : Third Edition is sent out in the prayerful hope that it may enrich the worship of congregations to the greater glory of God.

In the name of *The Church Hymnary* Revision Committee:

THOMAS H. KEIR, D.D.
Convener

R. STUART LOUDEN, D.D.
Vice-Convener

F. N. DAVIDSON KELLY, S.S.C.
Hon. Secretary

INTRODUCTION

Worship and Hymns

A Church hymn book is essentially designed for Christian worship.

Christ's earthly life and self-giving on the Cross was itself the one offering of perfect worship to the Father whose will he fulfilled. Through Word and Sacrament, as in daily obedience, his faithful disciples are united with him as his Body in the continuing offering of this worship.

Hence each action in Christian worship has a double significance. It is indeed Christ's people who pray and who praise the Father. Nevertheless they do so as the baptized community whose life is so grounded in Christ and bound up with his life that in worship he, as Head, exercises always his authoritative office as Prophet, High Priest and King.

Through the Church's worship, therefore, Christ fulfils today in the life of his people what he did on earth 'once and for all'. When Scripture is read and preached, it is not the words of the Minister the congregation awaits but the Word of Christ who is the Word of God. Through the rites of initiation, Holy Baptism and Confirmation together with Holy Communion, Christ calls his people and establishes them in the covenant of grace. In Baptism he makes the person, whether infant or adult, a member of his Body. In Confirmation he strengthens and blesses the baptized, who profess their faith, as members of his Body with both privileges and responsibilities. In the Holy Communion Christ's eternal self-giving is present still in and through his Church. So, in every action of worship, including what is sung, Christ fulfils his ministry as Prophet, Priest and King in order that through his Church he may be known as Lord by the world he came to save.

INTRODUCTION

Study of the hymns offered in this book will, it is hoped, make these points clear.

The Cultural Context

It has at all times been necessary for the Committee, in the selection of material, to be aware of the special nature of its responsibility: to provide the means for high and holy worship, and at the same time to recognize the cultural limits within which this can be done.

On the one hand Christ, the Lord of the Church, is active in the midst of his worshipping people. It follows that as the spoken language used in church must be true and faithful to the Word of Christ, so the musical language also must be true to it. The Committee therefore had to take care, with what success only experience will show, to ensure that tunes are true to the words to which they are set. It is hoped, moreover, that in many instances the offer of a different tune to already well-known words will enable the words to yield up their meaning more fully.

On the other hand, this faithfulness to the Divine in worship must be balanced by a concern that the music is appropriate to the variety of emotions involved in the people's worship as well as to their musical ability. The Committee therefore had to keep in view the requirements of a number of somewhat differing communities not only in Britain but overseas. It also found it necessary to include a number of hymns of more or less local provenance or use, to meet the specific needs of some particular branch of the Church. Thus it has tried to ensure that every congregation will find in the Hymnary a sufficient number of tunes it can use.

The Contents and their Order

In selecting the *contents* of the Hymnary every effort has been made to present the essential elements in the Biblical revelation as adequately as liturgical necessity demanded and available resources permitted. Since a Church hymnal is essentially a liturgical book, the Committee, in determining the *order* in which the hymns are arranged, has borne in mind that the Order of Holy Communion is normative for worship in the Reformed Church and that, where there is no regular weekly celebration of Holy Communion, the service should still follow the eucharistic pattern.

The Order of Common Worship

The central act of Christian worship from the beginning was understood as a unity, the structure of which involved a double action: (*a*) the 'Liturgy of the Word' based on the reading and exposition of the Scriptures; and (*b*) the 'Liturgy of the faithful', sometimes called 'the Liturgy of the Upper Room'—that is, the Holy Communion or Lord's Supper.

Part I: The approach to God

In the early centuries, Christian worship seems normally to have commenced with reading and preaching. Later, however, it became customary to commence the service with brief acts of approach to God. This comprises *the first part of the service* (Part I of the Hymnary).

Part II: The Word of God

Following his people's approach, God speaks to them through his Word in Holy Scripture and sermon. This 'Liturgy of the Word' is *the second part of the service* (Part II of the Hymnary).

Part III: Response to the Word of God

The third part, to which all else leads, is the 'Liturgy of the Upper Room'—the Holy Communion.

Even where the sacramental elements are not present, there follows response to the Word of God in the Church's outpouring of faith, adoration, thanksgiving, dedication and intercession, culminating in her rejoicing

in the communion of saints and the hope of glory
(Parts III and IV of the Hymnary). Thus, recommissioned, the Church returns to her work in the world.

Using the Book

It will be noted that there is a certain correspondence
both in style and content between the earlier portions
of Parts I and III of the Hymnary, the former acknowledging the greatness of God, the latter providing acts
of adoration and thanksgiving. Clearly certain hymns
in Part III may with perfect propriety be used for the
opening of worship, while some in Part I will provide
on occasion suitable acts of response to what God has
spoken in his Word. Nevertheless the distinction between the two parts of the book remains valid since
the hymns in Part III do on the whole express the
heightened adoration and thanksgiving which faithful
worshippers are more prepared to offer after the
Divine Word has been heard. This again is characteristic of the Communion Service.

The Table of Contents indicates the shape of the service
both in its broad pattern and in its variable details;
while cross-references at the end of the sub-sections in
the body of the book point out certain cognate hymns
to be found in other parts of the Hymnary.

The value of arranging a hymn-book in this way,
both to ministers in selecting a praise list and to congregations at worship, will, the Committee trusts,
prove itself in practice.

Psalms and Paraphrases

From the beginning the Psalter had an integral place
in Christian worship. Having regard to this and also
to the traditional use of metrical versions in the
Reformed Church, the Committee hopes, by including
a selection of psalms, both prose and metrical, to
promote a fuller use of the riches of the Psalter and
that the range of selection may be widened.

INTRODUCTION

The selections from the Psalter and Scottish Paraphrases are normally placed first in the appropriate section or sub-section of the Hymnary.

Hymns for Children

In selecting hymns for use by children, it should not be forgotten that in this, as in other fields, it is better that a child's reach should exceed his grasp than that he should be encouraged to sing what is banal or below his best capacity. Many of the great hymns of the Church are admirably suited for children's enjoyment and use, so that their omission from children's worship is a serious lack.

Hymns suitable only for children and for younger children are placed according to the same principle as the other hymns, hymns of approach to God in Part I and so on, except that they are invariably last in the sub-section. These hymns are designated in a distinctive way in the Index of First Lines.

The Contribution of the Centuries

Each age, including our own, has contributed something new and of value to the rich treasury of the Church's hymnody, and this is reflected in the contents of the book, which contains a number of hymns and tunes written this century, as well as a significant corpus of specially commissioned music.

Congregations will gain both in the variety and the devotional fullness of their worship by extending the range of their hymnody.

So far as possible the dates of author, composer or source are given.

Thus the Church is constantly reminded that her inheritance and her promise are alike ageless, because they are from God the Eternal;

TO WHOM, FATHER, SON AND HOLY SPIRIT, ONE GOD,
BE GLORY IN THE CHURCH TO THE AGES OF AGES.

INTRODUCTORY NOTES TO
THE MUSIC

The Selection of the Music

IN the selection of music, three guiding principles have been followed:

1. that the tunes and settings should in general be easily learned and readily singable by the average congregation, and that tunes should be thoroughly suited to the words they are to serve;

2. that where a familiar tune has to be omitted, it should wherever possible be replaced by another familiar tune, or else a cross-reference given to such a tune occurring elsewhere in the book;

3. that a fine tune may well be employed more than once, thus bringing into use certain hymns previously unfamiliar because the tune was unknown or uninspiring, and also providing a known tune for special hymns only rarely required—for example at weddings, funeral services, consecration of churches and so on.

The Style and Interpretation of Congregational Music

SINGING

Every hymn has its own style, and the manner of its performance will vary, depending on a number of practical considerations—the occasion, the size of the congregation, the acoustics of the building. Consequently, few indications of *tempo* are offered, but it is hoped that the use of the crotchet instead of the minim as the standard pulse will assist towards lively musical interpretation.

The end of the verbal line in a hymn is generally indicated by the sign ⫽ in the musical setting.

Unison verses should be used at times to highlight the words.

Amen has been excluded where it is not appropriate, and should be sung only where it is printed.

ACCOMPANIMENT

It is recognized that the organ will not always be the accompanying instrument. The following points are for general guidance.

(*a*) *The congregation* will best hear notes of at least an octave higher, or lower, than their own voices. Hence organ upper-work and pedals, piano lower and upper octaves, double bass, and strings and woodwind in upper octaves will prove most helpful in leading singing.

(*b*) *The accompaniment* should clearly indicate the mood for each verse, while avoiding too precious an interpretation within the verse itself.

(*c*) *Tunes* should be played over at the speed intended for singing. Normally it is only necessary for the first phrase to be played over. The practice of playing first and final phrases is to be discouraged.

MUSICAL SETTINGS

Some tunes have been revised to a limited extent. Others have been strengthened by more sweeping alterations in the harmonic structure.

A few settings more suitable for a choir than for the average congregation have been included.

Children's hymns and those recommended for unison singing have generally been given accompaniments which are both effective and readily playable.

PROSE SETTINGS

To encourage a wider and more varied use of speech rhythms four musical styles have been included.

1. In *Anglican chanting* the spoken word should always be the guide, the words being sung at the speed

of clear speech with the stresses and rhythms of normal speech. Certain details of the pointing have been left to the individual choirmaster's own initiative and preference.

2. *Psalms or Canticles in the style of Gelineau* (e.g. No. 67) are designed to be sung with the rhythm of natural speech bound only by one slow pulse in each bar. The organist must be careful to supply this pulse clearly and regularly. Further details will be found in the introductions to *The Psalms of Joseph Gelineau*, published by the Grail Press.

3. By the introduction of *chanted psalms using only a few chords* (e.g. No. 66) it is hoped that congregations who have not yet attempted to sing prose settings will be encouraged to do so. The short series of chords or 'chant' is used once to each verse. The melodic note changes on the syllables or word marked with an acute accent. These settings may be sung in unison or in harmony.

4. In classical *plainchant* the syllables should be sung with even spacing, but without stiffness. Where possible the singing should be unaccompanied. If, however, a keyboard accompaniment is used it should contain as few chord changes as possible, and the choice of harmony should be governed by the accepted style for the accompaniment of modal music.[1]

The following symbols, occurring in the music or in the verbal text as the case may be, will be found sufficient to direct the singing of the tones.

[ ] Notes enclosed in a *bracket* are used only for the first verse of the psalm; succeeding verses commence on the reciting note.

A *vertical* indicates the point at which the reciting note is quitted. Occasionally it will be found

[1] Further guidance may be found in J. H. Arnold, *The Accompaniment of Plainsong* (O.U.P., reprinted by Waltham Forest Books); and in *A Manual of Plainsong* edited by H. B. Briggs and W. H. Frere, revised and enlarged by J. H. Arnold (Novello).

that at the end of the half-verse a note is left over, for which there is no verbal syllable remaining; in such instances the note is simply omitted. This is termed the 'abrupt mediation'. In No. 166 (Psalm 2) for instance, this happens a number of times. Notes are also omitted if necessary from the traditional endings.

:   A *colon* at the end of the half-verse corresponds with the bar-line in the music, at which point a short silence occurs, the duration of which is approximately equal to the two previous syllables. There should, however, be no break between verses, but the first syllable of each new verse should maintain without interruption the flow of notes from the last syllable of the previous verse.

⌒   A *tie* indicates that two syllables are to be sung at the same pitch. In other words, the note of the first syllable is simply repeated.

··   A *double dot* above the text is used where one syllable requires two notes of the chant.

—   A *long dash* indicates that the reciting note is omitted altogether.

The method of chanting is as follows. The first half-verse of a psalm should, if possible, be chanted by one or two solo voices, the second half of the verse being sung by the choir or congregation or both. Thereafter complete verses should be sung alternately by, for example, the choir (verse 2) and congregation (verse 3) and so on; or else by a chanter (verse 2) and choir (verse 3). Or some other similar pattern may be followed, such as the ladies' voices of the choir (verse 2) being answered by the men's voices (verse 3), always provided that the alternation is that of complete verses. Only the first verse should be divided between voices or sections of singers at the half-way point.

ACKNOWLEDGEMENTS

The Church Hymnary Trust wishes to thank the following who have given permission for copyright material to be printed. *A blank in the second column indicates that the author is also the owner of the copyright.*

WORDS

AUTHOR	COPYRIGHT OWNER	NO. OF HYMN
Adams, J.	National Adult School Union	444
Agnew, E.	© W. L. Jenkins 1953	230 lines 1–12 from *Songs & Hymns for Primary Children,*
	© The Geneva Press 1972	230 lines 13–16 from *Teachers' Guide Book Revised*
Alexander, J. N. S.		162, 203
Alington, C. A.	The Proprietors of *Hymns Ancient and Modern*	270, 120, 599, 555, 593
Alston, A. E.	Mr. C. Alston	31 (tr.)
Andrew, Father	A. R. Mowbray & Co. Ltd.	252
Arlott, J.		619
Armitage, E. S.	United Reformed Church	553
Baring-Gould, S.	Mr. G. Hitchcock	423, 480, 653
Barkley, J. M.		595
Barnard, W. E.		625
Bax, C.	A. D. Peters & Co.	84
Bayly, A. F.		554 (alt.), 141, 503 (alt.), 426, 458
Bell, G. K. A.	Oxford University Press	474
Blatchford, A. N.	Ascherberg, Hopwood & Crew Ltd.	148
Bourne, G. H.	Oxford University Press	583
Bowie, W. Russell	Abingdon Press	255, 509
Bridges, R.	Oxford University Press	55, 57, 119, 251, 335, 370, 403, 405, 408, 472 (i), 642
Briggs, G. W.	Oxford University Press	215, 219, 452, 505, 572
Brownlie, J.	Mr. A. Rutherford Brownlie	95
Buchanan, V.	Oxford University Press	327

ACKNOWLEDGEMENTS

AUTHOR	COPYRIGHT OWNER	NO. OF HYMN
Chesterton, G. K.	Oxford University Press	520, from *The English Hymnal*
Christierson, F. von	Hymn Society of America	133
Clarkson, E. M.	Inter-Varsity Press	337, 592
Cropper, M.		467, 228
Crum, J. M. C.	Oxford University Press	278, from *The Oxford Book of Carols*
Darbyshire, J. R.	Oxford University Press	260
Dearmer, P.	Oxford University Press	341, from *The Oxford Book of Carols* 43, 111, 515, 588, from *The English Hymnal* 128, 416, from *Songs of Praise*
Draper, W. H.	Roberton Publications	30
Dudley-Smith, T.		164
Dugmore, E. E.	Mr. E. M. Mills	451
East, J. T.	Methodist Youth Department	222
Editors of *The B.B.C. Hymn Book*	Oxford University Press	305
Ferguson, J. M. Macdougall	Religious Education Press	631, 654
Fletcher, F.	Oxford University Press	309
Fosdick, H. E.	Mrs. E. Fosdick Downs	88
Frere, M. Temple	The National Society	622
Gelineau, J.	A. P. Watt & Son Ltd.	67, 350, 389
Gill, D. M.		384
Gillett, G. G. S.	Oxford University Press	328
Green, F. Pratt	Oxford University Press	152
Greenaway, A. R.	The Proprietors of *Hymns Ancient and Modern*	244, 248
Head, B. P.	The Revd. A. Hanbury Head	339
Housman, L.	Oxford University Press	196, 507
Hoyle, R. Birch	World Student Christian Federation	279
Huey, M. E.	©W. L. Jenkins 1963	17, from *Songs and Hymns for Primary Children*
Hull, E.	Chatto & Windus Ltd.	87 (*coll.*)
Hunter, A. M.		399
Hunter Clare, T. C.		513
Ikeler, C. R.	©W. L. Jenkins 1963	427, from *Songs and Hymns for Primary Children*
Jackson, F. A.	National Christian Education Council	281, 621, 630, 633
Jeffries, C.	Joint Action for Christian Literature Overseas (Feed the Minds)	468

ACKNOWLEDGEMENTS

AUTHOR	COPYRIGHT OWNER	NO. OF HYMN
Jones, A. M.	United Society for Christian Literature	340
Kipling, R.	A. P. Watt & Son Ltd.	446
Kirkland, P. M.	The Misses Kirkland	283
Lacey, T. A.	Oxford University Press	472 (ii)
Littlewood, R. Wesley	Methodist Youth Department	528
Lowry, S. C.	Oxford University Press	454
Macalister, E. F. Boyle	National Christian Education Council	16, 557
Macalister, R. A. S.	Oxford University Press	129, 401
Macnicol, N.	Trustees of the late Helen Macnicol	82
Masterman, J. H. B.	The Proprietors of *Hymns Ancient and Modern*	508
Mathams, W. J.	Oxford University Press	100
Mathews, B. J.	Oxford University Press	501
Mealy, N. and M.	Seabury Press Inc.	155, from *Sing for Joy*
Merrill, W. P.	*The Presbyterian Outlook*	477
Milner-Barry, A. M.	The National Society	280
Moore, J. Boyd		601
Moore, J. E.	United Church Press	466, from *Pilgrim Bible Stories for Children*
Newbolt, M. R. and G. W. Kitchin	The Proprietors of *Hymns Ancient and Modern*	550
Niles, D. T.	East Asia Christian Conference	415
Oxenham, John	Westminster Bank Ltd. and Miss T. Dunkerley	425
Parker, W. H.	National Christian Education Council	124
Perkins, J. E.	United Church Press	157, from *As Children Worship*
Phillips, A. N.		506
Phillips, E. M.		690
Piggott, W. Charter	Oxford University Press	134, 538
Pitt-Watson, I.		126, 64, 68 (paraphrased from *The New English Bible*)
Quinn, J.	Geoffrey Chapman Ltd.	276, 308, 568 (adpt.), 581, 589, 175
Reed, E. M.	Evans Bros. Ltd.	186
Rees, T.	A. R. Mowbray & Co. Ltd.	334, 473
Roberts, K. E.	Oxford University Press	185, from *The Oxford Book of Carols*
Roberts, R. E.	Oxford University Press	330
Scott, R. B. Y.		511
Shields, E. McE.	©Presbyterian Board of Christian Education 1935 and 1963	229

ACKNOWLEDGEMENTS

AUTHOR	COPYRIGHT OWNER	NO. OF HYMN
Shillito, E.	Oxford University Press	292
Skemp, A.	National Christian Education Council	156
Smith, F. M.	The National Society	447
Snow, G.		91
Stevenson, L.	Oxford University Press	375
Struther, J.	Oxford University Press	92, 206
Terry, R. R.	Oxford University Press	652, from *The Oxford Book of Carols*
Tucker, F. Bland	The Church Pension Fund	586 (alt.), 297, 522, 242
Tweedy, H. Hallam	Hymn Society of America	499
Tynan-Hinkson, K.	Search Press Ltd.	524
Waddell, H.	The Girls' Auxiliary	486
Watt, L. MacLean	Mr. A. L. MacLean Watt	666
Wilkinson, K. Barclay	Mr. D. R. Gould	432
Winslow, J. C.		428, 51
Woodward, G. R.	A. R. Mowbray & Co. Ltd.	187, 271
Woodward, G. R.	Schott & Co. Ltd.	604, 640, from *The B.B.C. Hymn Book*
Wren, B.	Oxford University Press	469
Wright, W.	Young Men's Christian Association	614

The Church Hymnary Trust also wishes to thank Dr. Bernard Rose for carrying out the pointing of the psalms set to PLAINSONG CHANTS in this book: Nos. 63, 158, 166, 231, 232, 239, 262, 284, 310, 326.

CONTENTS

CONTENTS

I

APPROACH TO GOD

THE HOUSE OF GOD

1

PSALM 100

ALL people that on earth do dwell,
Sing to the Lord with cheerful voice.
Him serve with mirth, his praise forth tell,
Come ye before him and rejoice.

2 Know that the Lord is God indeed;
Without our aid he did us make;
We are his folk, he doth us feed,
And for his sheep he doth us take.

3 O enter then his gates with praise,
Approach with joy his courts unto:
Praise, laud, and bless his Name always,
For it is seemly so to do.

4 For why the Lord our God is good,
His mercy is for ever sure;
His truth at all times firmly stood,
And shall from age to age endure.

5 *To Father, Son, and Holy Ghost,*
The God whom earth and heaven adore,
Be glory, as it was of old,
Is now, and shall be evermore.
Amen.

2

BEFORE Jehovah's awesome throne,
Ye nations, bow with sacred joy;

Know that the Lord is God alone;
He can create, and he destroy.

2 His sovereign power, without our aid,
Made us of clay, and formed us men;
And, when like wandering sheep we strayed,
He brought us to his fold again.

3 We are his people, we his care,—
Our souls and all our mortal frame:
What lasting honours shall we rear,
Almighty Maker, to thy Name?

4 We'll crowd thy gates with thankful songs,
High as the heavens our voices raise;
And earth, with her ten thousand tongues,
Shall fill thy courts with sounding praise.

5 Wide as the world is thy command,
Vast as eternity thy love;
Firm as a rock thy truth must stand,
When rolling years shall cease to move.

ISAAC WATTS, 1674–1748, and
JOHN WESLEY, 1703–91
From Psalm 100

3

PSALM 100
Jubilate Deo

O BE joyful in the Lord ' all ye ' lands : serve the Lord with gladness and come before his ' presence ' with a ' song.

1

2 Be ye sure that the Lord ' he
is ' God : it is he that hath
made us and we are his '
own we are his ' people ·
and the ' sheep of his '
pasture.

3 O go your way into his gates
with thanksgiving and
into his ' courts with '
praise : be thankful unto him
and speak ' good ' of his '
Name.

4 For the Lord is gracious his
mercy is ' ever- ' lasting :
and his truth endureth from
gener- ' ation to ' gener- '
ation.

*Glory ' be to the ' Father : and to
the Son ' and to the ' Holy '
Ghost :*

*As it ' was in the be- ' ginning :
is now and ever shall be '
world without ' end.*
                    A- ' men.

4   PSALM 84, verses 1–5

H OW lovely is thy dwelling-
place,
O Lord of hosts, to me!
The tabernacles of thy grace
How pleasant, Lord, they be!

2 My   thirsty   soul   longs
vehemently,
Yea faints, thy courts to see:
My very heart and flesh cry
out,
O living God, for thee.

3 Behold, the sparrow findeth out
An house wherein to rest;
The swallow also for herself
Hath purchasèd a nest;

4 Even thine own altars, where
she safe
Her young ones forth may
bring,
O thou almighty Lord of hosts,
Who art my God and King.

5 Blest are they in thy house that
dwell,
They ever give thee praise.

Blest is the man whose strength
thou art,
In whose heart are thy ways.

6 *To Father, Son, and Holy Ghost,
The God whom we adore,
Be glory, as it was, and is,
And shall be evermore. Amen.*

5   PSALM 15

W ITHIN   thy   tabernacle,
Lord,
Who shall abide with thee?
And in thy high and holy hill
Who shall a dweller be?

2 The man that walketh up-
rightly,
And worketh righteousness,
And as he thinketh in his heart,
So doth he truth express.

3 Who doth not slander with his
tongue,
Nor to his friend doth hurt;
Nor yet against his neighbour
doth
Take up an ill report.

4 In whose eyes vile men are des-
pised ;
But those that God do fear
He honoureth; and changeth
not,
Though to his hurt he swear.

5 His coin puts not to usury,
Nor take reward will he
'Against the guiltless. Who doth
thus
Shall never movèd be.

6 *To Father, Son, and Holy Ghost,
The God whom we adore,
Be glory, as it was, and is,
And shall be evermore. Amen.*

6   PSALM 36, verses 5–9

T HY mercy, Lord, is in the
heavens;
Thy truth doth reach the
clouds:

Thy justice is like mountains great;
Thy judgments deep as floods:

2 Lord, thou preservest man and beast.
How precious is thy grace!
Therefore in shadow of thy wings
Men's sons their trust shall place.

3 They with the fatness of thy house
Shall be well satisfied;
From rivers of thy pleasures thou
Wilt drink to them provide.

4 Because of life the fountain pure
Remains alone with thee;
And in that purest light of thine
We clearly light shall see.

5 *To Father, Son, and Holy Ghost,*
The God whom we adore,
Be glory, as it was, and is,
And shall be evermore. Amen.

7   PSALM 43, verses 3–5

O SEND thy light forth and thy truth;
Let them be guides to me,
And bring me to thine holy hill,
Even where thy dwellings be.

2 Then will I to God's altar go,
To God my chiefest joy:
Yea, God, my God, thy Name to praise
My harp I will employ.

3 Why art thou then cast down, my soul?
What should discourage thee?
And why with vexing thoughts art thou
Disquieted in me?

4 Still trust in God; for him to praise
Good cause I yet shall have:
He of my countenance is the health,
My God that doth me save.

5 *To Father, Son, and Holy Ghost,*
The God whom we adore,
Be glory, as it was, and is,
And shall be evermore. Amen.

8   PSALM 116, verses 1–7

I LOVE the Lord, because my voice
And prayers he did hear.
I, while I live, will call on him,
Who bowed to me his ear.

2 The cords of death on every side
Encompassed me around;
The sorrows of the grave me seized,
I grief and trouble found.

3 Upon the Name of God the Lord
Then did I call, and say,
Deliver thou my soul, O Lord,
I do thee humbly pray.

4 God merciful and righteous is,
Yea, gracious is our Lord.
God saves the meek: I was brought low,
He did me help afford.

5 O thou my soul, do thou return
Unto thy quiet rest;
For largely, lo, the Lord to thee
His bounty hath expressed.

6 *To Father, Son, and Holy Ghost,*
The God whom we adore,
Be glory, as it was, and is,
And shall be evermore. Amen.

9   *Lobe den Herren*

P RAISE to the Lord, the Almighty, the King of creation;
O my soul, praise him, for he is thy health and salvation;
All ye who hear,
Now to his temple draw near,
Joining in glad adoration.

2 Praise to the Lord, who o'er all things so wondrously reigneth,

Shieldeth thee gently from
  harm, or when fainting
  sustaineth;
Hast thou not seen
How thy heart's wishes have
  been
Granted in what he ordaineth?

3 Praise to the Lord, who doth
    prosper thy work and de-
    fend thee;
Surely his goodness and mercy
  shall daily attend thee;
Ponder anew
  What the Almighty can do,
Who with his love doth befriend
  thee.

4 Praise to the Lord! O let all that
    is in me adore him!
All that hath life and breath,
  come now with praises be-
  fore him!
Let the Amen
  Sound from his people again:
Gladly for aye we adore him.

> JOACHIM NEANDER, 1650–80
> Tr. CATHERINE WINKWORTH
> 1827–78, and others
> From Psalms 103, 150

IO *Angularis fundamentum lapis*
      Christus missus est

CHRIST is made the sure
  foundation,
Christ the head and corner-
  stone,
Chosen of the Lord, and
  precious,
Binding all the Church in one,
Holy Zion's help for ever,
And her confidence alone.

2 To this temple, where we call
    thee,
Come, O Lord of Hosts, to-
    day:
With thy wonted loving-kind-
    ness,
Hear thy servants as they
    pray,
And thy fullest benediction
Shed within its walls alway.

3 Here vouchsafe to all thy ser-
    vants
What they ask of thee to
    gain,

What they gain from thee for
    ever
With the blessèd to retain,
And hereafter in thy glory
Evermore with thee to reign.

4 *Laud and honour to the Father,*
  Laud and honour to the Son,
Laud and honour to the Spirit,
  Ever Three and ever One,
One in might, and One in glory,
  While unending ages run.
                            Amen.

> Latin, 7th or 8th century
> Tr. JOHN MASON NEALE, 1818–66
> altered

II

JESUS, stand among us
  In thy risen power;
Let this time of worship
  Be a hallowed hour.

2 Breathe the Holy Spirit
    Into every heart;
Bid the fears and sorrows
  From each soul depart.

3 Thus with quickened footsteps
    We pursue our way,
Watching for the dawning
  Of eternal day.

> WILLIAM PENNEFATHER, 1816–73

I2 *Macht hoch die Thür, das Thor*
       macht weit

LIFT up your heads, ye
  mighty gates,
      Alleluia!
Behold, the King of glory waits;
      Alleluia!
The King of kings is drawing
  near,
The Saviour of the world is here.
      Alleluia!

2 O blest the land, the city blest,
      Alleluia!
Where Christ the ruler is confessed.
      Alleluia!
O happy hearts and happy
  homes
To whom this King in triumph
  comes.
      Alleluia!

3 Redeemer, come! with us abide,
Alleluia!
Our hearts to thee we open wide,
Alleluia!
Thy presence with us let us feel,
Thy grace and love in us reveal.
Alleluia!

GEORG WEISSEL, 1590–1635
Tr. CATHERINE WINKWORTH, 1827–78
altered

13   *Lux alma Jesu mentium*

LIGHT of the anxious
heart,
Jesus, thou dost appear,
To bid the gloom of guilt de-
part,
And shed thy sweetness here.

2 Joyous is he with whom,
God's Word, thou dost abide,
Sweet Light of our eternal
home,
To fleshly sense denied.

3 Brightness of God above,
Unfathomable grace,
Thy presence be a fount of love
Within thy chosen place.

c. 1200
Tr. JOHN HENRY NEWMAN, 1801–90

14

WE come unto our fathers'
God;
Their Rock is our Salvation;
The eternal arms, their dear
abode,
We make our habitation;
We bring thee, Lord, the praise
they brought;
We seek thee as thy saints have
sought
In every generation.

2 The fire divine their steps that
led
Still goeth bright before us;
The heavenly shield around
them spread
Is still high holden o'er us;

The grace those sinners that
subdued,
The strength those weaklings
that renewed,
Doth vanquish, doth restore
us.

3 Their joy unto their Lord we
bring;
Their song to us descendeth;
The Spirit who in them did sing
To us his music lendeth;
His song in them, in us, is one;
We raise it high, we send it
on,—
The song that never endeth.

4 Ye saints to come, take up the
strain,
The same sweet theme en-
deavour;
Unbroken be the golden chain;
Keep on the song for ever;
Safe in the same dear dwelling-
place,
Rich with the same eternal
grace,
Bless the same boundless
Giver.

THOMAS HORNBLOWER GILL
1819–1906

15

WE love the place, O God,
Wherein thine honour
dwells;
The joy of thine abode
All earthly joy excels.

2 It is the house of prayer,
Wherein thy servants meet;
And thou, O Lord, art there,
Thy chosen flock to greet.

3 We love the word of life,
The word that tells of peace,
Of comfort in the strife,
And joys that never cease.

4 We love to sing below
For mercies freely given;
But O we long to know
The triumph song of heaven!

5 Lord Jesus, give us grace,
   On earth to love thee more,
In heaven to see thy face,
   And with thy saints adore.

        WILLIAM BULLOCK, 1798–1874
        and HENRY WILLIAMS BAKER
             1821–77

16   *For younger children*

LORD Jesus, be thou with us
   now,
As in thy house in prayer we
   bow;
And when we sing, and when
   we pray,
Help us to mean the words we
   say,
Help us to listen to thy word,
And keep our thoughts from
   wandering, Lord.

EDITH FLORENCE BOYLE MACALISTER
           1873–1950

17   *For younger children*

SERVE the Lord with joy and
   gladness,
Come into his gates with song;
Serve the Lord with loving-
   kindness,
Love and praise him all day
   long.

        MARY ELIZABETH HUEY
    Based on Psalm 100, verse 2

18   *For younger children*

THIS is God's holy house
   And he is here today;
He hears each song of praise;
And listens while we pray.

        LOUISE M. OGELVEE

THE MAJESTY OF GOD

19   PSALM 95, verses 1–6

O COME, and let us to the
   Lord
In songs our voices raise,
With joyful noise let us the
   Rock
Of our salvation praise.

2 Let us before his presence come
   With praise and thankful
     voice;
Let us sing psalms to him with
    grace,
   And make a joyful noise.

3 The Lord's a great God and
    great King,
   Above all gods he is.
Depths of the earth are in his
    hand,
   The strength of hills is his.

4 To him the spacious sea belongs,
   For he the same did make;
The dry land also from his
    hands
   Its form at first did take.

5 O come and let us worship him,
   Let us bow down withal,
And on our knees before the
    Lord
   Our Maker let us fall.

6 *To Father, Son, and Holy Ghost,*
   The God whom we adore,
Be glory, as it was, and is,
   And shall be evermore. Amen.

20   PSALM 95, verses 1–7
       Venite, exultemus

O COME let us ' sing unto ·
   the ' Lord : let us heartily
rejoice in the ' strength of '
our sal- ' vation.

2 Let us come before his ' presence with ' thanksgiving :
and show ourselves ' glad in '
him with ' psalms.

3 For the Lord is a ' great '
   God : and a great ' King
a- ' bove all ' gods.

4 In his hand are all the '
   corners · of the ' earth : and
   the strength of the ' hills is '
   his ' also.

5 The sea is ' his and he ' made
   it : and his hands pre- '
   pared the ' dry ' land.

6 O come let us ' worship and
   fall ' down : and ' kneel
   be · fore the ' Lord our '
   Maker.

7 For he is our God and ' we
   are his ' people : he is our '
   shepherd and ' we are his '
   flock.

   Glory ' be to the ' Father : and
   to the Son ' and to the '
   Holy ' Ghost :

   As it ' was in the be- ' ginning '
   is now and ever shall be '
   world without ' end.
                         A- ' men.

21   PSALM 95, verses 1–7

*O COME let us sing unto the
   Lord:
   let us make a joyful noise to the
   rock of our salvation.
Let us come before his presence
   with thanksgiving,
   and make a joyful noise unto
   him with psalms.
For the Lord is a great God,
   and a great King above all gods.
In his hands are the deep places of
   the earth:
   the strength of the hills is his
   also.
The sea is his and he made it:
   and his hands formed the dry
   land.
O come let us worship and bow
   down:
   let us kneel before the Lord our
   maker.

For he is our God;
   and we are the people of his
   pasture and the sheep of his
   hand.

*Glory be to the Father,
   and to the Son, and to the Holy
   Ghost ;
As it was in the beginning, is now
   and ever shall be :
   world without end. Amen.*

   * *For pointing system, see p. xv.*

22   PSALM 96, verses 1, 2, 6–8

O SING a new song to the
   Lord:
   Sing all the earth to God.
To God sing, bless his Name,
   show still
   His saving health abroad.

2 Great honour is before his face,
   And majesty divine ;
   Strength is within his holy
   place,
   And there doth beauty shine.

3 Do ye ascribe unto the Lord,
   Of people every tribe,
   Glory do ye unto the Lord,
   And mighty power ascribe.

4 Give ye the glory to the Lord
   That to his Name is due ;
   Come ye into his courts, and
   bring
   An offering with you.

5 *To Father, Son, and Holy Ghost,
   The God whom we adore,
   Be glory, as it was, and is,
   And shall be evermore. Amen.*

23   PSALM 9, verses 7–11

G OD shall endure for aye ; he
   doth
   For judgment set his throne ;
   In righteousness to judge the
   world,
   Justice to give each one.

2 God also will a refuge be
    For those that are oppressed;
A refuge will he be in times
    Of trouble to distressed.

3 And they that know thy Name,
    in thee
    Their confidence will place:
For thou hast not forsaken them
    That truly seek thy face.

4 O sing ye praises to the Lord
    That dwells in Zion hill;
Among all nations of the earth
    His deeds record ye still.

5 *To Father, Son, and Holy Ghost,*
    The God whom we adore,
Be glory, as it was, and is,
    And shall be evermore. Amen.

24   PSALM 46, verses 1–5

GOD is our refuge and our
    strength,
In straits a present aid;
Therefore, although the earth
    remove,
We will not be afraid:

2 Though hills amidst the seas be
    cast;
    Though waters roaring make,
And troubled be; yea, though
    the hills
    By swelling seas do shake.

3 A river is, whose streams make
    glad
    The city of our God,
The holy place, wherein the
    Lord
    Most high hath his abode.

4 God in the midst of her doth
    dwell;
    Nothing shall her remove:
God unto her an helper will,
    And that right early, prove.

5 *To Father, Son, and Holy Ghost,*
    The God whom we adore,
Be glory, as it was, and is,
    And shall be evermore. Amen.

25   PSALM 62, verses 5–8

ONLY on God do thou, my
    soul,
    Still patiently attend;
My expectation and my hope
    On him alone depend.

2 He only my salvation is,
    And my strong rock is he;
He only is my sure defence:
    I shall not movèd be.

3 In God my glory placèd is,
    And my salvation sure;
In God the rock is of my
    strength,
    My refuge most secure.

4 Ye people, place your con-
    fidence
    In him continually;
Before him pour ye out your
    heart;
    God is our refuge high.

5 *To Father, Son, and Holy Ghost,*
    The God whom we adore,
Be glory, as it was, and is,
    And shall be evermore. Amen.

26   PSALM 27, verses 1, 3–5, 14

THE Lord's my light and
    saving health,
    Who shall make me dis-
    mayed?
My life's strength is the Lord,
    of whom
    Then shall I be afraid?

2 Against me though an host en-
    camp,
    My heart yet fearless is:
Though war against me rise, I
    will
    Be confident in this.

3 One thing I of the Lord desired,
    And will seek to obtain,
That all days of my life I may
    Within God's house remain;

4 That I the beauty of the Lord
    Behold may and admire,
And that I in his holy place
    May reverently enquire.

5 For he in his pavilion shall
   Me hide in evil days;
In secret of his tent me hide,
   And on a rock me raise.

6 Wait on the Lord, and be thou
   strong,
   And he shall strength afford
Unto thine heart; yea, do thou
   wait,
   I say, upon the Lord.

7 *To Father, Son, and Holy Ghost,*
   The God whom we adore,
Be glory, as it was, and is,
   And shall be evermore. Amen.

27   Psalm 33, verses 1–5

YE righteous, in the Lord rejoice;
   It comely is and right,
That upright men, with thankful voice,
   Should praise the Lord of
   might.

2 Praise God with harp, and unto
   him
   Sing with the psaltery;
Upon a ten-stringed instru-
   ment
   Make ye sweet melody.

3 A new song to him sing, and
   play
   With loud noise skilfully;
For right is God's word, all his
   works
   Are done in verity.

4 To judgment and to righteous-
   ness
   A love he beareth still;
The loving-kindness of the
   Lord
   The earth throughout doth
   fill.

5 *To Father, Son, and Holy Ghost,*
   The God whom we adore,
Be glory, as it was, and is,
   And shall be evermore. Amen.

28   Psalm 65, verses 1–4

PRAISE waits for thee in
   Zion, Lord:
   To thee vows paid shall be.
O thou that hearer art of prayer,
   All flesh shall come to thee.

2 Iniquities, I must confess,
   Prevail against me do:
But as for our transgressions
   all,
   Them purge away shalt thou.

3 Blest is the man whom thou
   dost choose
   And makest approach to
   thee,
That he within thy courts, O
   Lord,
   May still a dweller be:

4 We surely shall be satisfied
   With thy abundant grace,
And with the goodness of thy
   house,
   Even of thy holy place.

5 *To Father, Son, and Holy Ghost,*
   The God whom we adore,
Be glory, as it was, and is,
   And shall be evermore. Amen.

29   Psalm 92, verses 1–4

TO render thanks unto the
   Lord
   It is a comely thing,
And to thy Name, O thou most
   high,
   Due praise aloud to sing.

2 Thy loving-kindness to show
   forth
   When shines the morning
   light;
And to declare thy faithfulness
   With pleasure every night,

3 Upon a ten-stringed instru-
   ment,
   And on the psaltery,
Upon the harp with solemn
   sound
   And grave sweet melody.

4 For thou, Lord, by thy mighty
    works
 Hast made my heart right
  glad;
And I will triumph in the works
 Which by thine hands were
  made.

5 *To Father, Son, and Holy Ghost,*
 The God whom we adore,
Be glory, as it was, and is,
 And shall be evermore. Amen.

30 *Laudato sia Dio mio Signore*

ALL creatures of our God and
 King,
Lift up your voice and with us
 sing
 Alleluia, Alleluia!
Thou burning sun with golden
 beam,
Thou silver moon with softer
 gleam,
  O *praise him, O praise him,*
  Alleluia, Alleluia, Alleluia!

*2 Thou rushing wind that art so
 strong,
 Ye clouds that sail in heaven
  along,
 O praise him, Alleluia!
Thou rising morn, in praise
 rejoice,
Ye lights of evening, find a
 voice:

*3 Thou flowing water, pure and
 clear,
 Make music for thy Lord to
  hear,
 Alleluia, Alleluia!
Thou fire so masterful and
 bright,
That givest man both warmth
 and light:

4 Dear mother earth, who day by
 day
 Unfoldest blessings on our
  way,
 O praise him, Alleluia!
The flowers and fruits that in
 thee grow,
Let them his glory also show:

5 And all ye men of tender heart,
 Forgiving others, take your
  part,
  O sing ye, Alleluia!
Ye who long pain and sorrow
 bear,
Praise God and on him cast
 your care:

6 And thou, most kind and
 gentle death,
 Waiting to hush our latest
  breath,
  O praise him, Alleluia!
Thou leadest home the child
 of God,
And Christ our Lord the way
 hath trod:

7 *Let all things their Creator bless,*
 And worship him in humble-
 * ness,*
  O praise him, Alleluia!
Praise, praise the Father,
 praise the Son,
And praise the Spirit, Three in
 One: *Amen.*
   ST. FRANCIS OF ASSISI, 1182–1226
Tr. WILLIAM HENRY DRAPER, 1855–1933
 * *These verses may be omitted if desired.*

31 *O Pater sancte*

FATHER most holy, merciful
 and loving,
 Jesus, Redeemer, ever to be
  worshipped,
Life-giving Spirit, Comforter
 most gracious,
 God everlasting;

2 Three in a wondrous unity unbroken,
 One perfect Godhead, love
  that never faileth,
Light of the angels, succour of
 the needy,
 Hope of all living;

3 All thy creation serveth its
 Creator;
 Thee every creature praiseth
  without ceasing;
We too would sing thee psalms
 of true devotion;
 Hear, we beseech thee.

4 Lord God Almighty, unto *thee*
    be glory,
  One in Three Persons, over all
    exalted;
  Thine, as is meet, be honour,
    praise, and blessing,
  Now and for ever. Amen.

c. 10th century
Tr. ALFRED EDWARD ALSTON
1862–1927

32

IMMORTAL, invisible, God
    only wise,
In light inaccessible hid from
    our eyes,
Most blessèd, most glorious, the
    Ancient of Days,
Almighty, victorious, thy great
    Name we praise.

2 Unresting, unhasting, and silent
    as light,
  Nor wanting, nor wasting,
    thou rulest in might;
  Thy justice like mountains high
    soaring above
  Thy clouds, which are fountains
    of goodness and love.

3 To all, life thou givest—to both
    great and small;
  In all life thou livest, the true
    life of all;
  We blossom and flourish as
    leaves on the tree,
  And wither and perish—but
    naught changeth thee.

4 Great Father of Glory, pure
    Father of Light,
  Thine angels adore thee, all
    veiling their sight;
  All laud we would render: O
    help us to see
  'Tis only the splendour of light
    hideth thee.

WALTER CHALMERS SMITH, 1824–1908
Based on 1 Timothy 1:17

33

LET us with a gladsome mind
    Praise the Lord, for he is
    kind:
  For his mercies aye endure,
  Ever faithful, ever sure.

2 Let us blaze his Name abroad,
  For of gods he is the God:

3 He,   with   all-commanding
    might,
  Filled the new-made world with
    light:

4 He his chosen race did bless
  In the wasteful wilderness:

5 All things living he doth feed;
  His full hand supplies their
    need:

6 Let us then with gladsome mind
  Praise the Lord, for he is kind:

JOHN MILTON, 1608–74
From Psalm 136

34

LORD of all being, throned
    afar,
  Thy glory flames from sun and
    star;
  Centre and soul of every sphere,
  Yet to each loving heart how
    near!

2 Sun of our life, thy quickening
    ray
  Sheds on our path the glow of
    day;
  Star of our hope, thy softened
    light
  Cheers the long watches of the
    night.

3 Our midnight is thy smile with-
    drawn,
  Our noontide is thy gracious
    dawn,
  Our rainbow arch thy mercy's
    sign;
  All, save the clouds of sin, are
    thine.

4 Lord of all life, below, above,
  Whose light is truth, whose
    warmth is love,
  Before thy ever-blazing throne
  We ask no lustre of our own.

5 Grant us thy truth to make us
    free,
  And kindling hearts that burn
    for thee,

11   B

Till all thy living altars claim
One holy light, one heavenly
flame.

OLIVER WENDELL HOLMES, 1809–94

35

O WORSHIP the King all-
glorious above,
O gratefully sing his power and
his love,
Our Shield and Defender, the
Ancient of Days,
Pavilioned in splendour, and
girded with praise.

2 O tell of his might, O sing of his
grace,
Whose robe is the light, whose
canopy space.
His chariots of wrath the deep
thunder-clouds form,
And dark is his path on the
wings of the storm.

3 The earth with its store of
wonders untold,
Almighty, thy power hath
founded of old,
Hath stablished it fast by a
changeless decree,
And round it hath cast, like
a mantle, the sea.

4 Thy bountiful care what tongue
can recite?
It breathes in the air; it shines
in the light;
It streams from the hills; it
descends to the plain,
And sweetly distils in the dew
and the rain.

5 Frail children of dust, and
feeble as frail,
In thee do we trust, nor find
thee to fail;
Thy mercies how tender, how
firm to the end,
Our Maker, Defender, Re-
deemer, and Friend!

6 O measureless Might! ineffable
Love!
While angels delight to hymn
thee above,

The humbler creation, though
feeble their lays,
With true adoration shall sing
to thy praise.

ROBERT GRANT, 1779–1838
From Psalm 104

36

THE Lord is King! lift up
thy voice,
O earth, and all ye heavens,
rejoice;
From world to world the joy
shall ring,
"The Lord Omnipotent is King!"

2 The Lord is King! who then
shall dare
Resist his will, distrust his care,
Or murmur at his wise decrees,
Or doubt his royal promises?

3 The Lord is King! child of the
dust,
The Judge of all the earth is
just;
Holy and true are all his ways:
Let every creature speak his
praise.

4 Come, make your wants, your
burdens known;
Christ will present them at the
throne;
For he is at the Father's side,
The Man of Love, the Crucified.

5 One Lord, one empire, all
secures;
He reigns, and life and death
are yours:
Through earth and heaven one
song shall ring,
"The Lord Omnipotent is King!"

JOSIAH CONDER, 1789–1855
altered

37

PRAISE the Lord! ye
heavens, adore him;
Praise him, angels, in the
height;

Sun and moon, rejoice before
    Him,
  Praise Him, all ye stars and
    light.
Praise the Lord! for he hath
    spoken;
  Worlds his mighty voice
    obeyed;
Laws which never shall be
    broken
  For their guidance hath he
    made.

2 Praise the Lord! for he is
    glorious;
  Never shall his promise fail;
God hath made his saints
    victorious;
  Sin and death shall not pre-
    vail.
Praise the God of our salva-
    tion!
  Hosts on high, his power
    proclaim;
Heaven, and earth, and all
    creation,
  Laud and magnify his Name.
    Amen.

Foundling Hospital Hymns, c. 1796
From Psalm 148

38

SONGS of praise the angels
    sang,
  Heaven with alleluias rang,
When creation was begun,
When God spake, and it was
    done.

2 Songs of praise awoke the morn
  When the Prince of Peace was
    born;
Songs of praise arose when he
  Captive led captivity.

3 Heaven and earth must pass
    away;
  Songs of praise shall crown that
    day;
God will make new heavens,
    new earth;
  Songs of praise shall hail their
    birth.

4 And can man alone be dumb,
  Till that glorious Kingdom
    come?
No! the Church delights to raise
  Psalms, and hymns, and songs
    of praise.

5 Saints below, with heart and
    voice,
  Still in songs of praise rejoice,
Learning here, by faith and
    love,
  Songs of praise to sing above.

6 Borne upon their latest breath,
  Songs of praise shall conquer
    death;
Then, amidst eternal joy,
  Songs of praise their powers
    employ.
    JAMES MONTGOMERY, 1771–1854

39

STAND up, and bless the
    Lord,
  Ye people of his choice;
Stand up, and bless the Lord
    your God
  With heart and soul and
    voice.

2 Though high above all praise,
  Above all blessing high,
Who would not fear his holy
    Name,
  And laud and magnify?

3 O for the living flame
  From his own altar brought,
To touch our lips, our minds
    inspire,
  And wing to heaven our
    thought!

4 God is our strength and song,
  And his salvation ours;
When he his love in Christ pro-
    claimed
  With all our ransomed
    powers.

5 Stand up, and bless the Lord;
  The Lord your God adore;
Stand up, and bless his glorious
    Name
  Henceforth for evermore.
    JAMES MONTGOMERY, 1771–1854

40

WORSHIP the Lord in the
beauty of holiness;
Bow down before him, his
glory proclaim;
Gold of obedience and incense
of lowliness
Bring, and adore him; the
Lord is his Name!

2 Low at his feet lay thy burden
of carefulness;
High on his heart he will bear
it for thee,
Comfort thy sorrows, and
answer thy prayerfulness,
Guiding thy steps as may
best for thee be.

3 Fear not to enter his courts, in
the slenderness
Of the poor wealth thou
canst reckon as thine;

Truth in its beauty and love in
its tenderness,
These are the offerings to lay
on his shrine.

4 These, though we bring them in
trembling and fearfulness,
He will accept for the Name
that is dear,
Mornings of joy give for even-
ings of tearfulness,
Trust for our trembling, and
hope for our fear.

5 Worship the Lord in the beauty
of holiness;
Bow down before him, his
glory proclaim;
Gold of obedience and incense
of lowliness
Bring, and adore him; the
Lord is his Name!

JOHN SAMUEL BEWLEY MONSELL
1811-75

MORNING

41
PSALM 63, verses 1-4

LORD, thee my God, I'll
early seek:
My soul doth thirst for thee;
My flesh longs in a dry parched
land,
Wherein no waters be:

2 That I thy power may behold,
And brightness of thy face,
As I have seen thee heretofore
Within thy holy place.

3 Since better is thy love than
life,
My lips thee praise shall give.
I in thy Name will lift my hands,
And bless thee while I live.

4 To Father, Son, and Holy Ghost,
The God whom we adore,
Be glory, as it was, and is,
And shall be evermore. Amen.

42

AWAKE, my soul, and with the
sun
Thy daily stage of duty run;
Shake off dull sloth, and joyful
rise,
To pay thy morning sacrifice.

2 Wake, and lift up thyself, my
heart,
And with the angels bear thy
part,
Who all night long unwearied
sing
High praise to the eternal King.

3 Lord, I my vows to thee renew;
Disperse my sins as morning
dew;
Guard my first springs of
thought and will,
And with thyself my spirit fill.

4 Direct, control, suggest, this
    day,
All I design, or do, or say,
That all my powers, with all
    their might,
In thy sole glory may unite.

5 *Praise God, from whom all*
    blessings flow;
Praise him, all creatures here
    below;
Praise him above, ye heavenly
    host;
Praise Father, Son, and Holy
    Ghost. Amen.

THOMAS KEN, 1637–1711

43   *Nocte surgentes*

FATHER, we praise thee,
    now the night is over;
Active and watchful, stand we
    all before thee;
Singing, we offer prayer and
    meditation:
        Thus we adore thee.

2 Monarch of all things, fit us for
    thy mansions;
Banish our weakness, health
    and wholeness sending;
Bring us to heaven, where thy
    saints united
        Joy without ending.

3 *All-holy Father, Son, and equal*
    Spirit,
Trinity blessèd, send us thy
    salvation;
Thine is the glory, gleaming and
    resounding
        Through all creation. Amen.

10th century or earlier
Tr. PERCY DEARMER, 1867–1936

44

MOST glorious Lord of life,
    that on this day
    Didst make thy triumph over
        death and sin,
And having harrowed hell,
    didst bring away
    Captivity thence captive, us
        to win:

2 This joyous day, dear Lord,
    with joy begin,
    And grant that we, for whom
        thou diddest die,
Being with thy dear blood clean
    washed from sin,
    May live for ever in felicity:

3 And that thy love we, weighing
    worthily,
May likewise love thee for the
    same again;
And for thy sake, that all like
    dear didst buy,
    With love may one another
        entertain.

4 So let us love, dear Love, like as
    we ought,
    Love is the lesson which the
        Lord us taught.

EDMUND SPENSER, c. 1552–99

45   *Iam lucis orto sidere*

NOW that the daylight fills
    the sky,
We lift our hearts to God on
    high,
That he, in all we do or say,
Would keep us free from harm
    today:

2 Would guard our hearts and
    tongues from strife,
From anger's din would hide
    our life,
From all ill sights would turn
    our eyes,
Would close our ears from
    vanities:

3 Would keep our inmost con-
    science pure,
Our souls from folly would
    secure,
Would bid us check the pride of
    sense
With due and holy abstinence.

4 So we, when this new day is
    gone
And night in turn is drawing on,
With conscience by the world
    unstained,
Shall praise his Name for vic-
    tory gained.

Before 8th century
Tr. JOHN MASON NEALE, 1818–66

46

THIS is the day of light:
　Let there be light today;
O Dayspring, rise upon our
　night,
And chase its gloom away.

2　This is the day of prayer:
　Let earth to heaven draw
　near;
Lift up our hearts to seek thee
　there,
　Come down to meet us here.

3　This is the first of days:
　Send forth thy quickening
　breath,
And wake dead souls to love
　and praise,
　O Vanquisher of death!

JOHN ELLERTON, 1826–93

47

NEW every morning is the love
　Our wakening and uprising
　prove;
Through sleep and darkness
　safely brought,
Restored to life, and power, and
　thought.

2　New mercies, each returning
　day,
　Hover around us while we
　pray,—
New perils past, new sins for-
　given,
New thoughts of God, new
　hopes of heaven.

3　If, on our daily course, our mind
　Be set to hallow all we find,
New treasures still, of countless
　price,
God will provide for sacrifice.

4　The trivial round, the common
　task,
　Will furnish all we ought to
　ask,—
　Room to deny ourselves, a road
　To bring us daily nearer God.

5　Only, O Lord, in thy dear love
　Fit us for perfect rest above;
And help us, this and every day,
　To live more nearly as we pray.

JOHN KEBLE, 1792–1866

48

O LORD of life, thy quicken-
　ing voice
Awakes my morning song!
In gladsome words I would
　rejoice
That I to thee belong.

2　I see thy light, I feel thy wind;
　The world, it is thy word;
Whatever wakes my heart and
　mind
　Thy presence is, my Lord.

3　Therefore I choose my highest
　part,
　And turn my face to thee;
Therefore I stir my inmost
　heart
　To worship fervently.

4　Lord, let me live and will this
　day—
　Keep rising from the dead;
Lord, make my spirit good and
　gay—
　Give me my daily bread.

5　Within my heart speak, Lord,
　speak on,
　My heart alive to keep,
Till comes the night, and,
　labour done,
　In thee I fall asleep.

GEORGE MACDONALD, 1824–1905

49　*For younger children*

THE morning bright, with
　rosy light,
Has waked me up from sleep;
　Father, I own, thy love alone
　Thy little one doth keep.

2 All through the day, I humbly
    pray,
  Be thou my Guard and Guide;
  My sins forgive, and let me
    live,
  Blest Jesus, near thy side.

3 O make thy rest within my
    breast,
  Great Spirit of all grace;
  Make me like thee, then shall
    I be
  Prepared to see thy face.

THOMAS OSMOND SUMMERS
1812–82

EVENING

50   *Sol praeceps rapitur*

THE sun is sinking fast,
  The daylight dies;
Let love awake, and pay
  Her evening sacrifice.

2 As Christ upon the Cross
  His head inclined,
  And to his Father's hands
  His parting soul resigned,

3 So now herself my soul
  Would wholly give
  Into his sacred charge
  In whom all spirits live;

4 Thus would I live; yet now
  Not I, but he
  In all his power and love
  Henceforth alive in me:

5 One sacred Trinity,
  One Lord Divine;
  Myself for ever his,
  And he for ever mine.

Anonymous 18th century Latin Hymn
Tr. EDWARD CASWALL, 1814–78

51

AS now the day draws near its
    ending,
  While evening steals o'er
    earth and sky,
Once more to thee our hymns
    ascending
  Sound forth thy praises,
    Lord Most High.

Thine is the splendour of the
    morning,
  Thine is the evening's tran-
    quil light;
Thine too the veil which till the
    dawning
  Shrouds all the earth in
    peaceful night.

2 Maker of worlds beyond our
    knowing,
  Realms which no human eye
    can scan,
  Yet in thy wondrous love be-
    stowing
  Through Christ thy saving
    aid to man;
Lord, while the hymns of all
    creation
  Rise ever to thy throne above,
We too would join in adoration,
  Owning thee God of change-
    less love.

JACK COPLEY WINSLOW
Partly based on a hymn by
JOHN ELLERTON, 1826–93

52

AT even, when the sun was
    set,
  The sick, O Lord, around thee
    lay;
O in what divers pains they met!
  O with what joy they went
    away!

2 O Saviour Christ, our woes
    dispel:
  For some are sick, and some
    are sad,

And some have never loved thee
well,
And some have lost the love
they had.

3 O Saviour Christ, thou too art
Man;
Thou hast been troubled,
tempted, tried;
Thy kind but searching glance
can scan
The very wounds that shame
would hide.

4 Thy touch has still its ancient
power;
No word from thee can fruitless fall:
Hear in this solemn evening
hour,
And in thy mercy heal us all.

HENRY TWELLS, 1823–1900

Thine ear discerns, thy love
rejoices,
When hearts rise up to thee
in truth.

5 O Light all clear, O Truth most
holy,
O boundless Mercy pardoning
all,
Before thy feet, abashed and
lowly,
With fervent prayer thy
children fall:—

6 When we no more on earth
adore thee,
And others worship here in
turn,
O may we sing that song before
thee,
Which none but thy redeemed
can learn.

JOHN ELLERTON, 1826–93

53

BEFORE the day draws near
its ending,
And evening steals o'er earth
and sky,
Once more to thee our hymns
ascending
Shall speak thy praises, Lord
Most High.

2 Thy Name is blessed by countless numbers
In vaster worlds unseen, unknown,
Whose duteous service never
slumbers,
In perfect love and faultless
tone.

3 Yet thou wilt not despise the
weakest
Who here in spirit bend the
knee;
Thy Christ hath said, 'Thou,
Father, seekest
For such as these to worship
thee.'

4 And through the swell of chanting voices,
The blended notes of age and
youth,

54 Φῶς ἱλαρὸν ἁγίας δόξης

HAIL, gladdening Light, of
his pure glory poured
Who is the immortal Father,
heavenly, blest,
Holiest of Holies, Jesus Christ,
our Lord!

2 Now we are come to the sun's
hour of rest,
The lights of evening round us
shine.
We hymn the Father, Son, and
Holy Spirit Divine.

3 Worthiest art thou at all times
to be sung with undefilèd
tongue,
Son of our God, Giver of life,
alone:
Therefore in all the world, thy
glories, Lord, they own.
Amen.

Before 4th century
Tr. JOHN KEBLE, 1792–1866

55 Φῶς ἱλαρὸν ἁγίας δόξης

O GLADSOME Light, O
grace
Of God the Father's face,

18

The eternal splendour wearing;
  Celestial, holy, blest,
  Our Saviour Jesus Christ,
Joyful in thine appearing.

2 Now, ere day fadeth quite,
  We see the evening light,
Our wonted hymn outpouring;
  Father of might unknown,
  Thee, his incarnate Son,
And Holy Spirit adoring.

3 To thee of right belongs
  All praise of holy songs,
O Son of God, Lifegiver;
  Thee therefore, O Most High,
  The world doth glorify,
And shall exalt for ever.

Before 4th century
Tr. ROBERT BRIDGES, 1844–1930

56 *O Lux beata Trinitas*

O TRINITY, O blessèd
  Light,
O Unity, most principal,
The fiery sun now leaves our
  sight:
  Cause in our hearts thy
  beams to fall.

2 Let us with songs of praise
  divine
  At morn and evening thee
  implore;
And let our glory, bowed to
  thine,
  Thee glorify for evermore.

3 *To God the Father, glory great,*
  And glory to his only Son,
And to the Holy Paraclete,
  Both now and still while ages
  run. Amen.

Attributed to ST. AMBROSE
340–97
Tr. WM. DRUMMOND OF
HAWTHORNDEN, 1585–1649

57 *Nun ruhen alle Wälder*

THE duteous day now closeth,
  Each flower and tree re-
  poseth,
  Shade creeps o'er wild and
  wood:

Let us, as night is falling,
On God our Maker calling,
  Give thanks to him, the
  Giver good.

2 Now all the heavenly splendour
Breaks forth in starlight tender
  From myriad worlds un-
  known;
And man, the marvel seeing,
Forgets his selfish being,
  For joy of beauty not his own.

3 Awhile his mortal blindness
May miss God's loving-kindness,
  And grope in faithless strife:
But when life's day is over,
Shall death's fair night discover
  The fields of everlasting life.

PAUL GERHARDT, 1607–76
Par. ROBERT BRIDGES, 1844–1930

58 *For younger children*

IF I come to Jesus,
  He will make me glad;
He will give me pleasure
  When my heart is sad.
    If I come to Jesus,
      Happy shall I be;
    He is gently calling
      Little ones like me.

2 If I come to Jesus,
  He will hear my prayer;
He will love me dearly;
  He my sins did bear.

3 If I come to Jesus,
  He will take my hand,
He will kindly lead me
  To a better land.

FRANCES (CROSBY) VAN ALSTYNE
1820–1915

59 *For younger children*

JESUS Christ, our Lord and
  King,
Listen to the prayer we sing
Now the lovely light, that shone
Through our happy day, has
  gone.

2 Thou, by whom the birds were
 fed,
 Gavest us our daily bread;
 Thou the gentle dark hast sent—
 May we sleep in hushed content.

3 Bless thy grateful children now,
 As our sleepy heads we bow;
 May thy Holy Spirit's might
 Guard us through the hours of
 night.

4 Teach us, Lord, thy way to
 know,
 We must in thy pattern grow;
 And, when thou at last shalt
 come,
 Take us to thy heavenly home.

Based on a hymn by
EMILY MARY SHAPCOTE, 1828–1909

The following are also suitable:

No.
489 I joy'd when to the house of God
347 Praise ye the Lord. God's praise
 within
348 Sing a new song to Jehovah
143 The spacious firmament on high
236 Children of Jerusalem
359 Praise the Lord, his glories show
455 Angel voices, ever singing

*Certain hymns in Part III, Section 1
(Adoration, Thanksgiving), and Section 2
(Affirmation) are also suitable.*

CONFESSION AND SUPPLICATION

60
KYRIE ELEISON

First Form

Minister Lord have mercy
People Christ have mercy
Minister Lord have mercy

Second Form

*Lord, have mercy upon us
Christ have mercy upon us
Lord have mercy upon us

* *When sung, each line is repeated
three times.*

61
TRISAGION

Holy God, holy and mighty, holy
and immortal, have mercy upon
us.

For Trisagion *with* The Reproaches, *see*
No. 240.

62
GLORIA IN EXCELSIS

GLORY be to God on high,
 and in earth peace, good
will towards men.
We praise thee, we bless thee,
 we worship thee, we glorify
 thee,
We give thanks to thee for
 thy great glory,

O Lord God, heavenly King,
 God the Father Almighty.
O Lord, the only begotten Son,
 Jesus Christ;
O Lord God, Lamb of God,
 Son of the Father,
That takest away the sins of
 the world, have mercy upon
 us.
Thou that takest away the sins
 of the world, have mercy
 upon us.
Thou that takest away the
 sins of the world, receive
 our prayer.
Thou that sittest at the right
 hand of God the Father, have
 mercy upon us.
For thou only art holy, thou
 only art the Lord;
Thou only, O Christ, with the
 Holy Ghost, art most high
 in the glory of God the
 Father. Amen.

63
Psalm 51, verses 1–4, 6–12

HAVE mercy upon me O
 God according to thy '
loving-kindness : according
to the multitude of thy
tender mercies blot ' out my
transgressions.

Wash me throughly from "
mine iniquity :: and " cleanse
me from my sins.

For I acknowledge " my transgressions :: and my sin is "
ever before me.

Against thee thee only have I
sinned and done this evil "
in thy sight :: that thou
mightest be justified when
thou speakest   and be "
clear when thou judgest.

Behold thou desirest truth in
the " inward parts :: and in
the hidden part thou shalt
make " me to know wisdom.

Purge me with hyssop and I "
shall be clean :: wash me and
I " shall be whiter than snow.

Make me to hear " joy and
gladness :: that the bones
which thou hast " broken
may rejoice.

Hide thy face " from my sins ::
and blot out " all mine iniquities.

Create in me a clean " heart
O God : and renew a right "
spirit within me.

Cast me not away " from thy
presence :: and take not thy "
Holy Spirit from me.

Restore unto me the joy of "
thy salvation :: and uphold
me " with thy free spirit.

Glory be to the Father and " to
the Son : and " to the Holy
Ghost ::

As it was in the beginning is
now and " ever shall be ::
world " without end Amen.

64   Psalm 51, verses 1—12

O GOD be gracious to me in
thy love,
And in thy mercy pardon my
misdeeds ;;

Wash me from guilt and cleanse
me from my sin,
For well I know the evil I have
done.

2 Against thee, Lord, thee only
have I sinned,
And what to thee is hateful
have I done ;;
I own thy righteousness in
changing me,
I know thee justified should'st
thou condemn.

3 Take hyssop, sprinkle me and
make me clean,
Wash me and make me whiter
than the snow ;;
Fill me with gladness and rejoicing, Lord,
And let my broken frame know
joy once more.

4 Turn thou thy face, O God,
from my misdeeds,
And blot out all the sins that
sully me ;;
Create a clean and contrite
heart in me,
Renew my soul in faithfulness
and love.

5 Drive me not from thy presence, gracious Lord,
Nor keep thy Holy Spirit far
from me ;;
Restore my soul with thy salvation's joy,
And with a willing spirit
strengthen me.

Ian Pitt-Watson
From The New English Bible version
of Psalm 51

65   Psalm 130, verses 1—6a, 7b, 8

LORD, from the depths to
thee I cried.
My voice, Lord, do thou hear ::
Unto my supplications' voice
Give an attentive ear.

2 Lord, who shall stand, if thou,
O Lord,
Shouldest mark iniquity ?
But yet with thee forgiveness is,
That feared thou mayest be.

211

3 I wait for God, my soul doth
   wait,
   My hope is in his word.
   More than they that for morn-
   ing watch,
   My soul waits for the Lord;

4 Redemption also plenteous
   Is ever found with him.
   And from all his iniquities
   He Israel shall redeem.

5 To Father, Son, and Holy
   Ghost,
   The God whom we adore,
   Be glory, as it was, and is,
   And shall be evermore. Amen.

66　　PSALM 130

*OUT of the depths have I
   cried unto thee O Lord.
Lord hear my voice let
thine ears be attentive to
the voice of my supplica-
tions.

If thou Lord shouldest mark
iniquities   O Lord who
shall stand?

But there is forgiveness with
thee   that thou mayest be
feared.

I wait for the Lord my soul
doth wait   and in his
word do I hope.

My soul waiteth for the Lord
more than they that watch
for the morning   I say
more than they that watch
for the morning.

Let Israel hope in the Lord
for with the Lord there is
mercy   and with him is
plenteous redemption.

And he shall redeem Israel
from all his iniquities.

*Glory be to the Father and to
the Son   and to the Holy
Ghost:*

*As it was in the beginning is
now and ever shall be
world without end. Amen.*
   * See No. 21 footnote.

67　PSALM 130, Gelineau version

*OUT of the depths I cry to
   you, O Lord,
Lord, hear my voice!
O let your ears be attentive
To the voice of my pleading.

2 If you, O Lord, should mark our
   guilt,
   Lord, who would survive?
   But with you is found forgive-
   ness:
   For this we revere you.

3 My soul is waiting for the Lord,
   I count on his word.
   My soul is longing for the Lord
   More than watchman for day-
   break.

4 Because with the Lord there is
   mercy
   And fullness of redemption,
   Israel indeed he will redeem
   From all its iniquity.

5 To the Father Almighty give
   glory,
   Give glory to his Son,
   To the Spirit most Holy give
   praise,
   Whose reign is for ever.

*It is suggested that either of the following
Antiphons be sung by the congregation
after each verse of the psalm.*

Antiphon 1
I place all my trust in you, my God: all my hope is in your saving word.

Antiphon 2
With the Lord there is mercy without end.

* The accented words and syllables should be stressed rhythmically.

68 From PSALM 139

THOU art before me, Lord, thou art behind,
And thou above me hast spread out thy hand;
Such knowledge is too wonderful for me,
Too high to grasp, too great to understand.

2 Then whither from thy Spirit shall I go,
And whither from thy presence shall I flee?
If I ascend to heaven thou art there,
And in the lowest depths I meet with thee.

3 If I should take my flight into the dawn,
If I should dwell on ocean's farthest shore,
Thy mighty hand would rest upon me still,
And thy right hand would guard me evermore.

4 If I should say 'Darkness will cover me,
And I shall hide within the veil of night',
Surely the darkness is not dark to thee,
The night is as the day, the darkness light.

5 Search me, O God, search me and know my heart,
Try me, O God, my mind and spirit try;
Keep me from any path that gives thee pain,

And lead me in the everlasting way.

IAN PITT-WATSON
From *The New English Bible* version of Psalm 139

69 PARAPHRASE 30

COME, let us to the Lord our God
With contrite hearts return;
Our God is gracious, nor will leave
The desolate to mourn.

2 His voice commands the tempest forth,
And stills the stormy wave;
And though his arm be strong to smite,
'Tis also strong to save.

3 Long hath the night of sorrow reigned,
The dawn shall bring us light:
God shall appear, and we shall rise
With gladness in his sight.

4 Our hearts, if God we seek to know,
Shall know him, and rejoice;
His coming like the morn shall be,
Like morning songs his voice.

5 As dew upon the tender herb,
Diffusing fragrance round;
As showers that usher in the spring,
And cheer the thirsty ground:

6 So shall his presence bless our souls,
And shed a joyful light;
That hallowed morn shall chase away
The sorrows of the night.

Scottish Paraphrases, 1781
From Hosea 6: 1–4

70 PSALM 143 (ii), from verses 1, 6, 8

O, HEAR my prayer, Lord,
Unto me answer make,
And, in thy righteousness,
Upon me pity take.

23

Lo, I do stretch my hands
To thee, my help alone;
For thou well understands
All my complaint and moan:

2 My thirsting soul desires,
And longeth after thee,
As thirsty ground requires
With rain refreshed to be.
Because I trust in thee,
O Lord, cause me to hear
Thy loving-kindness free,
When morning doth appear:

3 Cause me to know the way
Wherein my path should be;
For why, my soul on high
I do lift up to thee.
Now glory be to God!
The Father, and the Son,
And to the Holy Ghost,
All-glorious Three in One.
Amen.

71 Psalm 61, verses 1-4

O GOD, give ear unto my cry;
Unto my prayer attend.
From the uttermost corner of the land
My cry to thee I'll send.

2 What time my heart is over-whelmed
And in perplexity,
Do thou me lead unto the Rock
That higher is than I.

3 For thou hast for my refuge been
A shelter by thy power;
And for defence against my foes
Thou hast been a strong tower.

4 Within thy tabernacle I
For ever will abide;
And under covert of thy wings
With confidence me hide.

5 To Father, Son, and Holy Ghost,
The God whom we adore,
Be glory, as it was, and is,
And shall be evermore. Amen.

72 Paraphrase 22

O GOD of Bethel! by whose hand
Thy people still are fed;
Who through this weary pilgrimage
Hast all our fathers led:

2 Our vows, our prayers, we now present
Before thy throne of grace:
God of our fathers! be the God
Of their succeeding race.

3 Through each perplexing path of life
Our wandering footsteps guide;
Give us each day our daily bread,
And raiment fit provide.

4 O spread thy covering wings around,
Till all our wanderings cease,
And at our Father's loved abode
Our souls arrive in peace.

5 Such blessings from thy gracious hand
Our humble prayers implore;
And thou shalt be our chosen God,
And portion evermore.

Scottish Paraphrases, 1781
From Genesis 28: 20-22

73 Psalm 40, verses 1-4

I WAITED for the Lord my God,
And patiently did bear;
At length to me he did incline
My voice and cry to hear.

2 He took me from a fearful pit,
And from the miry clay,
And on a rock he set my feet,
Establishing my way.

3 He put a new song in my mouth,
Our God to magnify:
Many shall see it, and shall fear,
And on the Lord rely.

4 O blessèd is the man whose trust
　　Upon the Lord relies;
Respecting not the proud, nor
　　such
　　As turn aside to lies.

5 *To Father, Son, and Holy Ghost,*
　　The God whom we adore,
Be glory, as it was, and is,
　　And shall be evermore. Amen.

74 PSALM 25, verses 4, 5a, 6–10

SHOW me thy ways, O Lord;
　　Thy paths, O teach thou me:
And do thou lead me in thy
　　truth,
　　Therein my teacher be:

2 Thy tender mercies, Lord,
　　I pray thee to recall,
And loving-kindnesses; for they
　　Have been through ages all.

3 My sins and faults of youth
　　Do thou, O Lord, forget:
After thy mercy think on me,
　　And for thy goodness great.

4 God good and upright is:
　　The way he'll sinners show.
The meek in judgment he will
　　guide,
　　And make his path to know.

5 The whole paths of the Lord
　　Are truth and mercy sure,
To those that do his covenant
　　keep,
　　And testimonies pure.

6 *To thee be glory, Lord,*
　　Whom heaven and earth adore,
To Father, Son, and Holy Ghost,
　　One God for evermore. Amen.

75 PSALM 85 (ii), verses 1, 2, 5–7

LORD, thine heart in love
　　hath yearned
On thy lost and fallen land;
Israel's race is homeward
　　turned,
　　Thou hast freed thy captive
　　band:

2 Thou hast borne thy people's
　　sin,
　　Covered all their deeds of ill;
All thy wrath is gathered in,
　　And thy burning anger still.

3 Wilt thou not in mercy turn?
　　Turn, and be our life again,
That thy people's heart may
　　burn
　　With the gladness of thy
　　reign.

4 Show us now thy tender love;
　　Thy salvation, Lord, impart;
I the voice divine would prove,
　　Listening in my silent heart:

5 Listening what the Lord will
　　say—
　　'Peace' to all that own his
　　will:
To his saints that love his way,
　　'Peace', and 'turn no more to
　　ill'.

6 *Glory to the Father be,*
　　Glory, Christ our Lord, to thee,
Glory to the Holy Ghost,
　　Praised by men and Heavenly
　　Host. Amen.

76

DEAR Lord and Father of
　　mankind,
　　Forgive our foolish ways;
Reclothe us in our rightful
　　mind;
In purer lives thy service find,
　　*In deeper reverence, praise.

2 In simple trust like theirs who
　　heard,
　　Beside the Syrian sea,
The gracious calling of the Lord,
Let us, like them, without a
　　word
　　Rise up and follow thee.

3 O Sabbath rest by Galilee!
　　O calm of hills above,
Where Jesus knelt to share with
　　thee
The silence of eternity,
　　Interpreted by love!

4 With that deep hush subduing all
    Our words and works that drown
The tender whisper of thy call,
    As noiseless let thy blessing fall
    As fell thy manna down.

5 Drop thy still dews of quietness,
    Till all our strivings cease;
Take from our souls the strain and stress,
    And let our ordered lives confess
    The beauty of thy peace.

6 Breathe through the heats of our desire
    Thy coolness and thy balm;
Let sense be dumb, let flesh retire;
    Speak through the earthquake, wind, and fire,
    O still small voice of calm!

JOHN GREENLEAF WHITTIER, 1807–92

    * The last line of each verse is to be repeated, when Tune (ii) REPTON is sung.

77

FATHER of heaven, whose love profound
A ransom for our souls hath found,
Before thy throne we sinners bend;
To us thy pardoning love extend.

2 Almighty Son, Incarnate Word,
Our Prophet, Priest, Redeemer, Lord,
Before thy throne we sinners bend;
To us thy saving grace extend.

3 Eternal Spirit, by whose breath
The soul is raised from sin and death,
Before thy throne we sinners bend;
To us thy quickening power extend.

4 Jehovah—Father, Spirit, Son—
Mysterious Godhead, Three in One,
Before thy throne we sinners bend;
Grace, pardon, life to us extend.

EDWARD COOPER, 1770–1833

78

JESUS, Lover of my soul,
    Let me to thy bosom fly,
While the nearer waters roll,
    While the tempest still is high;
Hide me, O my Saviour, hide,
    Till the storm of life is past;
Safe into the haven guide,
    O receive my soul at last!

2 Other refuge have I none;
    Hangs my helpless soul on thee;
Leave, ah! leave me not alone;
    Still support and comfort me.
All my trust on thee is stayed;
    All my help from thee I bring;
Cover my defenceless head
    With the shadow of thy wing.

3 Thou, O Christ, art all I want;
    More than all in thee I find;
Raise the fallen, cheer the faint,
    Heal the sick, and lead the blind.
Just and holy is thy Name,
    I am all unrighteousness;
False and full of sin I am,
    Thou art full of truth and grace.

4 Plenteous grace with thee is found,
    Grace to cover all my sin;
Let the healing streams abound;
    Make and keep me pure within.
Thou of life the fountain art,
    Freely let me take of thee;
Spring thou up within my heart,
    Rise to all eternity.

CHARLES WESLEY, 1707–88

79

JUST as I am, without one plea
But that thy blood was shed for me,
And that thou bidd'st me come to thee,
O Lamb of God, I come.

2 Just as I am, though tossed about
With many a conflict, many a doubt,
Fightings and fears within, without,
O Lamb of God, I come.

3 Just as I am, thou wilt receive,
Wilt welcome, pardon, cleanse, relieve;
Because thy promise I believe,
O Lamb of God, I come.

4 Just as I am—thy love unknown
Has broken every barrier down—
Now to be thine, yea, thine alone,
O Lamb of God, I come.

5 Just as I am, of that free love
The breadth, length, depth, and height to prove,
Here for a season, then above,—
O Lamb of God, I come.

CHARLOTTE ELLIOTT, 1789–1871

80

Μνώεο Χριστέ

LORD Jesus, think on me,
And purge away my sin;
From earthborn passions set me free,
And make me pure within.

2 Lord Jesus, think on me,
With care and woe oppressed;
Let me thy loving servant be,
And taste thy promised rest.

3 Lord Jesus, think on me,
Amid the battle's strife;
In all my pain and misery
Be thou my health and life.

4 Lord Jesus, think on me,
Nor let me go astray;
Through darkness and perplexity
Point thou the heavenly way.

5 Lord Jesus, think on me,
When flows the tempest high:
When on doth rush the enemy,
O Saviour, be thou nigh.

6 Lord Jesus, think on me,
That, when the flood is past,
I may the eternal brightness see,
And share thy joy at last.

SYNESIUS OF CYRENE, c. 375–430
Tr. ALLEN WILLIAM CHATFIELD
1808–96

81

MY faith looks up to thee,
Thou Lamb of Calvary,
Saviour Divine;
Now hear me while I pray;
Take all my guilt away;
O let me from this day
Be wholly thine.

2 May thy rich grace impart
Strength to my fainting heart,
My zeal inspire;
As thou hast died for me,
O may my love to thee
Pure, warm, and changeless be,
A living fire.

3 While life's dark maze I tread,
And griefs around me spread,
Be thou my Guide;
Bid darkness turn to day,
Wipe sorrow's tears away,
Nor let me ever stray
From thee aside.

4 When ends life's transient dream,
When death's cold, sullen stream
Shall o'er me roll,
Blest Saviour, then, in love,
Fear and distrust remove;
O bear me safe above,
A ransomed soul.

RAY PALMER, 1808–87

82 *Śiṣyahī ganāyā nahī yogya jo tayālā*

ONE who is all unfit to
count
As scholar in thy school,
Thou of thy love hast named a
friend—
O kindness wonderful!

2 So weak am I, O gracious Lord,
So all unworthy thee,
That even the dust upon thy
feet
Outweighs me utterly.

3 Thou dwellest in unshadowed
light,
All sin and shame above—
That thou shouldst bear our
sin and shame,
How can I tell such love?

4 Ah, did not he the heavenly
throne
A little thing esteem,
And not unworthy for my sake
A mortal body deem?

5 When in his flesh they drove
the nails,
Did he not all endure?
What name is there to fit a life
So patient and so pure?

6 So, Love itself in human form,
For love of me he came;
I cannot look upon his face
For shame, for bitter shame.

7 If there is aught of worth in me,
It comes from thee alone;
Then keep me safe, for so, O
Lord,
Thou keepest but thine own.

From the Marathi of
NARAYAN VAMAN TILAK
1862–1919
Tr. NICOL MACNICOL
1870–1952

83

ROCK of Ages, cleft for me,
Let me hide myself in thee;
Let the water and the blood,
From thy riven side which
flowed,
Be of sin the double cure,
Cleanse me from its guilt and
power.

2 Not the labours of my hands
Can fulfil thy law's demands;
Could my zeal no respite know,
Could my tears for ever flow,
All for sin could not atone:
Thou must save, and thou alone.

3 Nothing in my hand I bring,
Simply to thy cross I cling;
Naked, come to thee for dress;
Helpless, look to thee for grace;
Foul, I to the fountain fly;
Wash me, Saviour, or I die.

4 While I draw this fleeting
breath,
When mine eyelids close in
death,
When I soar through tracts un-
known,
See thee on thy judgment
throne,
Rock of Ages, cleft for me,
Let me hide myself in thee.

AUGUSTUS MONTAGUE TOPLADY
1740–78

84

TURN back, O man, forswear
thy foolish ways;
Old now is earth, and none may
count her days,
Yet thou, her child, whose head
is crowned with light,
Still wilt not hear thine inner
God proclaim—
'Turn back, O man, forswear
thy foolish ways.'

2 Earth might be fair and all
men glad and wise:
Age after age their tragic empires rise,
Built while they dream, and in
that dreaming weep:
Would man but wake from out
his haunted sleep,
Earth might be fair and all
men glad and wise.

3 Earth shall be fair, and all her
people one:
Nor till that hour shall God's
whole will be done.

Now, even now, once more from
   earth to sky,;
Peals forth in joy man's old un-
   daunted cry—
'Earth shall be fair, and all her
   folk be one.'

CLIFFORD BAX, 1886–1962

85

O FOR a heart to praise my
   God!
A heart from sin set free;
A heart that always feels thy
   blood,
So freely shed for me;

2 A heart resigned, submissive,
   meek,
My great Redeemer's throne,
Where only Christ is heard to
   speak,
Where Jesus reigns alone;

3 A humble, lowly, contrite heart,
Believing, true, and clean,
Which neither life nor death
   can part
From him that dwells within;

4 A heart in every thought re-
   newed,
And full of love divine,
Perfect and right and pure and
   good,
A copy, Lord, of thine!

5 Thy nature, gracious Lord,
   impart;
Come quickly from above;
Write thy new Name upon my
   heart,
Thy new, best Name of Love.

CHARLES WESLEY, 1707–88

86

Je te salue, mon certain Redempteur

I GREET thee, who my sure
   Redeemer art,
My only Trust and Saviour of
   my heart,
Who pain didst undergo for my
   poor sake;
I pray thee from our hearts all
   cares to take.

2 Thou art the King of mercy and
   of grace,
Reigning omnipotent in every
   place:
So come, O King, and our whole
   being sway;
Shine on us with the light of thy
   pure day.

3 Thou art the Life, by which
   alone we live,
And all our substance and our
   strength receive;
Sustain us by thy faith and by
   thy power,
And give us strength in every
   trying hour.

4 Thou hast the true and perfect
   gentleness,
No harshness hast thou and no
   bitterness:
O grant to us the grace we
   find in thee,
That we may dwell in perfect
   unity.

5 Our hope is in no other save in
   thee;
Our faith is built upon thy
   promise free;
Lord, give us peace, and make
   us calm and sure,
That in thy strength we evermore endure.

Attributed to JOHN CALVIN
1509–64
Tr. ELIZABETH LEE SMITH
1817–98; altered

87

Slane, an old Irish air

B E thou my Vision, O Lord of
   my heart;
Naught be all else to me, save
   that thou art,—
Thou my best thought, by day
   or by night,
Waking or sleeping, thy presence my light.

2 Be thou my Wisdom, thou my
   true Word;
I ever with thee, thou with me,
   Lord;

Thou my great Father, I thy
  true son;
Thou in me dwelling, and I
  with thee one.

3 Be thou my battle-shield,
    sword for the fight;
Be thou my dignity, thou my
    delight,
Thou my soul's shelter, thou
    my high tower:
Raise thou me heaven-ward,
    O Power of my power.

4 Riches I heed not, nor man's
    empty praise,
Thou mine inheritance, now
    and always:
Thou and thou only, first in my
    heart,
High King of Heaven, my
    treasure thou art.

5 High King of Heaven, after
    victory won,
May I reach heaven's joys, O
    bright heaven's Sun!
Heart of my own heart, what-
    ever befall,
Still be my Vision, O Ruler of
    all.

Ancient Irish, tr. MARY BYRNE
1880–1931
versified ELEANOR HULL
1860–1935

88

GOD of grace and God of
  glory,
    On thy people pour thy
    power;
Now fulfil thy Church's story;
    Bring her bud to glorious
    flower.
Grant us wisdom, grant us
    courage,
    For the facing of this hour.

2 Lo, the hosts of evil round us
    Scorn thy Christ, assail his
    ways;
From the fears that long have
    bound us
    Free our hearts to faith and
    praise.

Grant us wisdom, grant us
    courage,
    For the living of these days.

3 Cure thy children's warring
    madness,
    Bend our pride to thy control;
Shame our wanton selfish glad-
    ness,
    Rich in goods and poor in
    soul.
Grant us wisdom, grant us
    courage,
    Lest we miss thy kingdom's
    goal.

4 Set our feet on lofty places,
    Gird our lives that they may
    be
Armoured with all Christ-like
    graces
    In the fight to set men free.
Grant us wisdom, grant us
    courage,
    That we fail not man nor
    thee.

HARRY EMERSON FOSDICK
1878–1969, and Compilers
of The BBC Hymn Book

89

Arglwydd, arwain trwy'r anialwch

GUIDE me, O thou great
  Jehovah,
    Pilgrim through this barren
    land;
I am weak, but thou art mighty;
    Hold me with thy powerful
    hand:
    Bread of heaven, Bread of
    heaven,
  *Feed me till my want is o'er.

2 Open now the crystal fountain,
    Whence the healing stream
    doth flow;
Let the fire and cloudy pillar
    Lead me all my journey
    through:
    Strong Deliverer, strong
    Deliverer,
  Be thou still my strength and
    shield.

3 When I tread the verge of Jor-
    dan,
    Bid my anxious fears subside!

Death of death, and hell's De-
    struction,
  Land me safe on Canaan's
    side!
      Songs of praises, songs of
        praises,
  I will ever give to thee.

        WILLIAM WILLIAMS, 1717–91
        Tr. PETER WILLIAMS, 1727–96

* *When tune (ii)* CWM RHONDDA *is used,
the last line of each verse must be repeated.*

90

L EAD us, heavenly Father,
    lead us
O'er the world's tempestuous
    sea;
Guard us, guide us, keep us, feed
    us,
  For we have no help but thee;
  Yet possessing every blessing
  If our God our Father be.

2 Saviour, breathe forgiveness
    o'er us,
  All our weakness thou dost
    know;
Thou didst tread this earth
    before us,
  Thou didst feel its keenest
    woe;
Lone and dreary, faint and
    weary,
  Through the desert thou didst
    go.

3 Spirit of our God, descending,
  Fill our hearts with heavenly
    joy,
Love with every passion blend-
    ing,
  Pleasure that can never cloy;
Thus provided, pardoned,
    guided,
  Nothing can our peace de-
    stroy.

        JAMES EDMESTON, 1791–1867

91

D EFEND me, Lord, from
    hour to hour,
  And bless thy servant's way;

Increase thy Holy Spirit's
    power
  Within me day by day.

2 Help me to be what I should be,
    And do what I should do,
And ever with thy Spirit free
    My daily life renew.

3 Grant me the courage from
    above
  Which thou dost give to all
Who hear thy word and know
    thy love
  And answer to thy call.

4 So may I daily grow in grace,
    Continuing thine alone,
Until I come to sing thy
    praise
  With saints around thy
    throne.

        GEORGE SNOW

92

L ORD of all hopefulness
    Lord of all joy,
Whose trust, ever childlike, no
    cares could destroy,
Be there at our waking, and
    give us, we pray,
Your bliss in our hearts, Lord,
    at the break of the day.

2 Lord of all eagerness, Lord of
    all faith,
Whose strong hands were
    skilled at the plane and the
    lathe,
Be there at our labours, and
    give us, we pray,
Your strength in our hearts,
    Lord, at the noon of the day.

3 Lord of all kindliness, Lord of
    all grace,
Your hands swift to welcome,
    your arms to embrace,
Be there at our homing, and
    give us, we pray,
Your love in our hearts, Lord,
    at the eve of the day.

4 Lord of all gentleness, Lord of
  all calm,
    Whose voice is contentment,
    whose presence is balm,
  Be there at our sleeping, and
  give us, we pray,
  Your peace in our hearts, Lord,
  at the end of the day.

  JAN STRUTHER, 1901–53

93

LOVING Shepherd of thy
  sheep,
  Keep me, Lord, in safety keep;
  Nothing can thy power with-
  stand;
  None can pluck me from thy
  hand.

2 Loving Shepherd, thou didst
  give
  Thine own life that I might live;
  May I love thee day by day,
  Gladly thy sweet will obey.

3 Loving Shepherd, ever near,
  Teach me still thy voice to hear;
  Suffer not my feet to stray
  From the straight and narrow
  way.

4 Where thou leadest may I go,
  Walking in thy steps below;
  Then, before thy Father's
  throne,
  Jesus, claim me for thine own.

  JANE ELIZA LEESON, 1809–81, altered
  From St. John 10: 11, 27, 28

94

O JESUS, strong and pure
  and true,
  Before thy feet we bow;
  The grace of earlier years re-
  new,
  And lead us onward now.

2 The joyous life that year by
  year
  Within these walls is stored,
  The golden hope, the gladsome
  cheer,
  We bring to thee, O Lord.

3 Our faith endow with keener
  powers,
    With warmer glow our love;
  And draw these halting hearts
  of ours
  From earth to things above.

4 In paths our bravest ones have
  trod,
    O make us strong to go,
  That we may give our lives to
  God,
    In serving man below.

5 So hence shall flow fresh
  strength and grace,
    As from a full-fed spring,
  To make the world a better
  place,
  And life a worthier thing.

  WILLIAM WALSHAM HOW, 1823–97

95

Keep dignity temperance

O LIGHT that knew no
  dawn,
    That shines to endless day,
  All things in earth and heaven
  Are lustred by thy ray;
  No eye can to thy throne as-
  cend,
  Nor mind thy brightness com-
  prehend.

2 Thy grace, O Father, give,
    That I may serve in fear;
  Above all boons, I pray,
    Grant me thy voice to
    hear;
  From sin thy child in mercy
  free,
  And let me dwell in light with
  thee.

3 That, cleansed from stain of
  sin,
    I may meet homage give,
  And, pure in heart, behold
    Thy beauty while I live;
  Clean hands in holy worship
  raise,
  And thee, O Christ my Saviour,
  praise.

4 In supplication meek
    To thee I bend the knee;
  O Christ, when thou shalt
  come,
    In love remember me,

322

And in thy Kingdom, by thy grace,
Grant me a humble servant's place.

5   Thy grace, O Father, give,
    I humbly thee implore;
And let thy mercy bless
    Thy servant more and more.
All grace and glory be to thee,
From age to age eternally.

ST. GREGORY NAZIANZEN, 329–89
Tr. JOHN BROWNLIE, 1857–1925

96   *Verborgne Gottesliebe du*

THOU hidden Love of God, whose height,
    Whose depth unfathomed, no man knows,
I see from far thy beauteous light,
    Inly I sigh for thy repose;
My heart is pained, nor can it be
At rest till it finds rest in thee.

2 Thy secret voice invites me still
    The sweetness of thy yoke to prove;
And fain I would; but, though my will
    Seem fixed, yet wide my passions rove;
Yet hindrances strew all the way;
I aim at thee, yet from thee stray.

3 'Tis mercy all, that thou hast brought
    My mind to seek her peace in thee;
Yet, while I seek but find thee not,
    No peace my wandering soul shall see.
O when shall all my wanderings end,
And all my steps to thee-ward tend?

4 Is there a thing beneath the sun
    That strives with thee my heart to share?

Ah! tear it thence, and reign alone,
    The Lord of every motion there;
Then shall my heart from earth be free,
When it has found repose in thee.

GERHARD TERSTEEGEN, 1697–1769
Tr. JOHN WESLEY, 1703–91

97   *For children*

FATHER, lead me, day by day,
Ever in thy perfect way;
Teach me to be pure and true;
Show me what I ought to do.

2 When in danger, make me brave;
Make me know that thou canst save;
Keep me safe by thy dear side;
Let me in thy love abide.

3 When I'm tempted to do wrong,
Make me steadfast, wise, and strong;
And, when all alone I stand,
Shield me with thy mighty hand.

4 When my heart is full of glee,
Help me to remember thee,
Happy most of all to know
That my Father loves me so.

5 May I do the good I know,
Be thy loving child below,
Then at last go home to thee,
Evermore thy child to be.

JOHN PAGE HOPPS, 1834–1912
altered

98   *For children*

JESUS, Saviour ever mild,
    Born for us a little Child
Of the Virgin undefiled:
    Hear us, Holy Jesus.

2 Jesus, Son of God most high,
Who didst in the manger lie,
Who upon the cross didst die,
            Hear us, Holy Jesus.

3 From all pride and vain conceit,
From all spite and angry heat,
From all lying and deceit,
            Save us, Holy Jesus.

4 From refusing to obey,
From the love of our own way,
From forgetfulness to pray,
            Save us, Holy Jesus.

5 By the Name we bow before,
Human Name, which evermore
All the hosts of heaven adore,
            Save us, Holy Jesus.
            RICHARD FREDERICK LITTLEDALE
            1833–90, and others

99   *For younger children*

FATHER, we thank thee for
    the night,
And for the pleasant morning
    light;
For rest and food and loving
    care,
And all that makes the day so
    fair.

2 Help us to do the things we
    should,
To be to others kind and good;
In all we do at work or play
To grow more loving every day.
            Ascribed to REBECCA J. WESTON
            19th century

100   *For younger children*

JESUS, Friend of little children,
    Be a friend to me;
Take my hand and ever keep
    me
    Close to thee.

2 Teach me how to grow in goodness
    Daily as I grow;
Thou hast been a child, and surely
    Thou dost know.

3 Never leave me nor forsake me,
    Ever be my Friend;
For I need thee from life's dawning
    To its end.
            WALTER JOHN MATHAMS
            1853–1931

INVOCATION

101   PSALM 106, verses 1–5, 48

GIVE praise and thanks unto
    the Lord,
    For bountiful is he;
His tender mercy doth endure
    Unto eternity.

2 God's mighty works who can
    express?
    Or show forth all his praise?
Blessèd are they that judgment
    keep,
    And justly do always.

3 Remember me, Lord, with that
    love
    Which thou to thine dost bear;
With thy salvation, O my God,
    To visit me draw near:

4 That I thy chosen's good may
    see,
    And in their joy rejoice;
And may with thine inheritance
    Triumph with cheerful voice.

5 Blest be Jehovah, Israel's God,
    To all eternity:
Let all the people say, Amen.
    Praise to the Lord give ye.

102 PSALM 90, verses 1, 2, 14, 16, 17

LORD, thou hast been our
dwelling-place
In generations all.
Before thou ever hadst brought
forth
The mountains great or
small;

2 Ere ever thou hadst formed the
earth,
And all the world abroad;
Even thou from everlasting art
To everlasting God.

3 O with thy tender mercies,
Lord,
Us early satisfy;
So we rejoice shall all our days,
And still be glad in thee.

4 O let thy work and power ap-
pear
Thy servants' face before;
And show unto their children
dear
Thy glory evermore:

5 And let the beauty of the Lord
Our God be us upon:
Our handy-works establish
thou,
Establish them each one.

6 *To Father, Son, and Holy Ghost,*
The God whom we adore,
Be glory, as it was, and is,
And shall be evermore. Amen.

103

BREATHE on me, Breath
of God;
Fill me with life anew,
That I may love what thou dost
love,
And do what thou wouldst
do.

2 Breathe on me, Breath of
God,
Until my heart is pure,
Until with thee I will one will,
To do and to endure.

3 Breathe on me, Breath of
God,
Till I am wholly thine,
Until this earthly part of me
Glows with thy fire divine.

4 Breathe on me, Breath of
God;
So shall I never die,
But live with thee the perfect
life
Of thine eternity.
EDWIN HATCH, 1835–89

104

COME, Holy Spirit, come;
Let thy bright beams
arise;
Dispel the darkness from our
minds,
And open all our eyes.

2 Cheer our desponding hearts,
Thou heavenly Paraclete;
Give us to lie with humble hope
At our Redeemer's feet.

3 Revive our drooping faith;
Our doubts and fears remove;
And kindle in our breasts the
flame
Of never-dying love.

4 Convince us of our sin;
Then lead to Jesus' blood,
And to our wondering view re-
veal
The secret love of God.

5 'Tis thine to cleanse the
heart,
To sanctify the soul,
To pour fresh life on every part,
And new create the whole.

6 Dwell, therefore, in our
hearts;
Our minds from bondage
free;
Then shall we know and praise
and love
The Father, Son, and thee.
JOSEPH HART, 1712–68

105

Veni, sancte Spiritus

COME, thou Holy Paraclete,
  And from thy celestial
    seat
  Send thy light and brilliancy.
Father of the poor, draw near;
Giver of all gifts, be here;
*Come, the soul's true radiancy.

2 Come, of comforters the best,
Of the soul the sweetest guest,
  Come in toil refreshingly.
Thou in labour rest most sweet,
Thou art shadow from the heat,
  Comfort in adversity.

3 O thou Light, most pure and
    blest,
  Shine within the inmost breast
Of thy faithful company.
  Where thou art not, man hath
    naught;
  Every holy deed and thought
Comes from thy Divinity.

4 What is soiled make thou pure;
  What is wounded, work its
    cure;
    What is parchèd fructify.
Fill thy faithful, who confide
In thy power to guard and
    guide,
  With thy sevenfold mystery.

13th century
Tr. JOHN MASON NEALE, 1818–66

* *The last line of each verse is repeated.*

106

HOLY Spirit, Truth Divine,
  Dawn upon this soul of
    mine;
  Word of God, and inward
    Light,
  Wake my spirit, clear my sight.

2 Holy Spirit, Love Divine,
Glow within this heart of mine;
Kindle every high desire;
Perish self in thy pure fire.

3 Holy Spirit, Power Divine,
Fill and nerve this will of mine;
By thee may I strongly live,
Bravely bear, and nobly strive.

4 Holy Spirit, Right Divine,
King within my conscience
    reign;
Be my law, and I shall be
Firmly bound, for ever free.

5 Holy Spirit, Peace Divine,
Still this restless heart of mine;
Speak to calm this tossing sea,
Stayed in thy tranquillity.

6 Holy Spirit, Joy Divine,
Gladden thou this heart of
    mine;
In the desert ways I sing,
"Spring, O Well, for ever
    spring!"

SAMUEL LONGFELLOW, 1819–92

107

SPIRIT Divine, attend our
    prayers,
  And make this house thy
    home;
Descend with all thy gracious
    powers;
  O come, great Spirit, come!

2 Come as the light: to us reveal
Our emptiness and woe;
And lead us in those paths of
    life
Where all the righteous go.

3 Come as the fire: and purge our
    hearts
Like sacrificial flame;
Let our whole soul an offering
    be
To our Redeemer's Name.

4 Come as the dove: and spread
    thy wings,
  The wings of peaceful love;
And let thy Church on earth
    become
Blest as the Church above.

5 Come as the wind, with rushing
    sound
  And Pentecostal grace,
That all of woman born may
    see
  The glory of thy face.

6 Spirit Divine, attend our
      prayers;
    Make a lost world thy home;
  Descend with all thy gracious
      powers;
    O come, great Spirit, come!!

ANDREW REED, 1787–1862

108

S PIRIT of God, descend upon
      my heart;
    Wean it from earth; through
      all its pulses move;
  Stoop to my weakness, mighty
      as thou art,
    And make me love thee as
      I ought to love.

2 I ask no dream, no prophet-
      ecstasies,
    No sudden rending of the
      veil of clay,
  No angel-visitant, no opening
      skies;
    But take the dimness of my
      soul away.

3 Hast thou not bid me love thee,
      God and King—
    All, all thine own, soul, heart,
      and strength, and mind?
  I see thy cross—there teach my
      heart to cling:
    O let me seek thee, and O let
      me find!!

4 Teach me to feel that thou art
      always nigh;
    Teach me the struggles of the
      soul to bear,
  To check the rising doubt, the
      rebel sigh;
    Teach me the patience of un-
      answered prayer.

5 Teach me to love thee as thine
      angels love,
    One holy passion filling all my
      frame—
  The baptism of the heaven-
      descended Dove,
    My heart an altar, and thy
      love the flame.

GEORGE CROLY, 1780–1860

109

S PIRIT of God, that moved of
      old
    Upon the waters' darkened
      face,
  Come, when our faithless hearts
      are cold,
    And stir them with an in-
      ward grace.

2 Thou that art power and peace
      combined,
    All highest strength, all
      purest love,
  The rushing of the mighty
      wind,
    The brooding of the gentle
      dove,

3 Come, give us still thy powerful
      aid,
    And urge us on, and keep us
      thine;
  Nor leave the hearts that once
      were made
    Fit temples for thy grace
      divine;

4 Nor let us quench thy sevenfold
      light;
    But still with softest breath-
      ings stir
  Our wayward souls, and lead us
      right,
    O Holy Ghost, the Com-
      forter.

CECIL FRANCES ALEXANDER
1818–95

110

O THOU who camest from
      above,
    The pure celestial fire to im-
      part,
  Kindle a flame of sacred love
    On the mean altar of my
      heart.

2 Jesus, confirm my heart's de-
      sire
    To work, and speak, and
      think for thee;
  Still let me guard the holy fire,
    And still stir up thy gift in
      me:

3 Ready for all thy perfect will,
My acts of faith and love repeat,
Till death thy endless mercies seal,
And make the sacrifice complete.

CHARLES WESLEY, 1707–88

III

JESUS, good above all other,
Gentle child of gentle mother,
In a stable born our brother,
Give us grace to persevere.

2 Jesus, cradled in a manger,
For us facing every danger,
Living as a homeless stranger,
Make we thee our King most dear.

3 Jesus, for thy people dying,
Risen Master, death defying,
Lord in heaven, thy grace supplying,
Keep us to thy presence near.

Jesus, who our sorrows bearest,
All our thoughts and hopes thou sharest;

Thou to man the truth declarest;
Help us all thy truth to hear.

5 Lord, in all our doings guide us;
Pride and hate shall ne'er divide us;
We'll go on with thee beside us,
And with joy we'll persevere!

PERCY DEARMER, 1867–1936

112 *For younger children*

JESUS Christ, I look to thee;
Thou shalt my example be;
Thou art holy, just, and mild;
Thou wast once a little child.

2 Make me, Jesus, what thou art;
Give me thy obedient heart;
Thou art merciful and kind;
Let me have thy loving mind.

3 I shall then show forth thy praise,
Serve thee all my happy days;
Then the world shall always see
Christ, the Holy Child, in me.

CHARLES WESLEY, 1707–88, altered

ILLUMINATION

113

BLEST are the pure in heart,
For they shall see their God:
The secret of the Lord is theirs;
Their soul is Christ's abode.

2 The Lord, who left the sky
Our life and peace to bring,
And dwelt in lowliness with men,
Their Pattern and their King,—

3 Still to the lowly soul
He doth himself impart,
And for his dwelling and his throne
Chooseth the pure in heart.

4 Lord, we thy presence seek;
Ours may this blessing be;
O give the pure and lowly heart,
A temple meet for thee.

vv. 1 and 3 JOHN KEBLE
1792–1866
vv. 2 and 4 from Hall's
Psalms and Hymns, 1836

114

CHRIST, whose glory fills the skies,
Christ, the true, the only Light,
Sun of Righteousness, arise,
Triumph o'er the shades of night.

Dayspring from on high, be near;
Daystar, in my heart appear.

2 Dark and cheerless is the morn
Unaccompanied by thee;
Joyless is the day's return,
Till thy mercy's beams I see,
Till they inward light impart,
Glad my eyes, and warm my heart.

3 Visit, then, this soul of mine;
Pierce the gloom of sin and grief;
Fill me, Radiancy Divine;
Scatter all my unbelief;
More and more thyself display,
Shining to the perfect day.

CHARLES WESLEY, 1707–88

115

Discendi, Amor santo

COME down, O Love Divine,
Seek thou this soul of mine,
And visit it with thine own ardour glowing;
O Comforter, draw near,
Within my heart appear,
And kindle it, thy holy flame bestowing.

2 O let it freely burn,
Till earthly passions turn
To dust and ashes, in its heat consuming;
And let thy glorious light
Shine ever on my sight,
And clothe me round, the while my path illuming.

3 Let holy charity
Mine outward vesture be,
And lowliness become mine inner clothing;
True lowliness of heart,
Which takes the humbler part,
And o'er its own shortcomings weeps with loathing.

4 And so the yearning strong,
With which the soul will long,
Shall far outpass the power of human telling;

For none can guess its grace,
Till he become the place
Wherein the Holy Spirit makes his dwelling.

BIANCO DA SIENA, ?–1434
Tr. RICHARD FREDERICK
LITTLEDALE, 1833–90

116

COME, gracious Spirit, heavenly Dove,
With light and comfort from above;
Be thou our Guardian, thou our Guide;
O'er every thought and step preside.

2 The light of truth to us display,
And make us know and choose thy way;
Plant holy fear in every heart,
That we from God may ne'er depart.

3 Lead us to Christ, the living Way;
Nor let us from his pastures stray:
Lead us to holiness, the road
That we must take to dwell with God.

4 Lead us to heaven, that we may share
Fullness of joy for ever there;
Lead us to God, our final rest,
To be with him for ever blest.

SIMON BROWNE, 1680–1732

117

COMMAND thy blessing from above,
O God, on all assembled here;

Behold us with a Father's love,
While we look up with filial fear.

2 Command thy blessing, Jesus, Lord;;
May we thy true disciples be;;
Speak to each heart the mighty word;;
Say to the weakest, 'Follow Me.'

3 Command thy blessing in this hour,
Spirit of truth, and fill this place
With humbling and exalting power,
With quickening and confirming grace.

4 O thou, our Maker, Saviour, Guide,
One true eternal God confessed,
May naught in life or death divide
The saints in thy communion blest.

5 With thee and these for ever bound,
May all who here in prayer unite,
With hearts and songs thy throne surround,
Rest in thy love, and reign in light.
JAMES MONTGOMERY, 1771–1854

118
Veni, Creator Spiritus

CREATOR Spirit! by whose aid
The world's foundations first were laid,
Come, visit every pious mind,
Come, pour thy joys on human kind;
From sin and sorrow set us free,
*And make thy temples worthy thee.

2 O Source of uncreated light,
The Father's promised Paraclete,

Thrice Holy Fount, thrice Holy Fire,
Our hearts with heavenly love inspire;;
Come, and thy sacred unction bring
To sanctify us while we sing.

3 Plenteous of grace, descend from high,
Rich in thy sevenfold energy;;
Thou Strength of his almighty hand,
Whose power does heaven and earth command,
Give us thyself, that we may see
The Father and the Son by thee.

4 Immortal Honour, endless fame
Attend the Almighty Father's Name;
The Saviour Son be glorified,
Who for lost man's redemption died;;
And equal adoration be,
Eternal Paraclete, to thee. Amen.

9th century
Tr. JOHN DRYDEN, 1631–1700
Adapted, JOHN WESLEY, 1703–91
** The last line of each verse is repeated.

119
ENTER thy courts, thou Word of life,
My joy and peace;;
Let the glad sound therein be heard,
Bid plaintive sadness cease.
Comfort my heart, thou Truth most fair;;
O enter in,
Chasing despair and earthborn care,
My woe and slothful sin.

2 Glad was the time when I would sing
The heavenly praise;;
Happy my heart when thou wert nigh,
Directing all my ways.
O let thy light, thy joy again
Return to me;;
Nor in disdain from me refrain,
Who lift my soul to thee.

In heaven and earth thy law
  endures,
Thy word abides:
My troubled flesh trembleth in
  awe,
My heart in terror hides.
Yet still on thee my hope is set;;
On thee, O Lord,
I will await and not forget
The promise of thy word.
ROBERT BRIDGES, 1844–1930

120

LORD of beauty, thine the
  splendour
    Shown in earth and sky and
    sea,
Burning sun and moonlight
  tender,
    Hill and river, flower and
    tree;
Lest we fail our praise to render,
    Touch our eyes that we may
    see!!

2 Lord of wisdom, whom obeying
    Mighty waters ebb and flow,,
    While unhasting, undelaying,,
    Planets on their courses go;;
  In thy laws thyself displaying,,
    Teach our minds thy truth to
    know!!

3 Lord of life, alone sustaining
    All below and all above,,
  Lord of love, by whose ordain-
    ing
    Sun and stars sublimely
    move,,
  In our earthly spirits reigning,,
    Lift our hearts, that we may
    love!!

4 Lord of beauty, bid us own
    thee,,
    Lord of truth, our footsteps
    guide,,
  Till as love our hearts enthrone
    thee,,
    And, with vision purified,,
  Lord of all, when all have
    known thee,,
    Thou in all art glorified!!
CYRIL ARGENTINE ALINGTON
1872–1955

121

THOU art the Way:: to thee
  alone
    From sin and death we flee;;
And he who would the Father
  seek
    Must seek him, Lord, by thee.

2 Thou art the Truth:: thy word
  alone
    True wisdom can impart;;
  Thou only canst inform the
    mind,,
    And purify the heart.

3 Thou art the Life:: the rending
  tomb
    Proclaims thy conquering
    arm;;
  And those who put their trust in
    thee
    Nor death nor hell shall harm.

4 Thou art the Way,, the Truth,,
  the Life::
    Grant us that way to know,,
  That truth to keep, that life to
    win,,
    Whose joys eternal flow.
GEORGE WASHINGTON DOANE
1799–1859

122

COME, Holy Ghost, our
  hearts inspire,,
    Let us thine influence prove,,
  Source of the old prophetic fire,,
    Fountain of life and love.

2 Come, Holy Ghost, for moved
  by thee
    The prophets wrote and
    spoke;;
  Unlock the truth, thyself the
    key;;
    Unseal the sacred book.

3 Expand thy wings, celestial
  Dove;;
    Brood o'er our nature's night;;
  On our disordered spirits move,,
    And let there now be light.

4 God through himself we them
  shall know,,
    If thou within us shine,,

And sound, with all thy saints below,
The depths of love divine.

CHARLES WESLEY, 1707–88

123 *For children*

HUSHED was the evening hymn,
The temple courts were dark,
The lamp was burning dim
Before the sacred ark,
When suddenly a voice Divine
Rang through the silence of the shrine.

2 The old man, meek and mild,
The priest of Israel, slept;
His watch the temple child,
The little Levite, kept;
And what from Eli's sense was sealed
The Lord to Hannah's son revealed.

3 O give me Samuel's ear,
The open ear, O Lord,
Alive and quick to hear
Each whisper of thy word,—
Like him to answer at thy call,
And to obey thee first of all.

4 O give me Samuel's heart,
A lowly heart, that waits
Where in thy house thou art,
Or watches at thy gates
By day and night,—a heart that still
Moves at the breathing of thy will.

5 O give me Samuel's mind,
A sweet unmurmuring faith,
Obedient and resigned
To thee in life and death,
That I may read, with child-like eyes,
Truths that are hidden from the wise.

JAMES DRUMMOND BURNS
1823–64

124 *For younger children*

HOLY Spirit, hear us;
Help us while we sing;
Breathe into the music
Of the praise we bring.

2 Holy Spirit, prompt us
When we kneel to pray;
Nearer come, and teach us
What we ought to say.

3 Holy Spirit, shine thou
On the book we read;
Gild its holy pages
With the light we need.

4 Holy Spirit, give us
Each a lowly mind;
Make us more like Jesus,
Gentle, pure, and kind.

5 Holy Spirit, help us
Daily, by thy might,
What is wrong to conquer,
And to choose the right.

WILLIAM HENRY PARKER
1845–1929

HOLY SCRIPTURE

125 PSALM 19, verses 7–10, 14

GOD'S law is perfect, and converts
The soul in sin that lies;
God's testimony is most sure,
And makes the simple wise.

2 The statutes of the Lord are right,
And do rejoice the heart:
The Lord's command is pure, and doth
Light to the eyes impart.

3 Unspotted is the fear of God,
  And doth endure for ever:
The judgments of the Lord are
  true
  And righteous altogether.

4 They more than gold, yea, much
  fine gold,
  To be desirèd are:
Than honey, honey from the
  comb
  That droppeth, sweeter far.

5 The words which from my
  mouth proceed,
  The thoughts sent from my
  heart,
Accept, O Lord, for thou my
  strength
  And my Redeemer art.

6 *To Father, Son, and Holy Ghost,*
  The God whom we adore,
Be glory, as it was, and is,
  And shall be evermore. Amen.

126 From PSALM 19, verses
  7–14

GOD'S perfect law revives the
  soul,
His word makes wise the simple;
God's clear commands rejoice
  the heart,
His light the eye enlightens;
God's fear is pure, his judg-
  ments just,
More to be sought than pure
  fine gold,
Sweeter by far than honey.

2 Lord, who can tell the secret
  faults
That have dominion o'er me?
Hold back thy servant from
  self-will
And break its power to bind me.
May all I think and all I say
Be now acceptable to thee,
My Rock and my Redeemer.

IAN PITT-WATSON
From *The New English Bible* version
of Psalm 19

127 PSALM 119, verses 33–40

TEACH me, O Lord, the perfect way
Of thy precepts divine,

And to observe it to the end
  I shall my heart incline.

2 Give understanding unto me,
  So keep thy law shall I;
Yea, even with my whole heart
  I shall
  Observe it carefully.

3 In thy law's path make me to
  go;
  For I delight therein.
My heart unto thy testimonies,
  And not to greed, incline.

4 Turn thou away my sight and
  eyes
  From viewing vanity;
And in thy good and holy way
  Be pleased to quicken me.

5 Confirm to me thy gracious
  word,
  Which I did gladly hear,
Even to thy servant, Lord, who
  is
  Devoted to thy fear.

6 Turn thou away my feared re-
  proach;
  For good thy judgments be.
Lo, for thy precepts I have
  longed;
  In thy truth quicken me.

7 *To Father, Son, and Holy Ghost,*
  The God whom we adore,
Be glory, as it was, and is,
  And shall be evermore. Amen.

128

BOOK of books, our people's
  strength,
  Statesman's, teacher's, hero's
  treasure,
Bringing freedom, spreading
  truth,
  Shedding light that none can
  measure—
  Wisdom comes to those
  who know thee,
  All the best we have we
  owe thee.

43   C

2 Thank we those who toiled in
    thought,
    Many diverse scrolls complet-
      ing,
Poets, prophets, scholars, saints,
    Each his word from God re-
      peating;
      Till they came, who told
        the story
      Of the Word, and showed
        his glory.

3 Praise we God, who hath in-
    spired
      Those whose wisdom still
        directs us;
Praise him for the Word made
    flesh,
    For the Spirit who protects
      us.
      Light of Knowledge, ever
        burning,
      Shed on us thy deathless
        learning.

             PERCY DEARMER, 1867–1936

129   *Liebster Jesu, wir sind hier*

LOOK upon us, blessèd Lord,
   Take our wandering thoughts
    and guide us:
We have come to hear thy
    word:
With thy teaching now provide
    us,
That, from earth's distrac-
    tions turning,
We thy message may be
    learning.

2   For thy Spirit's radiance
    bright
We, assembled here, are hop-
    ing:
If thou shouldst withhold the
    light,
In the dark our souls were
    groping:
    In word, deed, and thought
    direct us:
    Thou, none other, canst cor-
    rect us.

3   Brightness of the Father's
    face,
Light of Light, from God pro-
    ceeding,
Make us ready in this place:

Ear and heart await thy leading.
    In our study, prayers, and
    praising,
    May our souls find their
    upraising.

         TOBIAS CLAUSNITZER, 1619–84
         Tr. ROBERT MACALISTER
                 1870–1950

130

LORD, thy word abideth,
   And our footsteps guideth;
Who its truth believeth
Light and joy receiveth.

2 When our foes are near us,
Then thy word doth cheer us,
Word of consolation,
Message of salvation.

3 When the storms are o'er us,
And dark clouds before us,
Then its light directeth,
And our way protecteth.

4 Who can tell the pleasure,
Who recount the treasure,
By thy word imparted
To the simple-hearted?

5 Word of mercy, giving
Succour to the living;
Word of life, supplying
Comfort to the dying!

6 O that we, discerning
Its most holy learning,
Lord, may love and fear thee,
Evermore be near thee!

         HENRY WILLIAMS BAKER
                 1821–77

131

LIGHT of the world! for ever,
   ever shining,
    There is no change in thee;
True Light of Life, all joy and
    health enshrining,
    Thou canst not fade nor flee.

2 Thou hast arisen, but thou
    descendest never;
    Today shines as the past;
All that thou wast thou art, and
    shalt be ever,
    Brightness from first to last.

3 Night visits not thy sky, nor
    storm, nor sadness;—
  Day fills up all its blue,—
Unfailing beauty, and unfalter-
    ing gladness,
  And love for ever new.

4 Light of the world, undimming
    and unsetting!
  O shine each mist away;
Banish the fear, the falsehood,
    and the fretting;
  Be our unchanging Day.
        HORATIUS BONAR, 1808–89

132

TELL me the old, old story
  Of unseen things above,
Of Jesus and his glory,
  Of Jesus and his love.
Tell me the story simply,
  As to a little child;
For I am weak and weary,
  And helpless, and defiled.
   Tell me the old, old story,
   Tell me the old, old story,
   Tell me the old, old story,
   Of Jesus and his love.

2 Tell me the story slowly,
  That I may take it in,—
That wonderful redemption,
  God's remedy for sin.
Tell me the story often,
  For I forget so soon;
The early dew of morning
  Has passed away at noon.

3 Tell me the story softly,
  With earnest tones and grave;
Remember, I'm the sinner
  Whom Jesus came to save.
Tell me the story always,
  If you would really be,
In any time of trouble,
  A comforter to me.

4 Tell me the same old story
  When you have cause to fear
That this world's empty glory
  Is costing me too dear.
Yes, and when that world's
    glory
  Shall dawn upon my soul,

Tell me the old, old story,
  'Christ Jesus makes thee
    whole.'
    ARABELLA CATHERINE HANKEY
             1834–1911

133

BREAK forth, O living light
  of God,
Upon the world's dark hour!
Show us the way the Master
  trod;
Reveal his saving power.

2 Remove the veil of ancient
    words,
  Their message long obscure;
Restore to us thy truth, O God,
  And make its meaning sure.

3 O let thy Word be light anew
  To every nation's life;
Unite us in thy will, O Lord,
  And end all sinful strife.

4 O may one Lord, one Faith, one
    Word,
  One Spirit lead us still;
And one great Church go forth
    in might
  To work God's perfect will.
     FRANK VON CHRISTIERSON

134

HEAVENLY Father, may
  thy blessing
  Rest upon thy children now,
When in praise thy Name they
    hallow,
  When in prayer to thee they
    bow:
In the wondrous story reading
  Of the Lord of truth and
    grace,
May they see thy love reflected
  In the light of his dear face.

2 May they learn from this great
    story
  All the arts of friendliness;
Truthful speech and honest
    action,
  Courage, patience, steadfast-
    ness;

How to master self and temper,
  How to make their conduct
    fair;
When to speak and when be
    silent,
  When to do and when forbear.

3 May his Spirit wise and holy
  With his gifts their spirits
    bless,
Make them loving, joyous,
    peaceful,
  Rich in goodness, gentleness,
Strong in self-control, and
    faithful,
  Kind in thought and deed; for he
Sayeth, 'What ye do for others
  Ye are doing unto me'.

WILLIAM CHARTER PIGGOTT,
1872–1943

*See also certain hymns in Part II,
Section 3 (The Holy Spirit in the Church)*

*The following hymns are appropriate as
opening processional hymns on special
occasions:*

Advent: O come, O come, Emmanuel, 165
Christmas: Of the Father's love begotten,
  198
Palm Sunday: All glory, laud, and honour,
  233
Passiontide: Sing, my tongue, 256
Easter: 'Welcome, happy morning', 272
Ascension: The head that once, 286
Pentecost: Come, Holy Ghost, our souls
  inspire, 342
Trinity: Holy, holy, holy, 352
  I bind unto myself today, 402
All Saints: For all the saints, 534
Rogation and Harvest: We plough the
  fields, 620
Holy Communion: Deck thyself, my soul,
  567

II

THE WORD OF GOD:
HIS MIGHTY ACTS

CREATION AND PROVIDENCE

135   PSALM 148 (ii)

THE Lord of heaven confess,
  On high his glory raise.
Him let all angels bless,
  Him all his armies praise.
    Him glorify
      Sun, moon, and stars;
      Ye higher spheres,
    And cloudy sky.

2 From God your beings are,
    Him therefore famous make;
  You all created were,
    When he the word but spake.
      And from that place,
        Where fixed you be
        By his decree,
      You cannot pass.

3 Praise God from earth below,
    Ye dragons, and ye deeps:
  Fire, hail, clouds, wind, and
      snow,
    Whom in command he keeps.
      Praise ye his Name,
        Hills great and small,
        Trees low and tall;
      Beasts wild and tame;

4 All things that creep or fly.
    Ye kings, ye vulgar throng,
  All princes mean or high;
    Both men and virgins young,
      Even young and old,
        Exalt his Name;
        For much his fame
      Should be extolled.

5 O let God's Name be praised
    Above both earth and sky;

For he his saints hath raised,
  And set their horn on high;
    Even those that be
      Of Israel's race,
      Near to his grace.
    The Lord praise ye.

6 *To God the Father, Son,*
    And Spirit ever blest,
  Eternal Three in One,
    All worship be addressed,
      As heretofore
        It was, is now,
        And still shall be
      For evermore. Amen.

136   PSALM 147, verses 1–5

PRAISE ye the Lord; for it is
      good
  Praise to our God to sing:
For it is pleasant, and to praise
  It is a comely thing.

2 God doth build up Jerusalem;
    And he it is alone
  That the dispersed of Israel
    Doth gather into one.

3 Those that are broken in their
      heart,
    And grievèd in their minds,
  He healeth, and their painful
      wounds
    He tenderly up-binds.

4 He counts the number of the
      stars;
    He names them every one.
  Great is our Lord, and of great
      power;
    His wisdom search can none.

5 *To Father, Son, and Holy Ghost,*
  The God whom we adore,
Be glory, as it was, and is,
  And shall be evermore. Amen.

137 PSALM 136 (ii), verses 1–5,
          23–26

PRAISE God, for he is kind:
    His mercy lasts for aye.
Give thanks with heart and
    mind
To God of gods alway:
    For certainly
      His mercies dure
      Most firm and sure
    Eternally.

2 The Lord of lords praise ye,
  Whose mercies still endure.
  Great wonders only he
  Doth work by his great power:

3 Give praise to his great name,
  Who, by his wisdom high,
  The heaven above did frame,
  And built the lofty sky:

4 Who hath remembered us
  When in our low estate;
  And hath delivered us
  From foes who did us hate:

5 Who to all flesh gives food;
  For his grace faileth never.
  Give thanks to God most good,
  The God of heaven, for ever:

6 *To God the Father, Son,*
    And Spirit ever blest,
  Eternal Three in One,
    All worship be addressed,
      As heretofore
        It was, is now,
        And still shall be
      For evermore. Amen.

138 PSALM 8, verses 1, 3–5

HOW excellent in all the
    earth,
Lord, our Lord, is thy Name!
Who hast thy glory far advanced
  Above the starry frame.

2 When I look up unto the
    heavens,
    Which thine own fingers
      framed,
  Unto the moon, and to the
    stars,
    Which were by thee ordained;

3 Then say I, What is man, that
    he
    Remembered is by thee?
  Or what the son of man, that
    thou
    So kind to him should'st be?

4 For thou a little lower hast
    Him than the angels made;
  With glory and with dignity
    Thou crownèd hast his head.

5 *To Father, Son, and Holy Ghost,*
    The God whom we adore,
  Be glory, as it was, and is,
    And shall be evermore. Amen.

139 PSALM 121

I TO the hills will lift mine eyes.
    From whence doth come
      mine aid?
My safety cometh from the
    Lord,
    Who heaven and earth hath
      made.

2 Thy foot he'll not let slide, nor
    will
    He slumber that thee keeps.
  Behold, he that keeps Israel,
    He slumbers not, nor sleeps.

3 The Lord thee keeps, the Lord
    thy shade
    On thy right hand doth stay:
  The moon by night thee shall
    not smite,
    Nor yet the sun by day.

4 The Lord shall keep thy soul;
    he shall
    Preserve thee from all ill.
  Henceforth thy going out and
    in
    God keep for ever will.

5 *To Father, Son, and Holy Ghost,*
    The God whom we adore,
  Be glory, as it was, and is,
    And shall be evermore. Amen.

140 PSALM 93

THE Lord doth reign, and
    clothed is he
With majesty most bright;
His works do show him clothed
    to be,
And girt about with might.
The world is also stablishèd,
    That it cannot depart.
Thy throne is fixed of old, and
    thou
From everlasting art.

2 The floods, O Lord, have lifted
    up,
    They lifted up their voice;
The floods have lifted up their
    waves,
    And made a mighty noise.
But yet the Lord, that is on
    high,
    Is more of might by far
Than noise of many waters is,
    Or great sea-billows are.

3 Thy testimonies every one
    In faithfulness excel;
And holiness for ever, Lord,
    Thine house becometh well.
To Father, Son, and Holy Ghost,
*   The God whom we adore,*
Be glory, as it was, and is,
*   And shall be evermore. Amen.*

141

O LORD of every shining
    constellation
    That wheels in splendour
        through the midnight sky;
Grant us thy Spirit's true
    illumination
    To read the secrets of thy
        work on high.

2 And thou who mad'st the
    atom's hidden forces,
    Whose laws its mighty ener-
        gies fulfil;
Teach us, to whom thou giv'st
    such rich resources,
    In all we use, to serve thy
        holy will.

3 O Life, awaking life in cell and
    tissue,
    From flower to bird, from
        beast to brain of man;
O help us trace, from birth to
    final issue,
    The sure unfolding of thine
        ageless plan.

4 Thou who hast stamped thine
    image on thy creatures,
    And though they marred that
        image, lov'st them still;
Uplift our eyes to Christ, that
    in his features
    We may discern the beauty
        of thy will.

5 Great Lord of nature, shaping
    and renewing,
    Who mad'st us more than
        nature's sons to be;
Help us to tread, with grace our
    souls enduing,
    The road to life and immor-
        tality.
        ALBERT FREDERICK BAYLY

142   *Sei Lob und Ehr' dem*
           höchsten Gut

SING praise to God who reigns
    above,
    The God of all creation,
The God of power, the God of
    love,
    The God of our salvation;
With healing balm my soul he
    fills,
And every faithless murmur
    stills:
    To God all praise and glory!

2 The angel host, O King of kings,
    Thy praise for ever telling,
In earth and sky all living
    things
    Beneath thy shadow dwelling,
Adore the wisdom which could
    span,
And power which formed crea-
    tion's plan:

3 O ye who name Christ's holy
    Name,
    Give God all praise and glory:

All ye who own his power, pro-
claim
Aloud the wondrous story.
Cast each false idol from his
throne,
The Lord is God, and he alone:

JOHANN JAKOB SCHÜTZ, 1640–90
Tr. FRANCES ELIZABETH COX
1812–97

143

THE spacious firmament on
high,
With all the blue ethereal sky,
And spangled heavens, a shin-
ing frame,
Their great Original proclaim.
The unwearied sun, from day to
day,
Does his Creator's power dis-
play,
And publishes to every land
The work of an almighty hand.

2 Soon as the evening shades
prevail,
The moon takes up the won-
drous tale,
And nightly to the listening
earth
Repeats the story of her birth;
While all the stars that round
her burn,
And all the planets, in their
turn,
Confirm the tidings, as they roll,
And spread the truth from pole
to pole.

3 What though in solemn silence
all
Move round the dark terres-
trial ball?
What though no real voice nor
sound
Amidst their radiant orbs be
found?
In reason's ear they all rejoice,
And utter forth a glorious voice,
For ever singing, as they shine,
'The hand that made us is
divine.' Amen. (*Tune* ii)

JOSEPH ADDISON, 1672–1719

144

GOD is Love: his mercy
brightens
All the path in which we rove;
Bliss he wakes, and woe he
lightens:
God is Wisdom, God is Love.

2 Chance and change are busy
ever;
Man decays, and ages move;
But his mercy waneth never:

3 Even the hour that darkest
seemeth
Will his changeless goodness
prove;
From the mist his brightness
streameth:

4 He with earthly cares entwineth
Hope and comfort from
above;
Everywhere his glory shineth:

JOHN BOWRING, 1792–1872

145

O LORD of heaven and earth
and sea,
To thee all praise and glory be;
How shall we show our love to
thee,
Who givest all?

2 The golden sunshine, vernal air,
Sweet flowers and fruits thy
love declare;
Where harvests ripen, thou art
there,
Who givest all.

3 For peaceful homes and health-
ful days,
For all the blessings earth displays,
We owe thee thankfulness and
praise,
Who givest all.

4 Thou didst not spare thine only
Son,
But gav'st him for a world
undone,
And freely with that blessèd
One
Thou givest all.

5 For souls redeemed, for sins
    forgiven,
For means of grace and hopes
    of heaven,
Father, all praise to thee be
    given,
      Who givest all.
       CHRISTOPHER WORDSWORTH
       1807–85

146

MY God, I thank thee, who
    hast made
    The earth so bright,
So full of splendour and of joy,
    Beauty and light;
So many glorious things are
    here,
    Noble and right.

2 I thank thee, too, that thou
    hast made
    Joy to abound,
So many gentle thoughts and
    deeds
    Circling us round
That in the darkest spot of
    earth
    Some love is found.

3 I thank thee more that all our
    joy
    Is touched with pain,
That shadows fall on brightest
    hours,
    That thorns remain,
So that earth's bliss may be our
    guide,
    And not our chain.

4 I thank thee, Lord, that here
    our souls,
    Though amply blest,
Can never find, although they
    seek,
    A perfect rest,
Nor ever shall, until they lean
    On Jesus' breast.
       ADELAIDE ANNE PROCTER
       1825–64, altered slightly

147

GOD moves in a mysterious
    way,
    His wonders to perform;

He plants his footsteps in the
    sea,
    And rides upon the storm.

2 Deep in unfathomable mines
    Of never-failing skill
He treasures up his bright
    designs,
    And works his sovereign will.

3 Ye fearful saints, fresh courage
    take;
    The clouds ye so much dread
Are big with mercy, and shall
    break
    In blessings on your head.

4 Judge not the Lord by feeble
    sense,
    But trust him for his grace;
Behind a frowning providence
    He hides a smiling face.

5 Blind unbelief is sure to err,
    And scan his work in vain,
God is his own interpreter,
    And he will make it plain.
       WILLIAM COWPER, 1731–1800

148

A GLADSOME hymn of
    praise we sing,
    And thankfully we gather
To bless the love of God above,
    Our everlasting Father.
In him rejoice with heart and
    voice,
    Whose glory fadeth never,
Whose providence is our de-
    fence,
    Who lives and loves for ever.

2 Full in his sight his children
    stand,
    By his strong arm defended,
And he whose wisdom guides
    the world
    Our footsteps hath attended.
For nothing falls unknown to
    him,
    Or care or joy or sorrow,
And he whose mercy ruled the
    past
    Will be our stay tomorrow.
       AMBROSE NICHOLS BLATCHFORD
       1842–1924

149   *Rebus creatis nil egens*

O GOD, the joy of heaven
 above,
Thou didst not need thy creatures' love,
When from thy secret place
 was said
The word that earth's foundation laid.

2 Thou spakest:—worlds began
 to be;
They stand before thy majesty;
And all to their Creator raise
A wondrous harmony of praise.

3 But ere, O Lord, this lovely
 earth
From thy creative will had
 birth,
Thou in thy counsels didst unfold
Another world of fairer mould.

4 That world doth our Redeemer
 frame,
And build upon his mighty
 Name;
His Holy Church shall last for
 aye
Till time itself hath passed
 away.

CHARLES COFFIN, 1676–1749
Tr. Compilers of *Hymns Ancient
and Modern*, 1889, altered

150

WHEN all thy mercies, O my
 God!
My rising soul surveys,
Transported with the view, I'm
 lost
In wonder, love, and praise.

2 Unnumbered comforts to my
 soul
Thy tender care bestowed,
Before my infant heart conceived
From whom these comforts
 flowed.

3 When in the slippery paths of
 youth
With heedless steps I ran,

Thine arm, unseen, conveyed
 me safe,
And led me up to man.

4 Ten thousand thousand pre-
 cious gifts
My daily thanks employ;
Nor is the least a cheerful heart,
That tastes those gifts with
 joy.

5 Through every period of my
 life
Thy goodness I'll pursue;
And after death, in distant
 worlds,
The glorious theme renew.

JOSEPH ADDISON, 1672–1719

151   *For children*

GOD, who made the earth,
 The air, the sky, the sea,
Who gave the light its birth,
 Careth for me.

2 God, who made the grass,
 The flower, the fruit, the tree,
The day and night to pass,
 Careth for me.

3 God, who made the sun,
 The moon, the stars, is he
Who, when life's clouds come
 on,
 Careth for me.

4 God, who made all things,
 On earth, in air, in sea,
Who changing seasons brings,
 Careth for me.

5 God, who sent his Son
 To die on Calvary,
He, if I lean on him,
 Will care for me.

SARAH BETTS RHODES, 1829–1904

152   *For children*

HOW wonderful this world of
 thine,
A fragment of a fiery sun,
How lovely and how small!
Where all things serve thy
 great design,
Where life's adventure is begun
In thee, the life of all.

2 The smallest seed in secret
    grows,
    And thrusting upward answers
    soon
    The bidding of the light;
    The bud unfurls into a rose;
    The wings within the white
      cocoon
    Are perfected for flight.

3 The migrant bird, in winter
    fled,
    Shall come again with spring
      and build
    In this same shady tree;
    By secret wisdom surely led,
    Homeward across the clover-
      field
    Hurries the honey-bee.

4 O thou, whose greater gifts are
    ours:
    A conscious will, a thinking
      mind,
    A heart to worship thee—
    O take these strange unfolding
      powers
    And teach us through thy Son
      to find
    The life more full and free.

                FREDERICK PRATT GREEN

153   *For younger children*

A LITTLE child may know
  Our Father's name of 'Love';
'Tis written on the earth below,
And on the sky above.

2 Around me when I look,
    His handiwork I see;
    This world is like a picture-book
    To teach his Name to me.

3 The thousand little flowers
    Within our garden found,
    The rainbow and the soft spring
      showers,
    And every pleasant sound;

4 The birds that sweetly sing,
    The moon that shines by night,
    With every tiny living thing
    Rejoicing in the light;

5 And every star above,
    Set in the deep blue sky,
    All tell me that our God is Love,
    And tell me he is nigh.

          JANE ELIZA LEESON, 1809–81

154   *For younger children*

* A LL things bright and beautiful,
    All creatures great and
      small,
    All things wise and wonderful—
    The Lord God made them all.

2 Each little flower that opens,
    Each little bird that sings,—
    He made their glowing colours,
    He made their tiny wings.

3 The purple-headed mountain,
    The river running by,
    The sunset, and the morning
    That brightens up the sky,

4 The cold wind in the winter,
    The pleasant summer sun,
    The ripe fruits in the garden,—
    He made them every one:

5 He gave us eyes to see them,
    And lips that we might tell
    How great is God Almighty,
    Who has made all things well.

          CECIL FRANCES ALEXANDER
                    1818–95

* *Verse 1 is also sung as a refrain after
each other verse.*

155   *For younger children*

G OD who put the stars in
    space,
Who made the world we share,
In his making made a place
For me, and put me here.

2 Thank you, God, for stars in
    space
    And for the world we share.
    Thank you for my special place
    To love and serve you here.

          NORMAN and MARGARET MEALY
                based on a poem by
                LUCILE S. REID

156 *For younger children*

I LOVE to think that Jesus saw
The same bright sun that shines today;
It gave him light to do his work,
And smiled upon his play.

2 The same white moon, with silver face,
That sails across the sky at night,
He used to see in Galilee,
And watch it with delight.

3 The same great God that hears my prayers
Heard his, when Jesus knelt to pray;

He is my Father, who will keep
His child through every day.

ADA SKEMP, 1857–1927

157 *For younger children*

WE thank thee, God, for eyes to see
The beauty of the earth;
For ears to hear the words of love
And happy sounds of mirth;
For minds that find new thoughts to think,
New wonders to explore;
For health and freedom to enjoy
The good thou hast in store.

JEANNETTE PERKINS BROWN
1887–1960

THE PROMISE OF THE MESSIAH

158 PSALM 72, verses 1, 2, 5, 11, 17–19

GIVE the king thy judgments O ' God : and thy righteous-ness un ' to the king's son.

He shall judge thy people with ' righteousness : and thy ' poor with judgment.

They shall fear thee as long as the sun and moon en ' dure : throughout all ' generations.

Yea all kings shall fall down be ' fore him : all na ' tions shall serve him.

His Name shall endure for ever his Name shall be continued as long as the ' sun : and men shall be blessèd in him all nations shall ' call him blessèd.

Blessèd be the Lord God the God of ' Israel : who only ' doeth wondrous things.

And blessèd be his glorious Name for ' ever : and let the whole earth be filled with his glory ' A ' men and Amen.

Glory be to the Father and to the ' Son : and ' to the Holy Ghost :

As it was in the beginning is now and ever ' shall be : world with ' out end Amen.

159 PARAPHRASE 26, verses 5–10

BEHOLD he comes! your leader comes,
With might and honour crowned;
A witness who shall spread my Name
To earth's remotest bound.

2 See! nations hasten to his call
From every distant shore;
Isles, yet unknown, shall bow to him,
And Israel's God adore.

3 Seek ye the Lord while yet his
    ear
  Is open to your call;
While offered mercy still is near,
  Before his footstool fall.

4 Let sinners quit their evil ways,
  Their evil thoughts forgo:
And God, when they to him
    return,
  Returning grace will show.

5 He pardons with o'erflowing
    love:
  For, hear the voice divine!
My nature is not like to yours,
  Nor like your ways are mine:

6 But far as heaven's resplendent
    orbs
  Beyond earth's spot extend,
As far my thoughts, as far my
    ways,
  Your ways and thoughts
    transcend.

Scottish Paraphrases, 1781
From Isaiah 55:4–9

160 PARAPHRASE 39

HARK, the glad sound! the
    Saviour comes,
  The Saviour promised long;
Let every heart exult with joy,
  And every voice be song!

2 He comes, the prisoners to re-
    lieve,
  In Satan's bondage held;
The gates of brass before him
    burst,
  The iron fetters yield.

3 He comes, the broken hearts to
    bind,
  The bleeding souls to cure;
And with the treasures of his
    grace
  To enrich the humble poor.

4 The sacred year has now re-
    volved,
  Accepted of the Lord,
When heaven's high promise is
    fulfilled,
  And Israel is restored.

5 Our glad hosannas, Prince of
    Peace,
  Thy welcome shall proclaim;
And heaven's exalted arches
    ring
  With thy most honoured
    Name.

Scottish Paraphrases, 1781
From St. Luke 4:18, 19

161 BENEDICTUS

BLESSÈD be the Lord '
    God of ' Isra-el : for he
  hath visited ' and re-'
  deemed his ' people :
And hath raised up a mighty
  sal-' vation ' for us : in the '
  house of his ' servant '
  David.

2 As he spake by the mouth of
  his ' holy ' prophets : which
  have ' been since the ' world
  be-' gan :
That we should be ' saved
  from our ' enemies : and
  from the ' hands of ' all
  that ' hate us.

3 To perform the mercy ' promised to our ' forefathers :
  and to re-' member his '
  holy ' covenant :
To perform the oath which he
  sware to our ' forefather '
  Abraham : that ' he would '
  give ' us.

4 That we being delivered out
  of the ' hands of our '
  enemies : might ' serve him
  with-' out ' fear :
In holiness and ' righteousness
  be-' fore him : all the ' days '
  of our ' life.

5 And thou child shalt be called
  the ' prophet of the ' Highest :
  for thou shalt go before
  the face of the ' Lord to
  pre-' pare his ' ways :
To give knowledge of salvation ' unto his ' people : for
  the re-' mission ' of their '
  sins.

6 Through the tender ' mercy of
our ' God : whereby the '
dayspring from on ' high
hath ' visited us :
To give light to them that
sit in darkness and in the '
shadow of ' death : and to
guide our feet ' into the '
way of ' peace.

*Glory ' be to the ' Father : and to
the Son ' and to the ' Holy '
Ghost :
As it ' was in the be- ' ginning :
is now and ever shall be '
world without ' end.*
A- ' men.
From St. Luke 1: 68–79

*162

BEFORE all time the Word
existed ;
Before all time he was with God ;
With God in fellowship eternal,
In essence one with all God was.
Through him all things received
their birth ;
No thing without him came to
be.

2 The Word was life in all creation—
That life the Light of all mankind.
Through countless ages in the
darkness
The Light shone out, and still
it shines.
No matter how the dark
might strive,
Its force could not the Light
subdue.

3 To witness to the Light there
came,
Sent forth from God, a man
named John ;
That through him all men
might believe
The Light to whom he testi-
fied.
This True Light, lighting every
man,
Ev'n then was entering the
world.

4 The world he entered failed to
know him,
Although through him the
world was made:
To his own realm it was he
came,
Yet his own folk no welcome
gave.
But some there were who did
receive
The Light of men, the Word of
God.

5 To these, to all in him be-
lieving,
Who put their faith in his great
Name,
He gave authority and war-
rant—
The power God's children to
become.
No human blood or seed or will
Gave them this birth, but God
alone!

6 The Word became a human
being,
And made his dwelling in our
midst.
We saw his majesty and splen-
dour—
His glory, full of grace and
truth:
Such as to One alone belongs
Who is the Father's only Son.

JAMES N. S. ALEXANDER
From St. John 1: 1–7, 9–14

** When the whole paraphrase is not
sung, a selection of verses may be made as
follows: verses 1, 2, (3), and 6, or verses
3, 4, 5, and 6.*

163   MAGNIFICAT

MY soul doth magnify the
Lord   and my spirit
hath rejoiced in ' God my '
Saviour : for he hath re-
garded the ' lowliness ' of
his ' hand-maiden :
For be- ' hold from ' henceforth : all gener- ' ations
shall ' call me ' blessèd.

2 For he that is mighty hath '
magnified ' me : and ' holy '
is his ' Name :

And his mercy is on ' them
that ' fear him : through- '
out all ' gener- ' ations.

3 He hath showed ' strength
with his ' arm : he hath
scattered the proud in the
imagi- ' nation ' of their '
hearts :
He hath put down the '
mighty from their ' seat :
and hath ex- ' alted the '
humble and ' meek.

4 He hath filled the ' hungry
with ' good things : and the '
rich he hath sent ' empty
a- ' way :
He remembering his mercy
hath holpen his ' servant '
Isra-el : as he promised to
our forefathers ' Abraham
and his ' seed for ' ever.

Glory ' be to the ' Father : and to
the Son ' and to the ' Holy '
Ghost :
As it ' was in the be- ' ginning :
is now and ever shall be '
world without ' end.
A- ' men.
From St. Luke 1: 46–55

164

TELL out, my soul, the
greatness of the Lord!
Unnumbered blessings, give my
spirit voice;
Tender to me the promise of his
word;
In God my Saviour shall my
heart rejoice.

2 Tell out, my soul, the greatness
of his Name!
Make known his might, the
deeds his arm has done;
His mercy sure, from age to age
the same;
His holy Name—the Lord, the
Mighty One.

3 Tell out, my soul, the greatness
of his might!
Powers and dominions lay their
glory by.

Proud hearts and stubborn wills
are put to flight,
The hungry fed, the humble
lifted high.

4 Tell out, my soul, the glories of
his word!
Firm is his promise, and his
mercy sure.
Tell out, my soul, the greatness
of the Lord
To children's children and for
evermore!

TIMOTHY DUDLEY-SMITH
Based on the Magnificat as in *The*
New English Bible

165 *Veni, Emmanuel*

O COME, O come, Emmănuel,
And ransom captive Īsrael,
That mourns in lonely ěxile here
Until the Son of Gŏd appear.
Rejoice! rejoice! Emmănuel
Shall come to thee, O Īsrael.

2 O come, O come, thou Lŏrd of
might,
Who to thy tribes, on Sīnai's
height,
In ancient times didst gĭve the
law
In cloud and majestў and awe.

3 O come, thou Rod of Jěsse, free
Thine own from Satan's
tўranny;
From depths of hell thy pĕople
save,
And give them victory o'er the
grave.

4 O come, thou Dayspring, cŏme
and cheer
Our spirits by thine ădvent
here;
Disperse the gloomy cloŭds of
night,
And death's dark shadows pŭt
to flight.

5 O come, thou Key of David,
come,
And open wide our heavenly
home;

Make safe the way that leads on
high,
And close the path to misery:

18th century, based on the ancient
Advent Antiphons
Tr. JOHN MASON NEALE, 1818–66

CHRIST'S INCARNATION

166 PSALM 2, verses 1–3, 6–8,
10, 11, 12b

WHY do the heathen ' rage :
and the people i ' ma-gine
a vain thing?

The kings of the earth set
themselves and the rulers
take counsel to ' gether :
against the Lord and against
his a ' nointed saying,

Let us break their bonds a ' sunder:
and cast a ' way their cords
from us.

Yet have I set my ' king : upon
my holy ' hill of Zion.

I will declare the decree the
Lord hath said unto ' me :
thou art my son this day
have ' I begotten thee.

Ask of me and I shall give thee
the heathen for thine in- '
heritance : and the uttermost
parts of the earth for ' thy
possession.

Be wise now therefore O ye '
kings : be instructed ye '
judges of the earth.

Serve the Lord with ' fear : and
re ' joice with trembling.

Blessèd are ' all they : that ' put
their trust in him.

*Glory be to the Father and to the '
Son : and ' to the Holy Ghost.*

*As it was in the beginning is
now and ever ' shall be : world
with ' out end Amen.*

167 PSALM 72, verses 8, 10, 11,
17–19

HIS large and great dominion
shall
From sea to sea extend:
It from the river shall reach
forth
Unto earth's utmost end.

2 The kings of Tarshish, and the
isles,
To him shall presents bring;
And unto him shall offer gifts
Sheba's and Seba's king.

3 Yea, all the mighty kings on
earth
Before him down shall fall;
And all the nations of the world
Do service to him shall.

4 His Name for ever shall endure;
Last like the sun it shall:
Men shall be blest in him, and
blest
All nations shall him call.

5 Now blessèd be the Lord our
God,
The God of Israel,
For he alone doth wondrous
works,
In glory that excel.

6 And blessèd be his glorious
Name
To all eternity:
The whole earth let his glory
fill.
Amen, so let it be.

168 PARAPHRASE 19

THE race that long in darkness pined
Have seen a glorious light;

The people dwell in day, who
dwelt
In death's surrounding night.

2 To us a Child of hope is born;
To us a Son is given;
Him shall the tribes of earth
obey,
Him all the hosts of heaven.

3 His name shall be the Prince of
Peace,
For evermore adored,
The Wonderful, the Counsellor,
The great and mighty Lord.

4 His power increasing still shall
spread,
His reign no end shall know;
Justice shall guard his throne
above,
And peace abound below.

Scottish Paraphrases, 1781
From Isaiah 9: 2, 6, 7

169

HARK! the herald angels
sing,
'Glory to the new-born King,
Peace on earth, and mercy
mild,
God and sinners reconciled!'
Joyful, all ye nations, rise,
Join the triumph of the skies,
With the angelic host proclaim,
'Christ is born in Bethlehem'.
*Hark! the herald angels sing,
'Glory to the new-born King'.*

2 Christ, by highest heaven
adored,
Christ, the everlasting Lord,
Late in time behold him come,
Offspring of a virgin's womb.
Veiled in flesh the Godhead see;
Hail, the Incarnate Deity,
Pleased as Man with man to
dwell,
Jesus, our Immanuel!

3 Hail, the heaven-born Prince of
Peace!
Hail, the Sun of Righteousness!
Light and life to all he brings,
Risen with healing in his wings.

Mild he lays his glory by,
Born that man no more may die,
Born to raise the sons of earth,
Born to give them second birth:
CHARLES WESLEY, 1707–88
and others

170

IT came upon the midnight
clear,
That glorious song of old,
From angels bending near the
earth
To touch their harps of
gold :—
'Peace on the earth, good will to
men,
From heaven's all-gracious
King!'
The world in solemn stillness lay
To hear the angels sing.

2 Still through the cloven skies
they come
With peaceful wings un-
furled ;
And still their heavenly music
floats
O'er all the weary world ;
Above its sad and lowly plains
They bend on hovering wing,
And ever o'er its Babel sounds
The blessèd angels sing.

3 But with the woes of sin and
strife
The world has suffered long ;
Beneath the angel strain have
rolled
Two thousand years of
wrong ;
And man, at war with man,
hears not
The love song which they
bring ;
O hush the noise, ye men of
strife,
And hear the angels sing.

4 For, lo! the days are hastening
on,
By prophet bards foretold,
When with the ever-circling
years
Comes round the Age of Gold,

When peace shall over all the
    earth
  Its ancient splendours fling,
And the whole world give back
    the song
  Which now the angels sing.
EDMUND HAMILTON SEARS
1810–76

171 *Fröhlich soll mein Herze springen*

ALL my heart this night re-
  joices,
  As I hear, far and near,
  Sweetest angel voices;
'Christ is born!' their choirs are
    singing,
  Till the air, everywhere,
  Now with joy is ringing.

2 Hark! a voice from yonder
    manger,
  Soft and sweet, doth entreat:
  'Flee from woe and danger;
Brethren, come: from all doth
    grieve you
  You are freed; all you need
  I will surely give you'.

3 Come, then, let us hasten
    yonder;
  Here let all, great and small,
  Kneel in awe and wonder.
Love him who with love is
    yearning;
  Hail the Star that, from far,
  Bright with hope is burn-
    ing.
PAUL GERHARDT, 1607–76
Tr. CATHERINE WINKWORTH
1827–78

172

O LITTLE town of Bethle-
  hem,
  How still we see thee lie!
Above thy deep and dreamless
    sleep
  The silent stars go by:
Yet in thy dark streets shineth
  The everlasting Light;

The hopes and fears of all the
    years
  Are met in thee tonight.

2 O morning stars, together
  Proclaim the holy birth,
And praises sing to God the
    King,
  And peace to men on earth.
For Christ is born of Mary;
  And, gathered all above,
While mortals sleep, the angels
    keep
  Their watch of wondering
    love.

3 How silently, how silently,
  The wondrous gift is given!
So God imparts to human
    hearts
  The blessings of his heaven.
No ear may hear his coming;
  But in this world of sin,
Where meek souls will receive
    him, still
  The dear Christ enters in.

4 O Holy Child of Bethlehem,
  Descend to us, we pray;
Cast out our sin, and enter in;
  Be born in us today.
We hear the Christmas angels
  The great glad tidings tell;
O come to us, abide with us,
  Our Lord Immanuel.
PHILLIPS BROOKS, 1835–93

173

THE first Nowell the angel
  did say
Was to certain poor shepherds
    in fields as they lay:
In fields where they lay a-keep-
    ing their sheep
On a cold winter's night that
    was so deep.
  Nowell, Nowell, Nowell,
    Nowell,
  Born is the King of Israel.

2 They lookèd up and saw a star,
    Shining in the east, beyond
        them far;
And to the earth it gave great
    light,
And so it continued both day
    and night.

3 And by the light of that same
    star,
    Three wise men came from
        country far;
To seek for a King was their
    intent,
And to follow the star wherever
    it went.

4 This star drew nigh to the
    north-west,
    O'er Bethlehem it took its rest,
And there it did both stop and
    stay
Right over the place where
    Jesus lay.

5 Then entered in those wise men
    three,
    Full reverently upon their knee,
And offered there in his pre-
    sènce
Their gold and myrrh and
    frankincense.

6 Then let us all with one accord
    Sing praises to our Heavenly
        Lord,
That hath made heaven and
    earth of naught,
And with his blood mankind
    hath bought.

Traditional Carol

174   PARAPHRASE 37

WHILE humble shepherds
    watched their flocks
    In Bethlehem's plains by
        night,
An angel sent from heaven ap-
    peared,
And filled the plains with
    light.

2 'Fear not', he said, for sudden
    dread
    Had seized their troubled
        mind;
'Glad tidings of great joy I bring
    To you and all mankind.

3 'To you in David's town, this
    day,
    Is born, of David's line,
The Saviour, who is Christ the
    Lord;
And this shall be the sign:

4 'The heavenly Babe you there
    shall find
    To human view displayed,
All meanly wrapped in swath-
    ing-bands,
And in a manger laid.'

5 Thus spake the seraph; and
    forthwith
    Appeared a shining throng
Of angels praising God, and
    thus
Addressed their joyful song:

6 'All glory be to God on high,
    And to the earth be peace;
Good will is shown by heaven
    to men
And never more shall cease.'

Scottish Paraphrases, 1781
Based on St. Luke 2:8–14

175   *Quem pastores laudavere*

ANGEL voices, richly blend-
    ing,
Shepherds to the manger send-
    ing,
Sing of peace from heav'n
    descending!
Shepherds, greet your Shep-
    herd-King!

2 Lo! a star is brightly glowing!
    Eastern kings their gifts are
        showing
To the King whose gifts pass
    knowing!
Gentiles, greet the Gentiles'
    King!

3 To the manger come adoring,
    Hearts in thankfulness out-
        pouring
To the child, true peace re-
    storing,
Mary's Son, our God and King!

German, 14th century
Tr. JAMES QUINN

176

Stille Nacht, heilige Nacht

STILL the night, holy the
night!
Sleeps the world ; hid from sight,
Mary and Joseph in stable bare
Watch o'er the Child beloved
and fair,
Sleeping in heavenly rest,
Sleeping in heavenly rest.

2 Still the night, holy the night!
Shepherds first saw the light,
Heard resounding clear and
long,
Far and near, the angel-song,
'Christ the Redeemer is
here!
Christ the Redeemer is
here!'

3 Still the night, holy the night!
Son of God, O how bright
Love is smiling from thy face!
Strikes for us now the hour of
grace,
Saviour, since thou art
born!
Saviour, since thou art
born!

JOSEPH MOHR, 1792–1848
Tr. STOPFORD BROOKE, 1832–1916
and the Compilers of *The Church
Hymnary*, 1927 Edition

177

GLOOMY night embraced the
place
Where the noble Infant lay ;
The Babe looked up and showed
his face,
In spite of darkness it was
day!
It was thy day, Sweet, and did
rise,
Not from the East, but from
thine eyes.

2 We saw thee in thy balmy nest,
Bright dawn of our eternal
day!
We saw thine eyes break from
their east
And chase the trembling
shades away ;

We saw thee, and we blessed
the sight,
We saw thee by thine own sweet
light.

3 Welcome, all wonder in one
sight,
Eternity shut in a span,
Summer in winter, day in
night,
Heaven in earth, and God in
man!
Great Little One! whose all-
embracing birth
Lifts earth to heaven, stoops
heaven to earth.

RICHARD CRASHAW, c. 1613–49
From *Hymn in the Holy Nativity*
1648

178

IN the bleak mid-winter
Frosty wind made moan,
Earth stood hard as iron,
Water like a stone ;
Snow had fallen, snow on snow,
Snow on snow,
In the bleak mid-winter,
Long ago.

2 Our God, heaven cannot hold
him,
Nor earth sustain :
Heaven and earth shall flee
away
When he comes to reign :
In the bleak mid-winter
A stable-place sufficed
The Lord God Almighty,
Jesus Christ.

3 Angels and archangels
May have gathered there,
Cherubim and seraphim
Thronged the air ;
But only his mother,
In her maiden bliss,
Worshipped the Belovèd
With a kiss.

4 What can I give him,
Poor as I am ?
If I were a shepherd,
I would bring a lamb ;

If I were a wise man,
  I would do my part;
Yet what I can I give him—
  Give my heart.
                CHRISTINA ROSSETTI, 1830–94

179

SEE! in yonder manger low,
  Born for us on earth below,
See! the tender Lamb appears
Promised from eternal years.
  Hail, thou ever-blessèd morn!
  Hail, redemption's happy
    dawn!
  Sing through all Jerusalem,
  'Christ is born in Bethlehem!'

2 Lo! within a manger lies
He who built the starry skies,
He who, throned in height sub-
    lime,
Sits amid the cherubim.

3 Sacred Infant, all Divine,
What a tender love was thine,
Thus to come from highest bliss
Down to such a world as this!
                EDWARD CASWALL, 1814–78

180

Leanabh an aigh

CHILD in the manger,
  Infant of Mary;
Outcast and stranger,
  Lord of all!
Child who inherits
  All our transgressions,
All our demerits
  On him fall.

2 Once the most holy
  Child of salvation
Gently and lowly
  Lived below;
Now, as our glorious
  Mighty Redeemer,
See him victorious
  O'er each foe.

3 Prophets foretold him,
  Infant of wonder;
Angels behold him
  On his throne;

Worthy our Saviour
  Of all their praises;
Happy for ever
  Are his own.
                MARY MACDONALD, 1789–1872
                Tr. LACHLAN MACBEAN, 1853–1931

181

*ON Christmas night all Chris-
    tians sing,
To hear the news the angels
    bring—
News of great joy, news of great
    mirth,
News of our merciful King's
    birth.

2 Then why should men on earth
    be so sad,
Since our Redeemer made us
    glad,
When from our sin he set us
    free,
All for to gain our liberty?

3 When sin departs before his
    grace,
Then life and health come in its
    place;
Angels and men with joy may
    sing,
All for to see the new-born
    King.

4 All out of darkness we have
    light,
Which made the angels sing
    this night;
'Glory to God and peace to
    men,
Now and for evermore. Amen.'
                Traditional carol

* *The first two lines of each verse are
repeated.*

182

ANGELS from the realms of
    glory,
Wing your flight o'er all the
    earth;
Ye who sang creation's story,
  Now proclaim Messiah's
    birth;

Come and worship
Christ, the new-born King.
Come and worship,
    Worship Christ, the new-born
        King.

2 Shepherds, in the fields abiding,
    Watching o'er your flock by
        night,
  God with man is now residing,
    Yonder shines the infant
        Light;

3 Wise men, leave your contem-
        plations;
    Brighter visions beam afar;
  Seek the great Desire of
        nations;
    Ye have seen his natal star;

4 *All creation, join in praising*
    God the Father, Spirit, Son,
  Evermore your voices raising
    To the eternal Three in One:
        JAMES MONTGOMERY, 1771–1854

183

GOOD Christian men, rejoice
    With heart and soul and
        voice;
  Give ye heed to what we say,
  Jesus Christ is born today:
Ox and ass before him bow,
And he is in the manger now.
    Christ is born today!
    Christ is born today!

2 Good Christian men, rejoice
  With heart and soul and voice;
    Now ye hear of endless bliss,
    Jesus Christ was born for this:
  He hath oped the heavenly
        door,
  And man is blessèd evermore.
    Christ was born for this!
    Christ was born for this!

3 Good Christian men, rejoice
  With heart and soul and voice;
    Now ye need not fear the
        grave,
  Jesus Christ was born to save,
Calls you one, and calls you all,
To gain his everlasting hall.
    Christ was born to save!
    Christ was born to save!
        JOHN MASON NEALE, 1818–66

184

GOD rest you merry, gentle-
    men,
  Let nothing you dismay,
  For Jesus Christ our Saviour
  Was born upon this day,
  To save us all from Satan's
        power
  When we were gone astray:
  O *tidings of comfort and joy,*
    comfort and joy!
  O *tidings of comfort and joy!*

2 From God our Heav'nly Father
  A blessèd angel came,
  And unto certain shepherds
  Brought tidings of the same,
  How that in Bethlehem was
        born
  The Son of God by name:

3 The shepherds at those tidings
  Rejoicèd much in mind,
  And left their flocks a-feeding
  In tempest, storm and wind,
  And went to Bethlehem
        straightway
  This blessèd Babe to find:

4 But when to Bethlehem they
        came,
  Whereat this Infant lay,
  They found him in a manger,
  Where oxen feed on hay;
  His mother Mary kneeling
  Unto the Lord did pray:

5 Now to the Lord sing praises,
  All you within this place,
  And with true love and brother-
        hood
  Each other now embrace;
  This holy tide of Christmas
  All others doth deface:
        Traditional carol

185

O Deued Pob Cristion

ALL poor men and humble,
    All lame men who stumble,
  Come haste ye nor feel ye afraid;
  For Jesus, our treasure,
  With love past all measure,
  In lowly poor manger was laid.

*2 Though wise men who found
    him
  Laid rich gifts around him,
  Yet oxen they gave him their
    hay:
  And Jesus in beauty
  Accepted their duty;
  Contented in manger he lay.

3 Then haste we to show him
  The praises we owe him;
  Our service he ne'er can des-
    pise:
  Whose love still is able
  To show us that stable
  Where softly in manger he lies.
        KATHARINE EMILY ROBERTS, 1877–
           1962, based on a Welsh carol

  * Verses 2 and 3 are sung to the second
half of the tune.

186   W Żłobie Leży

INFANT holy,
  Infant lowly,
For his bed a cattle stall;
    Oxen lowing,
    Little knowing
Christ the babe is Lord of all.
    Swift are winging
    Angels singing,
    Nowells ringing,
    Tidings bringing,
Christ the babe is Lord of all,
Christ the babe is Lord of all.

2   Flocks were sleeping,
     Shepherds keeping
Vigil till the morning new
    Saw the glory,
    Heard the story,
Tidings of a gospel true.
    Thus rejoicing,
    Free from sorrow,
    Praises voicing,
    Greet the morrow,
Christ the babe was born for
    you!
Christ the babe was born for
    you!
            Polish carol
      Tr. EDITH M. G. REED, 1885–1933

187   Puer nobis nascitur

UNTO us is born a Son.
   King of Quires supernal:
See on earth his life begun,
Of lords the Lord eternal,
Of lords the Lord eternal.

2 Christ, from heav'n descending
    low,
  Comes on earth a stranger:
  Ox and ass their Owner know
  Becradled in the manger,
  Becradled in the manger.

3 This did Herod sore affray,
  And grievously bewilder;
  So he gave the word to slay,
  And slew the little childer,
  And slew the little childer.

4 Of his love and mercy mild
  This the Christmas story:
  And O that Mary's gentle
    Child
  Might lead us up to glory,
  Might lead us up to glory!

5 O and A and A and O,
  Cum cantibus in choro,
  Let our merry organ go,
  Benedicamus Domino,
  Benedicamus Domino.
              Piae Cantiones, 1582
      Tr. GEORGE RATCLIFFE WOODWARD
                       1848–1934

188   Vom Himmel hoch da
              komm ich her

GIVE heed, my heart, lift up
   thine eyes:
Who is it in yon manger lies?
Who is this child so young and
    fair?
The blessèd Christ-child lieth
    there.

2 Welcome to earth, thou noble
    Guest,
  Through whom even wicked
    men are blest!
  Thou com'st to share our
    misery;
  What can we render, Lord, to
    thee?

3 Were earth a thousand times as
    fair,
  Beset with gold and jewels rare,
  She yet were far too poor to be
  A narrow cradle, Lord, for
    thee.

4 Ah! dearest Jesus, Holy Child,
  Make thee a bed, soft, un-
    defiled,
  Within my heart, that it may
    be
  A quiet chamber kept for thee.

5 My heart for very joy doth leap;
  My lips no more can silence
    keep;
  I too must raise with joyful
    tongue
  That sweetest ancient cradle
    song.

6 'Glory to God in highest
    heaven,
  Who unto man his Son hath
    given!'
  While angels sing with pious
    mirth
  A glad New Year to all the
    earth.

MARTIN LUTHER, 1483–1546
Tr. CATHERINE WINKWORTH
1827–78

189

A solis ortus cardine

FROM east to west, from
    shore to shore,
  Let every heart awake and
    sing
The holy Child whom Mary bore,
  The Christ, the everlasting
    King.

2 Behold, the world's Creator
    wears
  The form and fashion of a
    slave;
  Our very flesh our Maker shares,
  His fallen creature, man, to
    save.

3 For this how wondrously he
    wrought!
  A maiden, in her lowly place,
  Became, in ways beyond all
    thought,
  The chosen vessel of his
    grace.

4 He shrank not from the oxen's
    stall,
  He lay within the manger
    bed,
  And he, whose bounty feedeth
    all,
  At Mary's breast himself was
    fed.

5 And while the angels in the sky
  Sang praise above the silent
    field,
  To shepherds poor the Lord
    most high,
  The one great Shepherd, was
    revealed.

6 *All glory for this blessèd morn*
  To God the Father ever be;
  All praise to thee, O Virgin-born,
  All praise, O Holy Ghost, to
    thee. Amen.

CAELIUS SEDULIUS, d. c. 450
Tr. JOHN ELLERTON, 1826–93

190

CHRISTIANS, awake, salute
    the happy morn,
Whereon the Saviour of the
    world was born;
Rise to adore the mystery of
    love,
Which hosts of angels chanted
    from above;
With them the joyful tidings
    first begun
Of God Incarnate and the Vir-
    gin's Son:

2 Then to the watchful shepherds
    it was told,
Who heard the angelic herald's
    voice, 'Behold,
I bring good tidings of a
    Saviour's birth
To you and all the nations upon
    earth;
This day hath God fulfilled his
    promised word,
This day is born a Saviour,
    Christ the Lord.'

3 To Bethl'em straight the en-
  lightened shepherds ran
To see the wonder God had
  wrought for man,
And found, with Joseph and the
  blessèd Maid,
Her Son, the Saviour, in a
  manger laid;
Joyful, the wondrous story they
  proclaim,
The first apostles of his infant
  fame.

4 O may we keep and ponder in
  our mind
God's wondrous love in saving
  lost mankind;
Trace we the Babe, who hath
  retrieved our loss,
From his poor manger to his
  bitter cross;
Saved by his love, incessant we
  shall sing
Eternal praise to heaven's
  almighty King.

> JOHN BYROM, 1691–1763
> and the Compilers of *The BBC
> Hymn Book*, 1951

191   *Adeste fideles*

O COME, all ye faithful,
    Joyful and triumphant,
O come ye, O come ye to
    Bethlehem;
Come and behold him
  Born the King of angels;
O come, let us adore him,
O come, let us adore him,
O come, let us adore him, Christ
    the Lord.

2 God of God,
    Light of Light,
Lo! he abhors not the Virgin's
    womb;
Very God,
  Begotten, not created;

3 Sing, choirs of angels,
    Sing in exultation,
Sing, all ye citizens of heaven
    above,
  'Glory to God
  In the highest':

For Christmas Day

4 Yea, Lord, we greet thee,
    Born this happy morning;
Jesus, to thee be glory given:
  Word of the Father,
  Now in flesh appearing;

> Possibly by JOHN WADE, c. 1711–86
> Tr. FREDERICK OAKELEY, 1802–80
> and others

192   *Μέγα καὶ παράδοξον θαῦμα*

A GREAT and mighty wonder
    A full and holy cure!
The Virgin bears the Infant
  With virgin-honour pure.
  Repeat the hymn again!
  'To God on high be glory,
  And peace on earth to men!'

2 The Word becomes incarnate
    And yet remains on high!
And Cherubim sing anthems
  To shepherds, from the sky:

3 While thus they sing your
    Monarch,
    Those bright angelic bands,
Rejoice, ye vales and moun-
    tains,
  Ye oceans, clap your hands:

4 Since all he comes to ransom,
    By all be he adored,
The Infant born in Bethl'em,
  The Saviour and the Lord:

5 And idol forms shall perish,
    And error shall decay,
And Christ shall wield his
    sceptre,
  Our Lord and God for aye:

> ST. GERMANUS, c. 634–c. 734
> Tr. JOHN MASON NEALE
> 1818–66, and others

193

O NCE in royal David's city
    Stood a lowly cattle-shed,
Where a mother laid her Baby
  In a manger for his bed.
Mary was that mother mild,
Jesus Christ her little Child.

2 He came down to earth from heaven
  Who is God and Lord of all,
And his shelter was a stable,
  And his cradle was a stall.
With the poor and mean and lowly
Lived on earth our Saviour holy.

3 And through all his wondrous childhood
  He would honour and obey,
Love, and watch the lowly maiden
  In whose gentle arms he lay.
Christian children all must be
Mild, obedient, good as he.

4 For he is our childhood's pattern:
  Day by day like us he grew;
He was little, weak, and helpless;
  Tears and smiles like us he knew;
And he feeleth for our sadness,
And he shareth in our gladness.

5 And our eyes at last shall see him,
  Through his own redeeming love;
For that Child so dear and gentle
  Is our Lord in heaven above;
And he leads his children on
To the place where he is gone.

6 Not in that poor lowly stable,
  With the oxen standing by,
We shall see him, but in heaven,
  Set at God's right hand on high,
When, like stars, his children crowned
All in white shall wait around.

CECIL FRANCES ALEXANDER
1818–95

194

LOVE came down at Christmas,
  Love all lovely, Love Divine;
Love was born at Christmas,
  Star and angels gave the sign.

2 Worship we the Godhead,
  Love Incarnate, Love Divine;
Worship we our Jesus:
  But wherewith for sacred sign?

3 Love shall be our token,
  Love be yours and love be mine,
Love to God and all men,
  Love for plea and gift and sign.

CHRISTINA ROSSETTI, 1830–94

195   *For younger children*

AWAY in a manger, no crib for a bed,
The little Lord Jesus laid down his sweet head.
The stars in the bright sky looked down where he lay,
The little Lord Jesus asleep on the hay.

2 The cattle are lowing, the Baby awakes,
But little Lord Jesus no crying he makes.
I love thee, Lord Jesus! look down from the sky,
And stay by my side until morning is nigh.

3 Be near me, Lord Jesus; I ask thee to stay
Close by me for ever, and love me, I pray.
Bless all the dear children in thy tender care,
And fit us for heaven, to live with thee there.

Anonymous

196   *Holy Innocents' Day*

WHEN Christ was born in Bethlehem,
  Fair peace on earth to bring,
In lowly state of love he came
  To be the children's King.

2 And round him, then, a holy
    band
  Of children blest was born,
Fair guardians of his throne to
    stand
  Attendant night and morn.

3 And unto them this grace was
    given
  A Saviour's Name to own,
And die for him who out of
    heaven
  Had found on earth a throne.

4 O blessèd babes of Bethlehem,
  Who died to save our King,
Ye share the martyrs' diadem,
  And in their anthem sing!
    LAURENCE HOUSMAN, 1865–1959

197

BEHOLD the great Creator
    makes
  Himself a house of clay,
A robe of human flesh he takes
  Which he will wear for aye.

2 Hark, hark, the wise eternal
    Word,
  Like a weak infant cries!
In form of servant is the Lord,
  And God in cradle lies.

3 Glad shepherds came to view
    this sight;
  A choir of angels sings,
And eastern sages with delight
  Adore this King of kings.

4 Join then, all hearts that are
    not stone,
  And all our voices prove,
To celebrate this holy One
  The God of peace and love.
    THOMAS PESTEL, 1584–1659
    altered

198

Corde natus ex Parentis

OF the Father's love begotten
  Ere the worlds began to
    be,
He is Alpha and Omega,
  He the source, the ending he,

Of the things that are, that have
    been,
  And that future years shall
    see,
    Evermore and evermore.

2 O that birth for ever blessèd,
  When the Virgin, full of grace,
By the Holy Ghost conceiving,
  Bare the Saviour of our race,
And the Babe, the world's
    Redeemer,
  First revealed his sacred face,

3 This is he whom seers in old
    time
  Chanted of with one accord,
Whom the voices of the pro-
    phets
  Promised in their faithful
    word;
Now he shines, the Long-
    expected;
  Let creation praise its Lord,

4 O ye heights of heaven, adore
    him;
  Angel hosts, his praises sing;
All dominions, bow before him,
  And extol our God and King;
Let no tongue on earth be
    silent,
  Every voice in concert ring,

5 *Christ, to thee, with God the
    Father,*
  And, O Holy Ghost, to thee,
*Hymn, and chant, and high
    thanksgiving,*
  And unwearied praises be,
Honour, glory, and dominion,
  And eternal victory,
Evermore and evermore. Amen.
    PRUDENTIUS, 348–c. 413
    Tr. JOHN MASON NEALE
    1818–66
    and HENRY WILLIAMS BAKER
    1821–77

199 *O sola magnarum urbium*

BETHLEHEM, of noblest
 cities
None can once with thee compare;
Thou alone the Lord from
  heaven
Didst for us incarnate bear.

2 Fairer than the sun at morning
  Was the star that told his
    birth;
To the world its God announc-
  ing,
Seen in fleshly form on earth.

3 Eastern sages at his cradle
  Make oblations rich and rare;
See them give, in deep devo-
  tion,
Gold and frankincense and
  myrrh.

4 Sacred gifts of mystic meaning:
  Incense doth their God dis-
  close,
Gold the King of kings pro-
  claimeth,
Myrrh his sepulchre fore-
  shows.

5 *Holy Jesu, in thy brightness*
  To the Gentile world displayed,
With the Father and the Spirit
  Endless praise to thee be paid.
    Amen.

PRUDENTIUS, 348–c. 413
Tr. EDWARD CASWALL, 1814–78

200

AS with gladness men of old
 Did the guiding star be-
  hold,
As with joy they hailed its light,
Leading onward, beaming
  bright,—
So, most gracious Lord, may we
Evermore be led to thee.

2 As with joyful steps they sped,
Saviour, to thy lowly bed,
There to bend the knee before
Thee, whom heaven and earth
  adore,—
So may we with willing feet
Ever seek thy mercy-seat.

3 As they offered gifts most rare
At thy cradle rude and bare,—
So may we with holy joy,
Pure, and free from sin's alloy,
All our costliest treasures bring,
Christ, to thee, our heavenly
  King.

4 Holy Jesus, every day
Keep us in the narrow way;
And, when earthly things are
  past,
Bring our ransomed souls at
  last
Where they need no star to
  guide,
Where no clouds thy glory
  hide.

5 In the heavenly country bright
Need they no created light;
Thou its light, its joy, its crown,
Thou its sun which goes not
  down;
There for ever may we sing
Alleluias to our King.

WILLIAM CHATTERTON DIX
1837–98

201

BRIGHTEST and best of the
 sons of the morning,
Dawn on our darkness, and
  lend us thine aid;
Star of the east, the horizon
  adorning,
Guide where our infant Redeemer is laid.

2 Cold on his cradle the dew-drops
  are shining;
Low lies his head with the
  beasts of the stall;
Angels adore him in slumber
  reclining,
Maker and Monarch and
  Saviour of all.

3 Say, shall we yield him, in
  costly devotion,
Odours of Edom, and offerings divine,
Gems of the mountains and
  pearls of the ocean,
Myrrh from the forest or gold
  from the mine?

4 Vainly we offer each ample
     oblation,
Vainly with gifts would his
     favour secure;
Richer by far is the heart's
     adoration;
Dearer to God are the prayers
     of the poor.

5 Brightest and best of the sons of
     the morning,
Dawn on our darkness, and
     lend us thine aid;
Star of the east, the horizon
     adorning,
Guide where our infant Re-
     deemer is laid.

REGINALD HEBER, 1783–1826

---

202   *Wie schön leuchtet der
                Morgenstern*

HOW brightly beams the
     morning star!
What sudden radiance from afar
     Doth glad us with its shin-
          ing?
Brightness of God, that breaks
     our night
And fills the darkened souls
     with light
Who long for truth were
     pining!
Thy word, Jesus, inly feeds us,
Rightly leads us,
Life bestowing.
Praise, oh praise such love
     o'erflowing!

2 O praise to him who came to
     save,
Who conquer'd death and burst
     the grave;
     Each day new praise re-
          soundeth
To him the Lamb who once
     was slain,
The friend whom none shall
     trust in vain,
     Whose grace for aye aboun-
          deth;
Sing, ye heavens, tell the story,
Of his glory,
Till his praises
Flood with light earth's darkest
     places!

PHILIPP NICOLAI, 1556–1608
and JOHANN SCHLEGEL, 1721–93
Tr. CATHERINE WINKWORTH, 1827–78

---

203   *Rājāono rājā ane sṛṣṭino sṛjnār*

KING of kings and Lord of
     lords, and Maker of all is
     he;
Leaving the glory of heav'n he
     comes, incarnate now to
     be,
     Incarnate now to be.

2 Lord of the world, he comes
     among us, bearing love
     and grace;
Born of the womb of Virgin
     Mary, there in David's
     place,
     There in David's place.

3 Angels clothed in robes of
     whiteness, far above the
     earth,
Filling the heav'ns with praise
     and wonder, sing of
     Jesus' birth,
     Sing of Jesus' birth.

4 Joyful, joyful, all you people,
     give the Saviour praise!
Welcome the new-born King
     with gladness, shouts of
     triumph raise!
     Shouts of triumph raise!

5 All for *your* sake, all for *my*
     sake; yes, for *all*, I say;
Now for the *world* comes news of
     salvation: 'Christ is born
     today!'
     'Christ is born today!'

6 Worship now, but do not leave
     him out in stable bare;
Give him your heart for home!
     Enthrone him, King of
     glory there!
     King of glory there!

From the Gujarati of KAHANJI
MADHAVJI RATNAGRAHI, 1869–1916
Tr. ROBERT H. S. BOYD,
adapted JAMES N. S. ALEXANDER

The following are also suitable
Nos. 40, 369, 399, 12, 158

204 NUNC DIMITTIS

LORD now lettest thou thy
    servant de- ' part in '
peace : ac- ' cording ' to thy '
word.

2 For mine eyes have ' seen thy
sal- ' vation : which thou
hast prepared before the '
face of ' all ' people.

3 To be a light to ' lighten
the ' Gentiles : and to be
the ' glory of thy ' people '
Isra-el.

*Glory ' be to the ' Father : and
to the Son ' and to the '
Holy ' Ghost :*

*As it ' was in the be- ' ginning :
is now and ever shall be '
world without ' end.*
          A- ' men.
From St. Luke 2: 29–32

205

'JESUS!' Name of wondrous
    love ;
Name all other names above,
Unto which must every knee
Bow in deep humility.

2 'Jesus!' Name of priceless worth
To the fallen sons of earth,
For the promise that it gave,—
'Jesus shall his people save'.

3 'Jesus!' Name of mercy mild,
Given to the Holy Child
When the cup of human woe
First he tasted here below.

4 'Jesus!' only Name that's given
Under all the mighty heaven
Whereby man, to sin enslaved,
Bursts his fetters, and is saved.

5 'Jesus!' Name of wondrous
    love ;
Human Name of God above ;
Pleading only this, we flee,
Helpless, O our God, to thee.
    WILLIAM WALSHAM HOW, 1823–97

206 Candlemas

WHEN Mary brought her
    treasure
Unto the holy place,
No eye of man could measure
The joy upon her face.
He was but six weeks old,
Her plaything and her pleasure,
Her silver and her gold.

2 Then Simeon, on him gazing
With wonder and with love,
His agèd voice up-raising
Gave thanks to God above:
'Now welcome sweet re-
lease!
For I, my Saviour praising,
May die at last in peace'.

3 And she, all sorrow scorning,
Rejoiced in Jesus' fame.
The child her arms adorning
Shone softly like a flame
That burns the long night
through,
And keeps from dusk till morn-
ing
Its vigil clear and true.

4 As by the sun in splendour
The flags of night are furled,
So darkness shall surrender
To Christ who lights the
world:
To Christ the Star of day,
Who once was small and tender,
A candle's gentle ray.
    JAN STRUTHER, 1901–53

207

BEHOLD a little Child,
    Laid in a manger bed ;
The wintry blasts blow wild
    around his infant head.
But who is this, so lowly laid ?
'Tis he by whom the worlds
    were made.

2   Where Joseph plies his trade,
     Lo, Jesus labours too;
  The hands that all things
     made an earthly craft
     pursue,
That weary men in him may
     rest,
And faithful toil through him
     be blest.

3   Among the doctors see
     The Boy so full of grace;
Say, wherefore taketh he the
     scholar's lowly place?
That Christian boys, with
     reverence meet,
May sit and learn at Jesus' feet.

4   Christ, once thyself a boy!
     Our boyhood guard and
     guide;
Be thou its light and joy, and
     still with us abide,
That thy dear love, so great and
     free,
May draw us evermore to thee.
       WILLIAM WALSHAM HOW
             1823–97

208   *Iordanis oras praevia*

ON Jordan's bank the Bap-
    tist's cry
Announces that the Lord is
    nigh;
Come then and hearken, for he
    brings
Glad tidings from the King of
    kings.

2 Then cleansed be every breast
    from sin;
Make straight the way for God
    within;
Prepare we in our hearts a
    home,
Where such a mighty Guest
    may come.

3 For thou art our salvation,
    Lord,
Our refuge, and our great
    reward;
Without thy grace we waste
    away,
Like flowers that wither and
    decay.

4 Stretch forth thine hand, to
    heal our sore,
And make us rise to fall no
    more;
Once more upon thy people
    shine,
And fill the world with love
    divine.

5 *All praise, eternal Son, to thee*
Whose advent sets thy people free,
Whom with the Father we adore,
And Holy Ghost, for evermore.
             Amen.
       CHARLES COFFIN, 1676–1749
       Tr. JOHN CHANDLER, 1806–76
               and others

209   *Hostis Herodes impie*

HOW vain the cruel Herod's
    fear,
When told that Christ the King
    is near!
He takes not earthly realms
    away,
Who gives the realms that ne'er
    decay.

2 The eastern sages saw from far
And followed on his guiding
    star;
By light their way to Light they
    trod,
And by their gifts confessed
    their God.

3 Within the Jordan's sacred
    flood
The heavenly Lamb in meek-
    ness stood,
That he, to whom no sin was
    known,
Might cleanse his people from
    their own.

4 And oh, what miracle divine,
When water reddened into wine!
He spake the word, and forth
    there flowed
A stream that nature ne'er be-
    stowed.

5 *All glory, Jesus, be to thee*
  For this thy glad Epiphany:
  Whom with the Father we adore,
  And Holy Ghost, for evermore.
  Amen.

CAELIUS SEDULIUS, d. c. 450
Tr. JOHN MASON NEALE, 1818–66
and Compilers of *Hymns Ancient and
Modern*, 1875 edn.

210

FORTY days and forty nights
  Thou wast fasting in the
  wild;
Forty days and forty nights
  Tempted still, yet undefiled.

*2 Sunbeams scorching day by
  day;
Chilly dewdrops nightly shed;
Prowling beasts about thy way;
Stones thy pillow; earth thy
  bed.

3 Shall not we thy sorrows share,
  Learn thy discipline of will,
And like thee, by fast and
  prayer
  Wrestle with the powers of
  ill?

4 What if Satan, vexing sore,
  Flesh and spirit shall assail,
Thou, his vanquisher before,
  Will not suffer us to fail.

5 Watching, praying, struggling
  thus,
  Victory ours at last shall be;
Angels minister to us
  As they ministered to thee.

GEORGE SMYTTAN, 1822–70
and FRANCIS POTT, 1832–1909
altered

* *This verse may be omitted if desired.*

211

JESUS calls us! O'er the
  tumult
Of our life's wild restless sea,
Day by day his voice is sounding,
  Saying, 'Christian, follow
  me':

2 As, of old, Saint Andrew heard
  it
  By the Galilean lake,
Turned from home and toil and
  kindred,
  Leaving all for his dear sake.

3 Jesus calls us from the worship
  Of the vain world's golden
  store,
From each idol that would keep
  us,
  Saying, 'Christian, love me
  more'.

4 In our joys and in our sorrows,
  Days of toil and hours of
  ease,
Still he calls, in cares and
  pleasures,
  'Christian, love me more than
  these'.

5 Jesus calls us! By thy mercies,
  Saviour, make us hear thy
  call,
Give our hearts to thy
  obedience,
  Serve and love thee best of
  all.

CECIL FRANCES ALEXANDER,
1818–95, altered

212

I HEARD the voice of Jesus
  say,
  'Come unto me and rest;
Lay down, thou weary one, lay
  down
  Thy head upon my breast':
I came to Jesus as I was,
  Weary, and worn, and sad;
I found in him a resting-place,
  And he has made me glad.

2 I heard the voice of Jesus say,
  'Behold, I freely give
The living water; thirsty one,
  Stoop down and drink, and
  live':
I came to Jesus, and I drank
  Of that life-giving stream;
My thirst was quenched, my
  soul revived,
  And now I live in him.

3 I heard the voice of Jesus say,
  'I am this dark world's Light;
Look unto me, thy morn shall
    rise,
  And all thy day be bright':
I looked to Jesus, and I found
  In him my Star, my Sun;
And in that light of life I'll
    walk,
  Till travelling days are done.
         HORATIUS BONAR, 1808–89

213

IT fell upon a summer day,
  When Jesus walked in
    Galilee,
The mothers from a village
    brought
  Their children to his knee.

2 He took them in his arms, and laid
  His hands on each remembered
    head;
'Suffer these little ones to come
  To me', he gently said.

3 'Forbid them not; unless ye bear
  The childlike heart your hearts
    within,
Unto my Kingdom ye may
    come,
  But may not enter in.'

4 Master, I fain would enter
    there;
O let me follow thee, and share
Thy meek and lowly heart, and
    be
  Freed from all worldly care.

5 O happy thus to live and move!
  And sweet this world, where I
    shall find
God's beauty everywhere, his
    love,
  His good in all mankind.

6 Then, Father, grant this child-
    like heart,
  That I may come to Christ, and
    feel
His hands on me in blessing
    laid,
  Love-giving, strong to heal.
    STOPFORD AUGUSTUS BROOKE
            1832–1916

214

THINE arm, O Lord, in days
  of old,
  Was strong to heal and save;
It triumphed o'er disease and
    death,
  O'er darkness and the grave.
To thee they went—the blind,
    the dumb,
  The palsied, and the lame,
The leper with his tainted life,
  The sick with fevered frame;

2 And, lo! thy touch brought life
    and health,
  Gave speech, and strength,
    and sight;
And youth renewed and frenzy
    calmed
  Owned thee, the Lord of
    light.
And now, O Lord, be near to
    bless,
  Almighty as of yore,
In crowded street, by restless
    couch,
  As by Gennesaret's shore.

3 Be thou our great Deliverer
    still,
  Thou Lord of life and death;
Restore and quicken, soothe
    and bless,
  With thine almighty breath;
To hands that work and eyes
    that see
  Give wisdom's heavenly lore,
That whole and sick, and weak
    and strong,
  May praise thee evermore.
     EDWARD HAYES PLUMPTRE
             1821–91

215

JESUS, whose all-redeeming
  love
  No penitent did scorn,
Who didst the stain of guilt
    remove,
  Till hope anew was born:

2 To thee, Physician of the soul,
  The lost, the outcast, came:
Thou didst restore and make
    them whole,
  Disburdened of their shame.

3 'Twas love, thy love, their
    bondage brake,
Whose fetters sin had bound:
For faith to love did answer
    make,
And free forgiveness found.

4 Jesus, that pardoning grace to
    find,
I too would come to thee:
O merciful to all mankind,
Be merciful to me.

GEORGE WALLACE BRIGGS
1875-1959

216

WHAT grace, O Lord, and
    beauty shone
Around thy steps below!
What patient love was seen in
    all
Thy life and death of woe!

2 Thy foes might hate, despise,
    revile,
Thy friends unfaithful prove:
Unwearied in forgiveness still,
Thy heart could only love.

3 O give us hearts to love like
    thee,
Like thee, O Lord, to grieve
Far more for others' sins than
    all
The wrongs that we receive.

4 One with thyself, may every
    eye
In us, thy brethren, see
That gentleness and grace that
    spring
From union, Lord, with
    thee.

EDWARD DENNY, 1796-1889

217   *For the Transfiguration*
Caelestis formam gloriae

O WONDROUS type, O
    vision fair
Of glory that the Church shall
    share,
Which Christ upon the moun-
    tain shows,
Where brighter than the sun he
    lows!

2 With shining face and bright
    array,
Christ deigns to manifest today
What glory shall be theirs,
    above,
Who joy in God with perfect
    love.

3 The law and prophets there
    have place,
The chosen witnesses of Grace;
The Father's voice from out the
    cloud
Proclaims his only Son aloud.

4 And Christian hearts are raised
    on high
By that great vision's mystery,
For which, in thankful strains,
    we raise
On this glad day the voice of
    praise.

5 O Father, with the eternal Son
And Holy Spirit ever One,
Vouchsafe to bring us, by thy
    grace,
To see thy glory face to face.

15th century
TR. JOHN MASON NEALE, 1818-66
and others

218

THERE'S a wideness in God's
    mercy,
Like the wideness of the sea;
There's a kindness in his justice,
Which is more than liberty.

2 There is no place where earth's
    sorrows
Are more felt than up in
    heaven:
There is no place where earth's
    failings
Have such kindly judgment
    given.

3 For the love of God is broader
Than the measures of man's
    mind;
And the heart of the Eternal
Is most wonderfully kind.

4 There is plentiful redemption
In the blood that has been
    shed;
There is joy for all the members
In the sorrows of the Head.

5 If our love were but more
simple,
We would take him at his
word;
And our lives be filled with
glory
From the glory of the Lord.

FREDERICK WILLIAM FABER
1814–63, altered

219

Son of the Lord Most High,
Who gave the worlds their
birth,
He came to live and die
The Son of Man on earth:
In Bethlem's stable born
was he,
And humbly bred in
Galilee.

2 Born in so low estate,
Schooled in a workman's
trade,
Not with the high and great
His home the Highest made:
But labouring by his
brethren's side,
Life's common lot he
glorified.

3 Then, when his hour was come,
He heard his Father's call:
And leaving friends and home,
He gave himself for all:
Glad news to bring, the
lost to find;
To heal the sick, the lame,
the blind.

4 Toiling by night and day,
Himself oft burdened sore,
Where hearts in bondage lay,
Himself their burden bore:
Till, scorned by them he
died to save,
Himself in death; as life, he
gave.

5 O lowly Majesty,
Lofty in lowliness!
Blest Saviour, who am I
To share thy blessedness?
Yet thou hast called me,
even me,
Servant Divine, to follow
thee.

GEORGE WALLACE BRIGGS
1875–1959

220

O sing a song of Bethlehem,
Of shepherds watching
there,
And of the news that came to
them
From angels in the air:
The light that shone on Bethle-
hem
Fills all the world today;
Of Jesus' birth and peace on
earth
The angels sing alway.

2 O sing a song of Nazareth,
Of sunny days of joy;
O sing of fragrant flowers'
breath,
And of the sinless Boy:
For now the flowers of Nazareth
In every heart may grow;
Now spreads the fame of his
dear Name
On all the winds that blow.

3 O sing a song of Galilee,
Of lake and woods and hill,
Of him who walked upon the
sea,
And bade its waves be still:
For though, like waves on
Galilee,
Dark seas of trouble roll,
When faith has heard the
Master's word,
Falls peace upon the soul.

4 O sing a song of Calvary,
Its glory and dismay;
Of him who hung upon the
tree,
And took our sins away:
For he who died on Calvary
Is risen from the grave,
And Christ, our Lord, by heaven
adored,
Is mighty now to save.

LOUIS FITZGERALD BENSON
1855–1930

221

Who is he in yonder stall,
At whose feet the shepherds
fall?
'Tis the Lord, O wondrous story!
'Tis the Lord, the King of glory!

2 Who is he in deep distress,
   Fasting in the wilderness?

3 Who is he the gathering throng
   Greet with loud triumphant
   song?

4 Lo, at midnight, who is he
   Prays in dark Gethsemane?

5 Who is he on yonder tree
   Dies in shame and agony?

6 Who is he that from the grave
   Comes to heal and help and
   save?

7 Who is he that from his throne
   Rules through all the world
   alone?

   BENJAMIN RUSSELL HANBY
   1833–67, altered

222

Wise men seeking Jesus
   Travelled from afar,
Guided on their journey
   By a beauteous star.

2 But if we desire him,
   He is close at hand;
For our native country
   Is our Holy Land.

3 Prayerful souls may find him
   By our quiet lakes,
Meet him on our hillsides
   When the morning breaks.

4 In our fertile cornfields
   While the sheaves are bound,
In our busy markets,
   Jesus may be found.

5 Fishermen talk with him
   By the great north sea,
As the first disciples
   Did in Galilee.

6 Every peaceful village
   In our land might be
Made by Jesus' presence
   Like sweet Bethany.

7 He is more than near us,
   If we love him well;
For he seeketh ever
   In our hearts to dwell.

   JAMES THOMAS EAST
   1860–1937

223   *O amor quam ecstaticus*

O Love, how deep, how
   broad, how high!
How passing thought and fan-
   tasy
That God, the Son of God,
   should take
Our mortal form for mortals'
   sake.

2 He sent no angel to our race
   Of higher or of lower place,
But wore the robe of human
   frame,
And he himself to this world
   came.

3 For us baptized, for us he bore
   His holy fast, and hungered
   sore;
For us temptations sharp he
   knew;
For us the tempter overthrew.

4 For us to wicked men betrayed,
   Scourged, mocked, in crown of
   thorns arrayed,
He bore the shameful cross and
   death;
For us at length gave up his
   breath.

5 For us he rose from death again,
   For us he went on high to reign,
For us he sent his Spirit here,
   To guide, to strengthen, and to
   cheer.

6 *To him whose boundless love has*
   won
Salvation for us through his Son,
To God the Father, glory be
Both now and through eternity.
   Amen.

   15th century
   Tr. BENJAMIN WEBB, 1820–85
   altered

224

My song is love unknown,
   My Saviour's love to me,
Love to the loveless shown, that
   they might lovely be.
O who am I, that for my sake
My Lord should take frail flesh
   and die?

2 He came from his blest throne,
　　Salvation to bestow:
But men made strange, and
　　none the longed-for Christ
　　would know.
　　　But O, my Friend, my
　　　Friend indeed,
Who at my need his life did
　　spend!

3 Sometimes they strew his way,
　　And his sweet praises sing;
Resounding all the day hosannas
　　to their King.
　　　Then 'Crucify!' is all their
　　　breath,
And for his death they thirst and
　　cry.

4 Why, what hath my Lord
　　done?
　　What makes this rage and
　　spite?
He made the lame to run, he
　　gave the blind their sight.
　　Sweet injuries! yet they at
　　these
Themselves displease and 'gainst
　　him rise.

5 They rise, and needs will have
　　My dear Lord done away;
A murderer they save, the Prince
　　of Life they slay.
　　Yet cheerful he to suffering
　　goes,
That he his foes from thence
　　might free.

6 In life, no house, no home
　　My Lord on earth might
　　have;
In death, no friendly tomb but
　　what a stranger gave.
What may I say? heav'n was
　　his home:
　　But mine the tomb wherein he
　　lay.

7 Here might I stay and sing,
　　No story so divine;
Never was love, dear King, never
　　was grief like thine!
　　This is my Friend, in whose
　　sweet praise
I all my days could gladly
　　spend.

　　　SAMUEL CROSSMAN, c. 1624–83

225 PARAPHRASE 52, verses 1,
　　　　　　3–6

YE who the Name of Jesus
　　bear,
　　His sacred steps pursue;
And let that mind which was in
　　him
　　Be also found in you.

2 His greatness he for us abased,
　　For us his glory veiled;
In human likeness dwelt on
　　earth,
　　His majesty concealed:

3 Nor only as a man appears,
　　But stoops a servant low;
Submits to death, nay, bears
　　the cross,
　　In all its shame and woe.

4 Hence God this generous love to
　　men
　　With honours just hath
　　crowned,
And raised the Name of Jesus
　　far
　　Above all names renowned:

5 That at this Name, with sacred
　　awe,
　　Each humble knee should
　　bow,
Of hosts immortal in the skies,
　　And nations spread below.

　　　Scottish Paraphrases, 1781
　　　　　　Phil. 2: 5, 7–10

226　　　*For children*

I CAN picture Jesus toiling,
　　Carpenter of Nazareth
　　town:
In his face a great love shining,
　　Working till the sun goes
　　down.
By his children still he stands,
Blessing labour of their hands.

2 I can picture Jesus stooping,
　　Lifting up a heavy weight;
Stiff with toil, his arms out-
　　stretching,
　　Weary, when the hour is late.
Still he stoops from heaven
　　above,
Drawing all men by his love.

3 Christ the Workman, make me
    holy,
  Christ the Saviour, make me
    true;
Make of me a thing of beauty,
    Show me how to labour too;
Fellow-worker would I be
Ever, blessèd Lord, with thee.

D. HELEN STONE

227 *For children*

I LOVE to hear the story
  Which angel voices tell,
How once the King of Glory
  *Came down on earth to
    dwell.

2 I am both weak and sinful,
    But this I surely know,
The Lord came down to save me
  Because he loved me so.

3 I'm glad my blessèd Saviour
    Was once a child like me,
To show how pure and holy
  His little ones might be;

4 And, if I try to follow
    His footsteps here below,
He never will forsake me,
  Because he loves me so.

5 To sing his love and mercy
    My sweetest songs I'll raise,
And, though I cannot see him,
    I know he hears my praise;

6 For he has kindly promised
    That even I may go
To sing among his angels,
  Because he loves me so.

EMILY HUNTINGTON MILLER
1833–1913

* The last line of each verse is repeated.

228 *For younger children*

JESUS' hands were kind
    hands, doing good to all,
Healing pain and sickness,
    blessing children small;
Washing tired feet, and saving
    those who fall;
Jesus' hands were kind hands,
    doing good to all.

2 Take my hands, Lord Jesus,
    let them work for you,
Make them strong and gentle,
    kind in all I do;
Let me watch you, Jesus, till
    I'm gentle too,
Till my hands are kind hands,
    quick to work for you.

MARGARET CROPPER

229 *For younger children*

I LIKE to think of Jesus
  So loving, kind, and true
That when he walked among
    his friends
His friends were loving too.

2 I like to think of Jesus
    With children at his knee;
And hear his gentle words
    again,
'Let children come to me'.

3 I like to think of Jesus
    So loving, kind, and true
That somehow when I think of
    him,
It makes me loving too.

ELIZABETH McEWEN SHIELDS

230 *For younger children*

WHEN Jesus saw the fisher-
    men
In boats upon the sea,
He called to them 'Come, leave
    your nets
And follow, follow me'.
They followed where he healed
    the sick
And gave the hungry bread,
And others joined them as they
    went
Wherever Jesus led.

2 And now his friends are every-
    where;
The circle once so small
Extends around the whole
    wide world,
For Jesus calls us all.

In this great circle we belong,
Wherever we may be,
If we will answer when he calls,
'Come, follow, follow me'.

EDITH AGNEW

The following are also suitable
No.
52 At even, when the sun was set
76 Dear Lord and Father of mankind

CHRIST'S PASSION AND CROSS

231 PSALM 42, verses 1–5,
8–11

AS the hart panteth after the water
brooks : so panteth my soul
after ' thee O God.

My soul thirsteth for God ' for
the living God : when shall
I come and appear ' before
God ?

My tears have been my ' meat
day and night : while they
continually say unto me
where ' is thy God ?

When I remember these things
I pour out ' my soul in me :
for I had gone with the
multitude I went with them
to the house of God with
the voice of joy and praise
with a multitude that kept '
holy day.

Why art thou cast down O
my soul ? and why art thou
dis ' quieted in me : hope
thou in God for I shall yet
praise him for the help of
his ' countenance.

Yet the Lord will command his
loving-kindness ' in the daytime : and in the night his
song shall be with me and
my prayer unto the God ' of
my life.

I will say unto God my rock
Why hast ' thou forgotten me :
why go I mourning because
of the oppression of the '
enemy ?

As with a sword in my bones
mine ene ' mies reproach me :
while they say daily unto me
where ' is thy God ?

Why art thou cast down O my
soul ? and why art thou
disquiet ' ed within me : hope
thou in God for I shall yet
praise him who is the
health of my countenance '
and my God.

232 PSALM 118, verses 19–29

OPEN to me the gates of righ-'
teousness : I will go into them
and I ' will praise the Lord.

This gate of ' the Lord : into which
the righ ' teous shall enter.

I will ' praise thee : for thou hast
heard me and art become ' my
salvation.

The stone which the builders '
refusèd : is become the head
stone ' of the corner.

This is the Lord's ' doing : it is
marvel ' lous in our eyes.

This is the day which the
Lord ' hath made : we will
rejoice and ' be glad in it.

Save now I beseech thee ' O
Lord : O Lord I beseech thee
send now ' prosperity.

Blessèd be he that cometh in
the Name of ' the Lord : we
have blessed you out of the '
house of the Lord.

God is ' the Lord which hath
showed ' us light : bind the
sacrifice with cords even unto
the horns ' of the altar.

Thou art my God and I will '
praise thee : thou art my God
I ' will exalt thee.

O give thanks unto the Lord
for he ' is good : for his mercy
endur ' eth for ever.

*Glory be to the Father and to '
the Son : and to ' the Holy
Ghost.*
*As it was in the beginning is
now and ever ' shall be : world
with ' out end Amen.*

233   *Gloria, laus et honor*

* *A*LL *glory, laud, and honour*
    To thee, Redeemer King,
To whom the lips of children
Made sweet hosannas ring!
Thou art the King of Israel,
Thou David's royal Son,
Who in the Lord's Name comest,
The King and Blessèd One.

2 The company of angels
    Are praising thee on high,
And mortal men and all things
Created make reply.

3 The people of the Hebrews
    With palms before thee went;
Our praise and prayer and an-
    thems
Before thee we present.

4 To thee before thy Passion
    They sang their hymns of
    praise;
To thee now high exalted
Our melody we raise.

5 Thou didst accept their praises;
    Accept the prayers we bring,
Who in all good delightest,
Thou good and gracious King.
    THEODULPH OF ORLEANS, *d.* 821
    Tr. JOHN MASON NEALE, 1818–66
    altered

* *This refrain is sung before each
verse and also after the final verse.*

234

R IDE on! ride on in majesty!
    Hark! all the tribes
'Hosanna!' cry;
O Saviour meek, pursue thy
    road
With palms and scattered gar-
    ments strowed.

2 Ride on! ride on in majesty!
In lowly pomp ride on to die;
O Christ, thy triumphs now
    begin
O'er captive death and con-
    quered sin.

3 Ride on! ride on in majesty!
The wingèd squadrons of the
    sky
Look down with sad and won-
    dering eyes
To see the approaching sacri-
    fice.

4 Ride on! ride on in majesty!
Thy last and fiercest strife is
    nigh;
The Father on his sapphire
    throne
Awaits his own anointed Son.

5 Ride on! ride on in majesty!
In lowly pomp ride on to die;
Bow thy meek head to mortal
    pain,
Then take, O God, thy power,
    and reign.
    HENRY HART MILMAN, 1791–1868

235   *For children*

H OSANNA, loud hosanna,
    The little children sang;
Through pillared court and
    temple
The joyful anthem rang;
To Jesus, who had blessed them
Close folded to his breast,
The children sang their praises,
The simplest and the best.

2 From Olivet they followed,
'Mid an exultant crowd,
The victor palm-branch waving,
And chanting clear and loud;

Bright angels joined the chorus,
Beyond the cloudless sky,—
'Hosanna in the highest!
Glory to God on high!'

3 Fair leaves of silvery olive
They strowed upon the
ground,
While Salem's circling moun-
tains
Echoed the joyful sound;
The Lord of men and angels
Rode on in lowly state,
Nor scorned that little children
Should on his bidding wait.

4 'Hosanna in the highest!'
That ancient song we sing,
For Christ is our Redeemer,
The Lord of heaven our
King.
O may we ever praise him
With heart and life and
voice,
And in his blissful presence
Eternally rejoice.

JEANNETTE THRELFALL, 1821–80

236   *For children*

CHILDREN of Jerusalem
Sang the praise of Jesus'
name:
Children, too, of modern days
Join to sing the Saviour's
praise.
Hark! while infant voices sing
Loud hosannas to our King.

2 We are taught to love the Lord,
We are taught to read his Word,
We are taught the way to
heaven:
Praise for all to God be given.

3 Parents, teachers, old and
young,
All unite to swell the song,
Higher and yet higher rise,
Till hosannas reach the skies.

JOHN HENLEY, 1800–42

237   *Thursday in Holy Week*
PARAPHRASE 35

'TWAS on that night when
doomed to know
The eager rage of every foe,
That night in which he was
betrayed,
The Saviour of the world took
bread;

2 And, after thanks and glory
given
To him that rules in earth and
heaven,
That symbol of his flesh he
broke,
And thus to all his followers
spoke:

3 'My broken body thus I give
For you, for all; take, eat, and
live:
And oft the sacred rite renew
That brings my wondrous love
to view.'

4 Then in his hands the cup he
raised,
And God anew he thanked and
praised,
While kindness in his bosom
glowed,
And from his lips salvation
flowed.

5 'My blood I thus pour forth,' he
cries,
'To cleanse the soul in sin that
lies;
In this the covenant is sealed,
And heaven's eternal grace
revealed.

6 'With love to man this cup is
fraught,
Let all partake the sacred
draught;
Through latest ages let it pour
In memory of my dying hour.'

Scottish Paraphrases, 1781
St. Matthew 26:26–29

238

PRAISE to the Holiest in the
height,
And in the depth be praise,—
In all his words most wonderful,
Most sure in all his ways.

2 O loving wisdom of our God!
    When all was sin and shame,
A second Adam to the fight
    And to the rescue came.

3 O wisest love! that flesh and blood,
    Which did in Adam fail,
Should strive afresh against the foe,
    Should strive and should prevail;

4 O generous love! that he who smote
    In Man, for man, the foe,
The double agony in Man,
    For man, should undergo,

5 And in the garden secretly,
    And on the cross on high,
Should teach his brethren, and inspire
    To suffer and to die.

6 Praise to the Holiest in the height,
    And in the depth be praise,—
In all his words most wonderful,
    Most sure in all his ways.

JOHN HENRY NEWMAN, 1801–90

239 PSALM 22, verses 1–9, 15–19, 22–24, 27, 30, 31

MY GOD my God why hast thou for ' saken me : why art thou so far from helping me and from the words of ' my roaring ?

O my God I cry in the daytime but thou ' hearest not : and in the night season and am ' not silent.

But thou art holy O thou that inhabitest the praises of Israel   Our fathers trusted in ' thee : they trusted and thou didst de ' liver them.

They cried unto thee and were de ' liver'd : they trusted in thee and were not ' confounded.

But I am a worm and ' no man : a reproach of men and despised of ' the people.

All they that see me laugh me to ' scorn : they shoot out the lip they shake the ' head saying,

He trusted on the Lord that he would de ' liver him: let him deliver him seeing he deligh ' ted in him.

But thou art he that took me out of the ' womb : thou didst make me hope when I was upon my ' mother's breasts.

Be not far from me for trouble is ' near : for there is ' none to help.

My strength is dried up like a potsherd   and my tongue cleaveth to my ' jaws : and thou hast brought me into the ' dust of death.

For dogs have ' compassed me : the assembly of the wicked have inclosed me they pierced my ' hands and my feet.

I may tell ' all my bones : they look and stare ' upon me.

They part my garments a ' mong them : and cast lots upon ' my vesture.

But be not thou far from me O ' Lord : O my strength haste thee ' to help me.

I will declare thy Name unto my ' brethren : in the midst of the congregation will ' I praise thee.

Ye that fear the Lord ' praise him : all ye the seed of Jacob glorify him and fear him all ye the seed ' of Israel.

For he hath not despised nor abhorred the affliction of the af ' flicted : neither hath he hid his face from him but when he cried unto ' him he heard.

All the ends of the world shall
remember and turn unto the '
Lord : and all the kindreds of
the nations shall worship '
before thee.

A seed shall ' serve him : it shall
be accounted to the Lord for
a ge ' neration.

They shall come and shall declare his righteousness unto
a people that shall be ' born :
that he ' hath done this.

240
TRISAGION
AND THE
REPROACHES

Choir or Cantor
Holy God, holy and mighty, holy
and immortal, have mercy
upon us.

Congregation
Holy God, holy and mighty, holy
and immortal, have mercy
upon us.

Choir or Cantor
O my people, what ' have I done to
thee ?
or wherein have I wear'ied thee ?
Answer me.
Because I brought thee forth out
of the land of Egypt, and led
thee to a land ex'ceeding good :
thou hast prepared a cross ' for
thy Saviour.

Congregation
Holy God, holy and mighty, holy
and immortal, have mercy
upon us.

Choir or Cantor
Before thee I o' pened the sea :
and with a spear thou hast
o' pened my side.
I went before thee in a pil ' lar of
cloud :
and thou hast brought me to
the judgment 'hall of Pilate.

Congregation
Holy God, holy and mighty, holy
and immortal, have mercy
upon us.

Choir or Cantor
I fed thee with manna ' in the
desert :
and thou hast beaten me with
' blows and stripes.
I made thee to drink the water of
salvation ' from the rock :
and thou hast made me to
drink ' gall and vinegar.

Congregation
Holy God, holy and mighty, holy
and immortal, have mercy
upon us.

Choir or Cantor
I gave thee a ' royal sceptre :
and thou hast given my head a
' crown of thorns.
I lifted thee up' with great power :
and thou hast hung me upon
the gibbet ' of the cross.

Congregation
Holy God, holy and mighty, holy
and immortal, have mercy
upon us.

EARLY GALLICAN CHURCH

241

THERE is a green hill far
away,
Outside a city wall,
Where the dear Lord was
crucified,
Who died to save us all.

2 We may not know, we cannot
tell
What pains he had to bear ;
But we believe it was for us
He hung and suffered there.

3 He died that we might be for-
given,
He died to make us good,
That we might go at last to
heaven,
Saved by his precious blood.

4 There was no other good enough
To pay the price of sin ;
He only could unlock the gate
Of heaven, and let us in.

5 O dearly, dearly has he loved,
  And we must love him too,
And trust in his redeeming
    blood,
  And try his works to do.

CECIL FRANCES ALEXANDER
1818–95

242 *Solus ad victimam procedis,*
        Domine

ALONE thou goest forth, O
    Lord,
  In sacrifice to die;
Is this thy sorrow naught to us
Who pass unheeding by?

2 Our sins, not thine, thou bearest,
      Lord;
  Make us thy sorrow feel,
Till through our pity and our
    shame
  Love answers love's appeal.

3 This is earth's darkest hour, but
      thou
  Dost light and life restore;
Then let all praise be given thee
  Who livest evermore.

4 Grant us to suffer with thee,
      Lord,
  That, as we share this hour,
Thy cross may bring us to thy
      joy
  And resurrection power.

PETER ABELARD, 1079–1142
Tr. FRANCIS BLAND TUCKER
altered

243

O COME and mourn with me
    awhile;
  O come ye to the Saviour's
    side;
O come, together let us mourn:
  Jesus, our Lord, is crucified!

2 Have we no tears to shed for
      him,
  While soldiers scoff and foes
    deride?
Ah! look how patiently he
  hangs:

3 Seven times he spake, seven
    words of love;
  And all three hours his silence
    cried
For mercy on the souls of men:

4 O break, O break, hard heart of
    mine!
  Thy weak self-love and guilty
    pride
His Pilate and his Judas were:

5 O love of God! O sin of man!
  In this dread act your
    strength is tried,
And victory remains with love:

FREDERICK WILLIAM FABER
1814–63, altered

244 *'Father, forgive them; for they*
        know not what they do.'

O WORD of pity, for our par-
    don pleading,
  Breathed in the hour of
    loneliness and pain;
O voice, which, through the ages
    interceding,
  Calls us to fellowship with
    God again.

2 O word of comfort, through the
    silence stealing,
  As the dread act of sacrifice
    began;
O infinite compassion, still re-
    vealing
  The infinite forgiveness won
    for man.

3 O word of hope, to raise us near-
    er heaven,
  When courage fails us, and
    when faith is dim;
The souls for whom Christ prays
    to Christ are given,
  To find their pardon and
    their joy in him.

4 O Intercessor, who art ever liv-
    ing
  To plead for dying souls that
    they may live,
Teach us to know our sin which
    needs forgiving,
  Teach us to know the love
    which can forgive.

ADA RUNDALL GREENAWAY
1861–1937

245 *Verily I say unto thee, Today shalt thou be with me in Paradise.'*

'LORD, when thy Kingdom
   comes, remember me!'
Thus spake the dying lips to
   dying ears.
O faith, which in that darkest
      hour could see
The promised glory of the
   far-off years!

2 Hark! through the gloom. the
      dying Saviour saith,
'Thou too shalt rest in Paradise today';
O words of love to answer
   words of faith!
O words of hope for those
   who live to pray!

3 Lord, when with dying lips my
      prayer is said,
Grant that in faith thy Kingdom I may see,
And, thinking on thy cross, and
   bleeding head,
May breathe my parting
   words, 'Remember me'.

4 Remember me; and, ere I pass
      away,
Speak thou the assuring
   word that sets us free,
And make thy promise to my
   heart, 'Today
Thou too shalt rest in Paradise with me'.

WILLIAM DALRYMPLE MACLAGAN
1826–1910

246 *'Woman, behold thy son!...
   Behold thy mother!'*

Stabat mater dolorosa

AT the cross, her station keep-
   ing,
Stood the mournful mother
   weeping,
   Where he hung, the dying
      Lord;
For her soul, of joy bereavèd,
Bowed with anguish, deeply
   grievèd,
   Felt the sharp and piercing
      sword.

2 O, how sad and sore distressèd
Now was she, that mother
   blessèd
   Of the sole-begotten One;
Deep the woe of her affliction,
When she saw the crucifixion
   Of her ever-glorious Son.

3 Who, on Christ's dear mother
      gazing,
Pierced by anguish so amazing,
   Born of woman, would not
      weep?
Who, on Christ's dear mother
      thinking,
Such a cup of sorrow drinking,
   Would not share her sorrows
      deep?

4 For his people's sins chastisèd,
She beheld her Son despisèd,
   Scourged, and crowned with
      thorns entwined;
Saw him then from judgment
   taken,
And in death by all forsaken,
   Till his spirit he resigned.

5 Jesus, may her deep devotion
Stir in me the same emotion,
   Fount of love, Redeemer
      kind,
That my heart, fresh ardour
   gaining,
And a purer love attaining,
   May with thee acceptance
      find.

13th century
Tr. EDWARD CASWALL, 1814–78
and others

247 *'My God, my God, why hast
   thou forsaken me?'*

THRONED upon the awe-
   some Tree,
King of grief, I watch with thee.
Darkness veils thine anguished
   face:
None its lines of woe can trace:
None can tell what pangs un-
   known
Hold thee silent and alone,—

2 Silent through those three dread
      hours,
Wrestling with the evil powers,
Left alone with human sin,

Gloom around thee and within,
Till the appointed time is nigh,
Till the Lamb of God may die.

3 Hark, that cry that peals aloud
Upward through the whelming
cloud!
Thou, the Father's only Son,
Thou, his own anointed One,
Thou dost ask him—can it
be?—
'Why hast thou forsaken me?'

4 Lord, should fear and anguish
roll
Darkly o'er my sinful soul,
Thou, who once wast thus bereft
That thine own might ne'er be
left,
Teach me by that bitter cry
In the gloom to know thee nigh.

JOHN ELLERTON, 1826–93

248   '*I thirst.*'

O PERFECT God, thy love
As perfect Man did share
Here upon earth each form of ill
Thy fellow-men must bear.

2 Now from the tree of scorn
We hear thy voice again;
Thou who didst take our mortal
flesh,
Hast felt our mortal pain.

3 Thy body suffers thirst,
Parched are thy lips and dry:
How poor the offering man can
bring
Thy thirst to satisfy!

4 O Saviour, by thy thirst
Borne on the cross of shame,
Grant us in all our sufferings
here
To glorify thy Name:

5 That through each pain and
grief
Our souls may onward move
To gain more likeness to thy
life,
More knowledge of thy love.

ADA RUNDALL GREENAWAY
1861–1937

249   '*It is finished.*'

O PERFECT life of love!
All, all is finished now,
All that he left his throne above
To do for us below.

2 No work is left undone
Of all the Father willed;
His toils and sorrows, one by
one,
The Scriptures have fulfilled.

3 No pain that we can share
But he has felt its smart;
All forms of human grief and
care
Have pierced that tender
heart.

4 And on his thorn-crowned
head,
And on his sinless soul,
Our sins in all their guilt were
laid,
That he might make us
whole.

5 In perfect love he dies;
For me he dies, for me!
O all-atoning Sacrifice,
I cling by faith to thee.

6 In every time of need,
Before the judgment throne,
Thy work, O Lamb of God, I'll
plead,
Thy merits, not my own.

7 Yet work, O Lord, in me,
As thou for me hast wrought;
And let my love the answer be
To grace thy love has brought.

HENRY WILLIAMS BAKER, 1821–77

250   '*Father, into thy hands
I commend my spirit.*'

A ND now, belovèd Lord, thy
soul resigning
Into thy Father's arms with
conscious will,
Calmly, with reverend grace,
thy head inclining,
The throbbing brow and
labouring breast grow still.

2 Freely thy life thou yieldest,
   meekly bending
Even to the last beneath our
   sorrows' load,
Yet strong in death, in perfect
   peace commending
Thy spirit to thy Father and
   thy God.

3 My Saviour, in mine hour of
   mortal anguish,
When earth grows dim, and
   round me falls the night,
O breathe thy peace, as flesh
   and spirit languish;
At that dread eventide let
   there be light.

4 To thy dear cross turn thou
   mine eyes in dying;
Lay but my fainting head
   upon thy breast;
Thine outstretched arms receive
   my latest sighing;
And then, O then, thine everlasting rest!

ELIZA SIBBALD ALDERSON
1818–89

251   *Herzliebster Jesu*

AH, holy Jesus, how hast thou
   offended,
That man to judge thee hath in
   hate pretended?
By foes derided, by thine own
   rejected,
     O most afflicted.

2 Lo, the good Shepherd for the
   sheep is offered;
The slave hath sinnèd, and the
   Son hath suffered;
For man's atonement, while he
   nothing heedeth,
     God intercedeth.

3 For me, kind Jesus, was thy
   incarnation,
Thy mortal sorrow, and thy
   life's oblation;
Thy death of anguish and thy
   bitter passion,
     For my salvation.

4 Therefore, kind Jesus, since I
   cannot pay thee,
I do adore thee, and will ever
   pray thee,
Think on thy mercy and thy
   love unswerving,
     Not my deserving.

JOHANN HEERMANN, 1585–1647
Par. ROBERT BRIDGES, 1844–1930

252

O DEAREST Lord, thy
   sacred head
With thorns was pierced for
   me;
O pour thy blessing on my head,
That I may think for thee.

2 O dearest Lord, thy sacred
   hands
With nails were pierced for
   me;
O shed thy blessing on my
   hands,
That they may work for thee.

3 O dearest Lord, thy sacred feet
With nails were pierced for
   me;
O pour thy blessing on my feet,
That they may follow thee.

4 O dearest Lord, thy sacred
   heart
With spear was pierced for
   me;
O pour thy spirit in my heart,
That I may live for thee.

FATHER ANDREW, 1869–1946

253   *O Haupt voll Blut und Wunden*

O SACRED Head, sore woun-
   ded,
With grief and shame weigh-
   ed down!
O Kingly Head, surrounded
With thorns, thine only
   crown!
How pale art thou with anguish,
   With sore abuse and scorn!
How does that visage languish,
   Which once was bright as
   morn!

2 O Lord of life and glory,
  What bliss till now was thine!
I read the wondrous story;
  I joy to call thee mine.
Thy grief and bitter passion
  Were all for sinners' gain;
Mine, mine was the trans-
    gression,
  But thine the deadly pain.

3 What language shall I borrow
  To praise thee, heavenly
    Friend,
For this thy dying sorrow,
  Thy pity without end?
O make me thine for ever,
  And, should I fainting be,
Lord, let me never, never
  Outlive my love to thee.

4 Be near me, Lord, when dying;
  O show thy cross to me;
And, for my succour flying,
  Come, Lord, to set me free;
These eyes, new faith receiving,
  From thee shall never move;
For he who dies believing
  Dies safely through thy love.

  PAUL GERHARDT, 1607–76
  Tr. JAMES WADDELL ALEXANDER
  1804–59

254

WHEN I survey the wondrous
    cross
  On which the Prince of Glory
    died,
My richest gain I count but loss,
  And pour contempt on all my
    pride.

2 Forbid it, Lord, that I should
    boast,
  Save in the death of Christ,
    my God;
All the vain things that charm
    me most,
  I sacrifice them to his blood.

3 See! from his head, his hands,
    his feet,
  Sorrow and love flow mingled
    down;

Did e'er such love and sorrow
    meet,
  Or thorns compose so rich a
    crown?

4 Were the whole realm of nature
    mine,
  That were an offering far too
    small;
Love so amazing, so divine,
  Demands my soul, my life,
    my all.

  ISAAC WATTS, 1674–1748

255

LORD Christ, when first thou
    cam'st to men,
  Upon a cross they bound
    thee,
And mocked thy saving king-
    ship then
  By thorns with which they
    crowned thee:
And still our wrongs may weave
    thee now
New thorns to pierce that
    steady brow,
  And robe of sorrow round
    thee.

2 New advent of the love of
    Christ,
  Shall we again refuse thee,
Till in the night of hate and war
  We perish as we lose thee?
From old unfaith our souls
    release
To seek the Kingdom of thy
    peace,
  By which alone we choose
    thee.

3 O wounded hands of Jesus,
    build
  In us thy new creation;
Our pride is dust, our vaunt is
    stilled,
  We wait thy revelation:
O Love that triumphs over loss,
We bring our hearts before thy
    cross,
  To finish thy salvation.

  WALTER RUSSELL BOWIE
  1882–1969

256 *Pange, lingua, gloriosi proelium certaminis*

* SING, my tongue, how glorious battle
Glorious victory became;
And above the cross, his trophy,
Tell the triumph and the fame:

Tell how he, the earth's Redeemer,
By his death for man o'ercame.

2 Thirty years fulfilled among us—
Perfect life in low estate—
Born for this, and self-surrendered,
To his Passion dedicate,
On the cross the Lamb is lifted,
For his people immolate.

3 His the nails, the spear, the spitting,
Reed and vinegar and gall;
From his patient body piercèd
Blood and water streaming fall:
Earth and sea and stars and mankind
By that stream are cleansèd all.

4 Faithful cross, above all other,
One and only noble tree,
None in foliage, none in blossom,
None in fruit compares with thee:
Sweet the wood and sweet the iron,
And thy load how sweet is he.

5 *Unto God be praise and honour:*
To the Father, to the Son,
To the mighty Spirit, glory—

Ever Three and ever One:
Power and glory in the highest
While eternal ages run. Amen.

VENANTIUS FORTUNATUS, c. 535–600
Tr. WILLIAM MAIR, 1830–1920
and
ARTHUR WELLESLEY WOTHERSPOON
1853–1936
and verse 4 JOHN MASON NEALE
1818–66

* *The pointing is for use with Tune* (i)
PANGE LINGUA *only.*

257 *Vexilla Regis prodeunt*

THE royal banners forward go;
The cross shines forth in mystic glow,
Where he, the Life, did death endure,
And yet by death did life procure.

2 His feet and hands outstretching there,
He willed the piercing nails to bear,
For us and our redemption's sake
A victim of himself to make.

3 There whilst he hung, his sacred side
By soldier's spear was opened wide,
To cleanse us in the precious flood
Of water mingled with his blood.

4 Fulfilled is now what David told
In true prophetic song of old,
To all the nations 'Lo', saith he,
'Our God is reigning from the tree'.

5 *Blest Three in One, our praise we sing*
To thee from whom all graces spring:

As by the cross thou dost restore,
So rule and guide us evermore.
Amen.

VENANTIUS FORTUNATUS
c. 535–600
Tr. JOHN MASON NEALE, 1818–66
and others

258

WE sing the praise of him
who died,
Of him who died upon the
cross;
The sinner's hope let men
deride,
For this we count the world
but loss.

2 Inscribed upon the cross we
see,
In shining letters, 'God is
love';
He bears our sins upon the
tree;
He brings us mercy from
above.

3 The cross! it takes our guilt
away;
It holds the fainting spirit
up;
It cheers with hope the gloomy
day,
And sweetens every bitter
cup;

4 It makes the coward spirit
brave,
And nerves the feeble arm for
fight;
It takes its terror from the
grave,
And gilds the bed of death
with light;

5 The balm of life, the cure of
woe,
The measure and the pledge
of love,
The sinner's refuge here below,
The angels' theme in heaven
above.

THOMAS KELLY, 1769–1855

259

IN the cross of Christ I glory,
Towering o'er the wrecks of
time;
All the light of sacred story
Gathers round its head sub-
lime.

2 When the woes of life o'ertake
me,
Hopes deceive and fears
annoy,
Never shall the cross forsake
me;
Lo! it glows with peace and
joy.

3 When the sun of bliss is beam-
ing
Light and love upon my way,
From the cross the radiance
streaming
Adds more lustre to the day.

4 Bane and blessing, pain and
pleasure,
By the cross are sanctified;
Peace is there that knows no
measure,
Joys that through all time
abide.

5 In the cross of Christ I glory,
Towering o'er the wrecks of
time;
All the light of sacred story
Gathers round its head sub-
lime.

JOHN BOWRING, 1792–1872

260   *Good Friday evening*

AT eve, when now he breathed
no more,
The faithful few in anguish sore
The Lord they loved to burial
bore.

2 To those who mourned him,
who can say
How long the hours of sullen
day,
How long the nights while hid
he lay?

3 O ye who shrink beneath the blow
That death can deal, henceforth ye know
Not hopeless is your human woe.

4 For then, before their tears had ceased,
Love woke to joy the crimson east,
And Jesus rose, from death released.

JOHN RUSSELL DARBYSHIRE
1880–1948

261 *Saturday in Holy Week*

BY Jesus' grave on either hand,
While night is brooding o'er the land,
The sad and silent mourners stand.

2 At last the weary life is o'er,
The agony and conflict sore
Of him who all our suffering bore.

3 Deep in the rock's sepulchral shade
The Lord, by whom the worlds were made,
The Saviour of mankind, is laid.

4 O hearts bereaved and sore distressed,
Here is for you a place of rest;
Here leave your griefs on Jesus' breast.

5 So, when the dayspring from on high
Shall chase the night and fill the sky,
Then shall the Lord again draw nigh.

ISAAC GREGORY SMITH, 1826–1920
The following is also suitable
No. 224 My song is love unknown

CHRIST'S RESURRECTION AND EXALTATION

262 PSALM 118, verses 15–24

THE voice of rejoicing and salvation is in the tabernacles of the ' righteous : the right hand of the Lord ' doëth valiantly.

The right hand of the Lord is ex ' alted : the right hand of the Lord ' doëth valiantly.

I shall not die ' but live : and declare ' the works of the Lord.

The Lord hath chastened ' me sore : but he hath not given me ' over unto death.

Open to me the gates of righ-' teousness : I will go into them and ' I will praise the Lord.

This gate of ' the Lord : into which the righ ' teous shall enter.

I will ' praise thee : for thou hast heard me and art become ' my salvation.

The stone which the builders ' refused : is become the head stone ' of the corner.

This is the Lord's ' doing : it is marvel ' lous in our eyes.

This is the day which the Lord ' hath made : we will rejoice ' and be glad in it.

Glory be to the Father and to ' the Son : and ' to the Holy Ghost.

As it was in the beginning is now and ever ' shall be : world with-' out end Amen.

263 PSALM 118, verses 19–25, 28, 29

O SET ye open unto me
  The gates of righteous-
ness;
Then will I enter into them,
  And I the Lord will bless.

2 This is the gate of God, by it
  The just shall enter in.
Thee will I praise, for thou me
  heard'st,
  And hast my safety been.

3 That stone is made head corner-
  stone,
  Which builders did despise:
This is the doing of the Lord,
  And wondrous in our eyes.

4 This is the day God made, in it
  We'll joy triumphantly.
Save now, I pray thee, Lord; I
  pray,
  Send now prosperity.

5 Thou art my God, I'll thee
  exalt;
  My God, I will thee praise.
Give thanks to God, for he is
  good:
  His mercy lasts always.

6 *To Father, Son, and Holy Ghost,*
  The God whom we adore,
Be glory, as it was, and is,
  And shall be evermore. Amen.

264

JESUS CHRIST is risen to-
  day, *Alleluia!*
Our triumphant holy day,
  Alleluia!
Who did once, upon the cross,
  Alleluia!
Suffer to redeem our loss.
  Alleluia!

2 Hymns of praise, then, let us sing
Unto Christ, our heavenly King,
Who endured the cross and
  grave,
Sinners to redeem and save.

3 But the anguish he endured
  Our salvation hath procured;
Now above the sky he's King,
  Where the angels ever sing.

4 *Sing we to our God above*
  Praise eternal as his love;
Praise him, all ye heavenly host,
  Father, Son, and Holy Ghost:
    Amen.
    Lyra Davidica, 1708

265

'THE Lord is risen indeed';
  Now is his work per-
  formed;
Now is the mighty Captive
  freed,
  And Death's strong castle
  stormed.

2 'The Lord is risen indeed':
  The grave has lost his prey;
With him is risen the ransomed
  seed,
  To reign in endless day.

3 'The Lord is risen indeed';
  He lives, to die no more;
He lives, the sinner's cause to
  plead,
  Whose curse and shame he
  bore.

4 Then, angels, tune your lyres,
  And strike each cheerful
  chord;
Join, all ye bright celestial
  choirs,
  To sing our risen Lord!
    THOMAS KELLY, 1769–1855

266 *Finita iam sunt proelia*

THE strife is o'er, the battle
  done;
Now is the Victor's triumph
  won;
Now be the song of praise
  begun,—
  Alleluia! Alleluia! Alleluia!

2 The powers of death have done
  their worst,

94

But Christ their legions hath
  dispersed;
Let shouts of holy joy out-
  burst,—

3 The three sad days have quickly
  sped;
He rises glorious from the dead;
All glory to our risen Head!.

4 He brake the age-bound chains
  of hell;
The bars from heaven's high
  portals fell;
Let hymns of praise his triumph
  tell.

5 Lord, by the stripes which
  wounded thee,
From death's dread sting thy
  servants free,
That we may live, and sing to
  thee:

17th century
Tr. FRANCIS POTT, 1832–1909, altered

267   *Ἀναστάσεως ἡμέρα*

THE day of resurrection!
  Earth, tell it out abroad;
The passover of gladness,
  The passover of God!
From death to life eternal,
  From earth unto the sky,
Our Christ hath brought us over
  With hymns of victory.

2 Our hearts be pure from evil,
  That we may see aright
The Lord in rays eternal
  Of resurrection light;
And, listening to his accents,
  May hear, so calm and plain,
His own 'All hail!' and, hearing,
  May raise the victor strain.

3 Now let the heavens be joyful!
  Let earth her song begin;
Let the round world keep
  triumph,
  And all that is therein;
Let all things seen and unseen
  Their notes of gladness blend,
For Christ the Lord hath risen,
  Our Joy that hath no end.

ST. JOHN OF DAMASCUS, d. c. 750
Tr. JOHN MASON NEALE, 1818–66
altered

268   *Christ lag in Todesbanden*

CHRIST Jesus lay in death's
  strong bands,
  For our offences given,
But now at God's right hand he
  stands,
  And brings us life from
  heaven:
Wherefore let us joyful be,
And sing to God right thank-
  fully
  Loud songs of Alleluia!
  Alleluia!

2 It was a strange and dreadful
  strife
  When life and death conten-
  ded;
The victory remained with life,
  The reign of death was ended:
Stripped of power, no more he
  reigns,
An empty form alone remains;
  His sting is lost for ever.

3 So let us keep the festival
  Whereto the Lord invites us;
Christ is himself the joy of all,
  The sun that warms and
  lights us;
By his grace he doth impart
Eternal sunshine to the heart;
  The night of sin is ended.

4 Then let us feast this Easter day
  On the true Bread of heaven.
The word of grace hath purged
  away
  The old and wicked leaven;
Christ alone our soul will feed,
He is our meat and drink indeed,
  Faith lives upon no other.

MARTIN LUTHER, 1483–1546
Tr. RICHARD MASSIE, 1800–87

269   *Αἴσωμεν πάντες λαοί*

COME, ye faithful, raise the
  strain
  Of triumphant gladness;
God hath brought his Israel
  Into joy from sadness;
Loosed from Pharaoh's bitter
  yoke
  Jacob's sons and daughters;

Led them with unmoistened
 foot
 Through the Red Sea waters.

2 'Tis the spring of souls today;
 Christ hath burst his prison,
And from three days' sleep in
 death
 As a sun hath risen:
All the winter of our sins,
 Long and dark, is flying
From his light, to whom we give
 Laud and praise undying.

3 Now the queen of seasons, bright
 With the day of splendour,
With the royal feast of feasts,
 Comes its joy to render;
Comes to gladden Christian
 men,
 Who with true affection
Welcome in unwearied strains
 Jesus' resurrection.

4 Neither might the gates of
 death,
 Nor the tomb's dark portal,
Nor the watchers, nor the seal,
 Hold thee as a mortal;
But arising, thou dost stand
 'Midst thine own, bestowing
Thine own peace, which ever-
 more
 Passeth human knowing.

  St. John of Damascus, d. c. 750
  Tr. John Mason Neale, 1818–66
  and others

270

GOOD Christian men, rejoice
 and sing!
Now is the triumph of our King!
To all the world glad news we
 bring:
 Alleluia! Alleluia! Alleluia!

2 The Lord of life is risen for aye;
Bring flowers of song to strew
 his way;
Let all mankind rejoice and say:

3 Praise we in songs of victory
That love, that life which cannot die,
And sing with hearts uplifted
 high:

4 Thy Name we bless, O risen
 Lord,
And sing today with one
 accord
The life laid down, the life re-
 stored:

  Cyril Argentine Alington
  1872–1955

271

THIS joyful Eastertide,
 Away with sin and sorrow.
My Love, the Crucified,
 Hath sprung to life this
 morrow:
  *Had Christ, that once was
   slain,
  Ne'er burst his three-day
   prison,
  Our faith had been in vain:
  But now hath Christ
   arisen,
  Arisen, arisen, arisen!*

2 My flesh in hope shall rest,
 And for a season slumber:
Till trump from east to west
 Shall wake the dead in
 number:

3 Death's flood hath lost his chill,
 Since Jesus crossed the river:
Lover of souls, from ill
 My passing soul deliver:

  George Ratcliffe Woodward
  1848–1934

272

    Salve, festa dies

'WELCOME, happy morn-
 ing!'—age to age shall
 say:
'Hell today is vanquished,
 heaven is won today.'
Lo! the Dead is living, God for
 evermore:
Him, their true Creator, all his
 works adore.

2 Earth with joy confesses, clothing her for spring,
All good gifts return with her
 returning King:
Bloom in every meadow, leaves
 on every bough,
Speak his sorrows ended, hail
 his triumph now.

3 Thou, of life the Author, death
    didst undergo,
Tread the path of darkness,
    saving strength to show.
Come then, True and Faithful,
    now fulfil thy word;
'Tis thine own third morning:
    rise, O buried Lord!

4 Loose the souls long prisoned,
    bound with Satan's chain:
All that now is fallen raise to
    life again:
Show thy face in brightness, bid
    the nations see:
Bring again our daylight: day
    returns with thee.

        VENANTIUS FORTUNATUS
             c. 535–600
    Par. JOHN ELLERTON, 1826–93

273

B LEST morning, whose first
    dawning rays
  Beheld the Son of God
Arise triumphant from the
    grave,
  And leave his dark abode!

2 Wrapt in the silence of the
    tomb
  The great Redeemer lay,
Till the revolving skies had
    brought
  The third, the appointed day.

3 Hell and the grave combined
    their force
To hold our Lord, in vain;
Sudden the Conqueror arose,
  And burst their feeble chain.

4 To thy great Name, Almighty
    Lord,
  We sacred honours pay,
And loud hosannas shall pro-
    claim
  The triumphs of the day.

5 Salvation and immortal praise
  To our victorious King!
Let heaven and earth, and rocks
    and seas,
  With glad hosannas ring.

6 To Father, Son, and Holy Ghost,
    The God whom we adore,
Be glory, as it was, and is,
    And shall be evermore. Amen.
          ISAAC WATTS, 1674–1748

274

T HE world itself keeps Easter
    Day,
  And Easter larks are singing;
And Easter flowers are bloom-
    ing gay,
  And Easter buds are spring-
    ing:
    Alléluia, Alléluia:
The Lord of all things lives
    anew,
And all his works are rising too:
    Hosanna in excelsis!

2 There stood the women by the
    tomb,
  On Easter morning early;
When day had scarcely chased
    the gloom,
  And dew was white and
    pearly:
    Alléluia, Alléluia:
With loving but with erring
    mind,
They came the Prince of Life to
    find:

3 But earlier still the angel sped,
  His news of comfort giving;
And 'Why', he said, 'among the
    dead
  Thus seek ye for the Living?'
    Alléluia, Alléluia:
The Lord hath risen, as all
    things tell:
Good Christians, see ye rise
    as well!

      JOHN MASON NEALE, 1818–66
                 altered

275

' C HRIST the Lord is risen to-
    day',
Sons of men and angels say;
Raise your joys and triumphs
    high;
Sing, ye heavens, and earth
    reply.

2 Love's redeeming work is done,
 Fought the fight, the battle
   won;
 Lo! our Sun's eclipse is o'er;
 Lo! he sets in blood no more.

3 Vain the stone, the watch, the
   seal;
 Christ has burst the gates of
   hell:
 Death in vain forbids his rise;
 Christ has opened Paradise.

4 Lives again our glorious King;
 Where, O Death, is now thy
   sting?
 Once he died, our souls to save;
 Where thy victory, O grave?

5 Soar we now where Christ has
   led,
 Following our exalted Head;
 Made like him, like him we rise;
 Ours the cross, the grave, the
   skies.

6 Hail, the Lord of earth and
   heaven!
 Praise to thee by both be given;
 Thee we greet triumphant now;
 Hail, the Resurrection thou!

CHARLES WESLEY, 1707–88

276

EASTER glory fills the sky!
 Christ now lives, no more to
   die!
 Darkness has been put to flight
 By the living Lord of light!
   Alleluia!

2 See, the stone is rolled away
 From the tomb where once he
   lay!
 He has risen as he said,
 Glorious Firstborn from the
   dead!

3 Seek not life within the tomb;
 Christ stands in the upper room!
 Risen glory he conceals,
 Risen Body he reveals!

4 Though we see his face no more,
 He is with us as before!
 Glory veiled, he is our Priest,
 His own flesh and blood our
   feast!

5 Christ, the Victor over death,
 Breathes on us the Spirit's
   breath!
 Paradise is our reward,
 Endless Easter with our Lord!

JAMES QUINN

277   *O filii et filiae*

*ALLELUIA! ALLELUIA! ALLELUIA

O SONS and daughters, let
   us sing!
 The King of heaven, the
   glorious King,
 O'er death today rose trium-
   phing.
   Alleluia!

2 That Easter morn, at break of
   day,
 The faithful women went their
   way
 To seek the tomb where Jesus
   lay:

3 An angel clad in white they see,
 Who sat, and spake unto the
   three,
 'Your Lord doth go to Galilee.'

4 That night the apostles met in
   fear;
 Amidst them came their Lord
   most dear,
 And said, 'My peace be on all
   here.'

5 When Thomas first the tidings
   heard,
 He doubted if it were their
   Lord,
 Until he came and spake the
   word:

6 'My piercèd side, O Thomas,
   see;
 Behold my hands, my feet,'
   said he,
 'Not faithless, but believing be.'

7 No longer Thomas then denied;
 He saw the feet, the hands, the
   side;
 'Thou art my Lord and God', he
   cried:

8 How blest are they who have
    not seen,
And yet whose faith hath con-
    stant been,
For they eternal life shall win:

9 On this most holy day of days,
To God your hearts and voices
    raise
In laud and jubilee and praise:

JEAN TISSERAND, ? –1494
Tr. JOHN MASON NEALE, 1818–66
altered

* These Alleluias are sung before the
first verse only.

278

NOW the green blade riseth
    from the buried grain,
Wheat that in dark earth many
    days has lain;
  Love lives again, that with
    the dead has been:
  Love is come again,
  Like wheat that springeth
  green.

2 In the grave they laid him,
    Love whom men had
    slain,
Thinking that never he would
    wake again,
  Laid in the earth like grain
    that sleeps unseen:

3 Forth he came at Easter, like
    the risen grain,
He that for three days in the
    grave had lain,
  Quick from the dead my
    risen Lord is seen:

4 When our hearts are wintry,
    grieving, or in pain,
Thy touch can call us back to
    life again,
  Fields of our hearts that
    dead and bare have
    been:

JOHN MACLEOD CAMPBELL CRUM
1872–1958

279

A toi la gloire, O Ressuscité

THINE be the glory, risen,
    conquering Son,
Endless is the victory thou o'er
    death hast won;
Angels in bright raiment rolled
    the stone away,
Kept the folded grave-clothes,
    where thy body lay.
  Thine be the glory, risen, con-
    quering Son,
  Endless is the victory thou o'er
    death hast won.

2 Lo! Jesus meets us, risen from
    the tomb;
Lovingly he greets us, scatters
    fear and gloom;
Let the Church with gladness
    hymns of triumph sing,
For her Lord now liveth; death
    hath lost its sting.

3 No more we doubt thee, glorious
    Prince of Life;
Life is naught without thee:
    aid us in our strife;
Make us more than conquerors,
    through thy deathless love:
Bring us safe through Jordan to
    thy home above.

EDMOND BUDRY, 1854–1932
Tr. R. BIRCH HOYLE, 1875–1939

280

For children

GOOD Joseph had a garden,
  Close by that sad green hill
Where Jesus died a bitter
    death
To save mankind from ill.

2 One evening in that garden,
Their faces dark with gloom,
They laid the Saviour's body
Within good Joseph's tomb.

3 There came the holy women
With spices and with tears;
The angels tried to comfort
    them,
But could not calm their fears.

4 Came Mary to that garden
And sobbed with heart forlorn;
She thought she heard the gar-
  dener ask,
'Whom   seekest   thou   this
  morn?'

5 She   heard   her   own   name
  spoken,
And then she lost her care:
All in his strength and beauty
The risen Lord stood fair!

6 Good Joseph had a garden;
Amid its trees so tall
The Lord Christ rose on Easter
  Day;
He lives to save us all.

7 And as he rose at Easter
He is alive for aye.
The   very   same   Lord   Jesus
  Christ
Who hears us sing today.

8 Go tell the Lord Christ's mes-
  sage,
The Easter triumph sing,
Till all his waiting children
  know
That Jesus is their King.

ALDA M. MILNER-BARRY
1877–1941

281   *For younger children*

AT Easter-time the lilies fair
 And lovely flowers bloomed
everywhere.
*At Eastertime, at Eastertime,
How glad the world at Eastertime!*

2 At Eastertime the angels said
That Christ had risen from the
  dead:

FREDERICK JACKSON, 1867–1942

282   *For younger children*

COME, ye children, sing to
  Jesus
On this happy Easter Day;

All the bells are gladly ringing,
Come, ye children, praise and
  pray.
All the flowers are gaily spring-
  ing,
All the birds with joy are sing-
  ing;
*Come, ye children, sing to Jesus,
Come, ye children, praise and
pray.*

2 'Christ   our   Saviour   now   is
  risen',
Let his little children say.
All the bells are gladly ringing
On this happy Easter Day;
All the flowers are gaily spring-
  ing,
All the birds with joy are sing-
  ing;

FREDERICK SMITH, 1800–73
altered by compilers

283   *For Easter evening*

JESUS, Lord, Redeemer,
 Once for sinners slain,
Crucified in weakness,
 Raised in power, to reign,
Dwelling with the Father,
 Endless in thy days,
Unto thee be glory,
 Honour, blessing, praise.

2 Faithful ones, communing,
 Towards the close of day,
Desolate and weary,
 Met thee in the way.
So, when sun is setting,
 Come to us, and show
All the truth; and in us
 Make our hearts to glow.

3 In the upper chamber,
 Where the ten, in fear,
Gathered sad and troubled,
 There thou didst appear.
So, O Lord, this evening,
 Bid our sorrows cease;
Breathing on us, Saviour,
 Say, 'I give you peace'.

PATRICK MILLER KIRKLAND
1857–1943

284 PSALM 47

O CLAP your hands all ye '
people : shout unto God
with the ' voice of triumph.

For the Lord most high is '
terri-ble : he is a great
King ' over all the earth.

He shall subdue the people
under us : and the nations '
under our feet.

He shall choose our inheritance ' for us : the excellency of
Jacob ' whom he lov'd.

God is gone up with a ' shout :
the Lord with the sound ' of
a trumpet.

Sing praises to God sing '
praises : sing praises unto our '
King sing praises.

For God is the King of all
the ' earth :' sing ye praises
with ' understanding.

God reigneth over the ' heathen :
God sitteth upon the throne '
of his holi-ness.

The princes of the people are
gathered together even
the people of the God of '
Abraham : for the shields of
the earth belong unto God he
is great ' ly exalted.

*Glory be to the Father and to the '
Son : and ' to the Holy Ghost.*

*As it was in the beginning is
now and ever ' shall be : world
with ' out end Amen.*

285 PSALM 68, verses 18a,
19, 20

T HOU hast, O Lord, most
glorious,
Ascended up on high ;
And in triumph victorious led
Captive captivity.

2 Blest be the Lord, who is to us
Of our salvation God ;
Who daily with his benefits
Us plenteously doth load.

3 He of salvation is the God,
Who is our God most strong ;
And unto God the Lord from
death
The issues do belong.

4 *To Father, Son, and Holy Ghost,
The God whom we adore,
Be glory, as it was, and is,
and shall be evermore. Amen.*

286

T HE Head that once was
crowned with thorns
Is crowned with glory now ;
A royal diadem adorns
The mighty Victor's brow.

2 The highest place that heaven
affords
Is his, is his by right,
The King of kings, and Lord of
lords,
And heaven's eternal Light ;

3 The joy of all who dwell above,
The joy of all below
To whom he manifests his love,
And grants his Name to know.

4 To them the cross, with all its
shame,
With all its grace, is given,
Their name an everlasting
name,
Their joy the joy of heaven.

5 They suffer with their Lord
below,
They reign with him above,
Their profit and their joy to
know
The mystery of his love.

6 The cross he bore is life and
health,
Though shame and death to
him,
His people's hope, his people's
wealth,
Their everlasting theme.

THOMAS KELLY, 1769–1855

287

THE Lord ascendeth up on
    high,
  The Lord hath triumphed
    gloriously,
  In power and might excell-
    ing;
The grave and hell are captive
    led,
Lo! he returns, our glorious
    Head,
  To his eternal dwelling.

2 The heavens with joy receive
    their Lord,
  By saints, by angel hosts
    adored;
  O day of exultation!
O earth, adore thy glorious
    King!
His rising, his ascension sing
  With grateful adoration!

3 Our great High Priest hath
    gone before,
  Now on his Church his grace to
    pour,
  And still his love he giveth:
O may our hearts to him ascend;
May all within us upward tend
  To him who ever liveth!
        ARTHUR TOZER RUSSELL, 1806–74

288

THE eternal gates are lifted
    up,
  The doors are opened wide;
The King of Glory is gone in
  Unto his Father's side.

2 Thou art gone up before us,
    Lord,
  To make for us a place,
That we may be where now thou
    art,
  And look upon God's face.

3 And ever on our earthly path
  A gleam of glory lies;
A light still breaks behind the
    cloud
  That veiled thee from our
    eyes.

4 Lift up our hearts, lift up our
    minds,
  And let thy grace be given,
That, while we live on earth
    below,
  Our treasure be in heaven;

5 That where thou art, at God's
    right hand,
  Our hope, our love may be.
Dwell thou in us, that we may
    dwell
  For evermore in thee.
        CECIL FRANCES ALEXANDER
                1818–95, altered

289

LOOK, ye saints! the sight is
    glorious;
  See the Man of Sorrows now;
From the fight returned vic-
    torious,
  Every knee to him shall bow:
Crown him! crown him! crown
    him! crown him!
  Crowns become the Victor's
    brow.

2 Crown the Saviour! angels,
    crown him!
  Rich the trophies Jesus
    brings;
In the seat of power enthrone
    him,
  While the vault of heaven
    rings:
Crown him! crown him! crown
    him! crown him!
Crown the Saviour King of
    kings!

3 Sinners in derision crowned him,
  Mocking thus the Saviour's
    claim;
Saints and angels crowd around
    him,
  Own his title, praise his
    Name:
Crown him! crown him! crown
    him! crown him!
Spread abroad the Victor's
    fame.

4 Hark, those bursts of ac-
    clamation!
Hark, those loud triumphant
    chords!
Jesus takes the highest station:
    O what joy the sight affords!
Crown him! crown him! crown
    him! crown him
King of kings, and Lord of
    lords!
                THOMAS KELLY, 1769–1855

290

Gen Himmel aufgefahren ist

GOD is ascended up on high,
    With merry noise of trum-
        pet's sound,
And princely seated in the sky,
Rules over all the world around:
        Alléluia!

2 In human shape and flesh he
    went,
    Adornèd with his Passion's
        scars,
Which in heaven's sight he did
    present
More glorious than the glitter-
    ing stars:

3 Lord, raise our sinking minds
    therefore
Up to our proper country dear,
And purify us evermore,
To fit us for those regions clear:
                HENRY MORE, 1614–87
                from the German carol

291

AGAIN the morn of gladness,
    The morn of light, is here,
And earth itself looks fairer,
    And heaven itself more near:
The bells, like angel voices,
    Speak peace to every breast;
And all the land lies quiet,
    To keep the day of rest.
        'Glory be to Jesus!'
            Let all his children say;
        'He rose again, he rose again,
            On this glad day!'

2 Again, O loving Saviour,
    The children of thy grace
Prepare themselves to seek thee
    Within thy chosen place.

Our song shall rise to greet thee,
    If thou our hearts wilt raise;
If thou our lips wilt open,
    Our mouth shall show thy
        praise.

3 Tell out, sweet bells, his
        praises!
    Sing, children, sing his Name!
Still louder and still farther
    His mighty deeds proclaim,
Till all whom he redeemèd
    Shall own him Lord and King,
Till every knee shall worship,
    And every tongue shall sing.
        'Glory be to Jesus!'
            Let all creation say;
        'He rose again, he rose again,
            On this glad day!'
                JOHN ELLERTON, 1826–93

292

AWAY with gloom, away with
        doubt!
    With all the morning stars we
        sing;
With all the sons of God we
        shout
    The praises of a King,
        Alleluia! Alleluia!
    Of our returning King.

2 Away with death, and welcome
        life;
    In him we died and live
        again;
And welcome peace, away with
        strife!
    For he returns to reign.
        Alleluia! Alleluia!
    The Crucified shall reign.

3 Then welcome beauty, he is
        fair;
    And welcome youth, for he is
        young;
And welcome spring; and every-
        where
    Let merry songs be sung!
        Alleluia! Alleluia!
    For such a King be sung!
                EDWARD SHILLITO, 1872–1948

The following are also suitable
No.
  11 Jesus, stand among us
  44 Most glorious Lord of life
605 Jesus lives! thy terrors now

CHRIST'S REIGN AND PRIESTHOOD

293 PARAPHRASE 48, verses
5–9

THE Saviour died, but rose
again
Triumphant from the grave;
And pleads our cause at God's
right hand,
Omnipotent to save.

2 Who then can e'er divide us
more
From Jesus and his love,
Or break the sacred chain that
binds
The earth to heaven above?

3 Let troubles rise, and terrors
frown,
And days of darkness fall;
Through him all dangers we'll
defy,
And more than conquer all.

4 Nor death nor life, nor earth
nor hell,
Nor time's destroying sway,
Can e'er efface us from his
heart,
Or make his love decay.

5 Each future period that will
bless,
As it has blessed the past;
He loved us from the first of
time,
He loves us to the last.

Scottish Paraphrases, 1781
From Romans 8:34–end

294 PARAPHRASE 20, verses
1–5

HOW glorious Zion's courts
appear,
The city of our God!
His throne he hath established
here,
Here fixed his loved abode.

2 Its walls, defended by his grace,
No power shall e'er o'erthrow,
Salvation is its bulwark sure
Against the assailing foe.

3 Lift up the everlasting gates,
The doors wide open fling;
Enter, ye nations, who obey
The statutes of our King.

4 Here shall ye taste unmingled
joys,
And dwell in perfect peace,
Ye, who have known Jehovah's
Name,
And trusted in his grace.

5 Trust in the Lord, for ever trust,
And banish all your fears;
Strength in the Lord Jehovah
dwells
Eternal as his years.

Scottish Paraphrases, 1781
From Isaiah 26:1–4

295 PARAPHRASE 58

WHERE high the heavenly
temple stands,
The house of God not made with
hands,
A great High Priest our nature
wears,
The Guardian of mankind appears.

2 He who for men their surety
stood,
And poured on earth his precious blood,
Pursues in heaven his mighty
plan,
The Saviour and the Friend of
man.

3 Though now ascended up on
high,
He bends on earth a brother's
eye;
Partaker of the human name,
He knows the frailty of our
frame.

4 Our fellow-sufferer yet retains
A fellow-feeling of our pains;
And still remembers in the skies
His tears, his agonies, and cries.

5 In every pang that rends the
    heart
  The Man of Sorrows had a
    part;
  He sympathizes with our grief,
  And to the sufferer sends relief.

6 With boldness, therefore, at the
    throne,
  Let us make all our sorrows
    known;
  And ask the aids of heavenly
    power
  To help us in the evil hour.

Scottish Paraphrases, 1781
From Hebrews 4:14–end

296

REJOICE, the Lord is
  King;
  Your Lord and King adore;
  Mortals, give thanks and sing
  And triumph evermore:
Lift up your heart, lift up your
    voice;
Rejoice; again I say, 'Rejoice'.

2 Jesus, the Saviour, reigns,
    The God of truth and love;
  When he had purged our
    stains,
    He took his seat above:
Lift up your heart, lift up your
    voice;
Rejoice; again I say, 'Rejoice'.

3 His Kingdom cannot fail;
    He rules o'er earth and
    heaven;
  The keys of death and hell
    Are to our Jesus given:
Lift up your heart, lift up your
    voice;
Rejoice; again I say, 'Rejoice'.

4 He sits at God's right hand
    Till all his foes submit,
    And bow to his command,
    And fall beneath his feet:
Lift up your heart, lift up your
    voice;
Rejoice; again I say, 'Rejoice'.

5 Rejoice in glorious hope;
    Jesus, the Judge, shall
    come,
  And take his servants up
    To their eternal home;

We then shall hear the arch-
    angel's voice;
The trump of God shall sound,
    'Rejoice'.

CHARLES WESLEY, 1707–88, altered

297

ALL praise to thee, for thou,
  O King divine,
Didst yield the glory that of
  right was thine,
That in our darkened hearts thy
  grace might shine:
    Alleluia!

2 Thou cam'st to us in lowliness of
  thought;
By thee the outcast and the
  poor were sought,
And by thy death was God's
  salvation wrought:

3 Let this mind be in us which
  was in thee,
Who wast a servant that we
  might be free,
Humbling thyself to death on
  Calvary:

4 Wherefore, by God's eternal
  purpose, thou
Art high exalted o'er all
  creatures now,
And given the Name to which
  all knees shall bow:

5 Let every tongue confess with
  one accord
In heaven and earth that Jesus
  Christ is Lord;
And God the Father be by all
  adored:

FRANCIS BLAND TUCKER
Based on Philippians 2:5–11

298

CROWN him with many
  crowns,
The Lamb upon his throne:
Hark how the heavenly anthem
  drowns
All music but its own.
Awake, my soul, and sing
Of him who died for thee,

And hail him as thy matchless King
Through all eternity.

2 Crown him the Lord of life,
Who triumphed o'er the grave,
And rose victorious in the strife
For those he came to save.
His glories now we sing
Who died and rose on high,
Who died eternal life to bring,
And lives that death may die.

3 Crown him the Lord of love;
Behold his hands and side,
Rich wounds yet visible above,
In beauty glorified.
All hail, Redeemer, hail!
For thou hast died for me:
Thy praise shall never, never fail
Throughout eternity.

MATTHEW BRIDGES, 1800–94
and GODFREY THRING, 1823–1903

299

BLESSING and honour and glory and power,
Wisdom and riches and strength evermore
Give ye to him who our battle hath won,
Whose are the Kingdom, the crown, and the throne.

2 Into the heaven of the heavens hath he gone;
Sitteth he now in the joy of the throne;
Weareth he now of the Kingdom the crown;
Singeth he now the new song with his own.

3 Soundeth the heaven of the heavens with his Name;
Ringeth the earth with his glory and fame;
Ocean and mountain, stream, forest, and flower
Echo his praises and tell of his power.

4 Ever ascendeth the song and the joy;
Ever descendeth the love from on high;
Blessing and honour and glory and praise,—
This is the theme of the hymns that we raise.

5 Give we the glory and praise to the Lamb;
Take we the robe and the harp and the palm;
Sing we the song of the Lamb that was slain,
Dying in weakness, but rising to reign.

HORATIUS BONAR, 1808–89

300

AT the Name of Jesus
Every knee shall bow,
Every tongue confess him
King of Glory now;
'Tis the Father's pleasure
We should call him Lord,
Who from the beginning
Was the mighty Word.

2 Humbled for a season,
To receive a name
From the lips of sinners,
Unto whom he came,
Faithfully he bore it
Spotless to the last;
Brought it back victorious,
When from death he passed.

3 Name him, brothers, name him
With love strong as death,
But with awe and wonder
And with bated breath!
He is God the Saviour,
He is Christ the Lord,
Ever to be worshipped,
Trusted, and adored.

4 In your hearts enthrone him;
There let him subdue
All that is not holy,
All that is not true:
Crown him as your Captain
In temptation's hour;
Let his will enfold you
In its light and power.

5 Brothers, this Lord Jesus
   Shall return again,
With his Father's glory,
   With his angel train;
For all wreaths of empire
   Meet upon his brow,
And our hearts confess him
   King of Glory now.

      CAROLINE MARIA NOEL, 1817–77

301   *Christus Redemptor gentium*

CHRIST is the world's Re-
   deemer,
The lover of the pure,
The fount of heav'nly wisdom,
   Our trust and hope secure;
The armour of his soldiers,
   The Lord of earth and sky;
Our health while we are living,
   Our life when we shall die.

2 Christ hath our host surrounded
   With clouds of martyrs
      bright,
Who wave their palms in
      triumph,
   And fire us for the fight.
For Christ the cross ascended
   To save a world undone,
And, suffering for the sinful,
   Our full redemption won.

3 Down in the realm of darkness
   He lay a captive bound,
But at the hour appointed
   He rose, a Victor crowned;
And now, to heav'n ascended,
   He sits upon the throne,
In glorious dominion,
   His Father's and his own.

4 *Glory to God the Father,*
   The unbegotten One;
All honour be to Jesus,
   His sole-begotten Son;
And to the Holy Spirit—
   The perfect Trinity.
Let all the worlds give answer,
   'Amen—so let it be'.

      ST. COLUMBA, 521–97
      Tr. DUNCAN MACGREGOR
      1854–1923, altered

302   *Jesu, nostra redemptio*

JESUS, our hope, our heart's
   desire,
Thy work of grace we sing;
Redeemer of the world art thou,
   Its Maker and its King.

2 How vast the mercy and the love
   Which laid our sins on thee,
And led thee to a cruel death
   To set thy people free!

3 But now the bonds of death are
      burst;
   The ransom has been paid;
And thou art on thy Father's
      throne,
   In majesty arrayed.

4 Jesus, our only joy be thou,
   As thou our prize wilt be;
In thee be all our glory now,
   And through eternity.

      7th–8th century
   Tr. JOHN CHANDLER, 1806–76
and Compilers of *Hymns Ancient and
      Modern*

303

GOD is working his purpose
   out, as year succeeds to
   year:
God is working his purpose out,
   and the time is drawing
   near—
Nearer and nearer draws the
   time—the time that shall
   surely be,
When the earth shall be filled
   with the glory of God, as
   the waters cover the sea.

2 What can we do to work God's
   work, to prosper and increase
The brotherhood of all mankind
   —the reign of the Prince of
   Peace?
What can we do to hasten the
   time—the time that shall
   surely be,
When the earth shall be filled
   with the glory of God, as
   the waters cover the sea?

3 March we forth in the strength
  of God, with the banner of
  Christ unfurled,
That the light of the glorious
  Gospel of truth may shine
  throughout the world:
Fight we the fight with sorrow
  and sin, to set their cap-
  tives free,
That the earth may be filled
  with the glory of God, as
  the waters cover the sea.

4 All we can do is nothing worth,
  unless God blesses the deed;
Vainly we hope for the harvest-
  tide, till God gives life to
  the seed;
Yet nearer and nearer draws
  the time—the time that
  shall surely be,
When the earth shall be filled
  with the glory of God, as
  the waters cover the sea.

ARTHUR CAMPBELL AINGER
1841–1919

304

JOIN all the glorious names
  Of wisdom, love, and
  power,
That ever mortals knew,
  That angels ever bore:
All are too mean to speak his
  worth,
Too mean to set my Saviour
  forth.

2 Great Prophet of my God,
  My tongue would bless thy
  Name;
By thee the joyful news
  Of our salvation came,—
The joyful news of sins for-
  given,
Of hell subdued, and peace
  with heaven.

3 Jesus, my great High Priest,
  Offered his blood and died;
My guilty conscience seeks
  No sacrifice beside:
His powerful blood did once
  atone,
And now it pleads before the
  throne.

4 My dear Almighty Lord,
  My Conqueror and my
  King,
Thy sceptre and thy sword,
  Thy reigning grace, I sing:
Thine is the power: behold, I sit
In willing bonds before thy feet.

5 Now let my soul arise,
  And tread the tempter
  down;
My Captain leads me forth
  To conquest and a crown:
A feeble saint shall win the day,
Though death and hell obstruct
  the way.

ISAAC WATTS, 1674–1748

305 *Hymnum canamus gloriae*

SING we triumphant hymns
  of praise,
New hymns to heaven exulting
  raise:
Christ, by a road before untrod,
Ascendeth to the throne of
  God.

2 O grant that we may thither
  tend,
And with unwearied hearts
  ascend
Toward thy kingdom's throne,
  where thou,
Our great high priest, art
  seated now.

3 Be thou our joy and strong
  defence,
Who art our future recompense:
So shall the light that springs
  from thee
Be ours through all eternity.

4 *O risen Christ, ascended Lord,*
  All praise to thee let earth
  accord,
Who art, while endless ages
  run,
With Father and with Spirit
  One. Amen.

THE VENERABLE BEDE 673–735
Tr. BENJAMIN WEBB, 1820–85
and Compilers of *The BBC*
Hymn Book

108

306

IMMORTAL Love, for ever
full,
  For ever flowing free,
For ever shared, for ever whole,
  A never-ebbing sea!

2 Blow, winds of God, awake and
  blow
  The mists of earth away:
Shine out, O Light Divine, and
  show
  How wide and far we stray.

3 We may not climb the heavenly
  steeps
  To bring the Lord Christ
  down;
In vain we search the lowest
  deeps,
  For him no depths can drown.

4 And not for signs in heaven
  above,
  Or earth below, they look
Who know with John his smile
  of love,
  With Peter his rebuke.

5 In joy of inward peace, or sense
  Of sorrow over sin,
He is his own best evidence;
  His witness is within.

6 And, warm, sweet, tender, even
  yet
  A present help is he;
And faith has still its Olivet,
  And love its Galilee.

7 The healing of his seamless
  dress
  Is by our beds of pain;
We touch him in life's throng
  and press,
  And we are whole again.
      JOHN GREENLEAF WHITTIER
                        1807–92

307

'LIFT up your hearts': I hear
  the summons calling
  Forth from the heavenly
  altar where he stands—
Our great High Priest, the
  Father's love revealing,
  In priestly act, with pleading
  outspread hands.

2 'Lift up your hearts': with
  hearts to heaven soaring
  The Church exulting makes
  her glad reply—
'We lift them up unto the Lord',
  adoring;
  Our God and thine, through
  thee, we glorify.

3 'Lift up your hearts': alas, O
  Lord, I cannot
  Lift up aright my burdened
  heart to thee;
Thou knowest, Lord, the cares
  that weigh upon it,
  The chains that bind it
  struggling to be free.

4 O Love divine! thy promise
  comes to cheer me,
  O Voice of pity! blessing and
  thrice blest—
'Come unto me, ye laden hearts
  and weary;
  Take up my yoke, and learn:
  I pledge you rest'.

5 I dare not waver by such grace
  invited,
  I yield my heart, dear Lord:
  I close the strife.
Lift thou my heart until, with
  thine united,
  I taste anew the joy of endless
  life.
      JOHN MACLEOD, 1840–98, altered

308

NOW at last he takes his
  throne; *Alleluia!*
From all ages his alone!
  Alleluia!
With his praise creation rings,
Lord of lords and King of kings.

2 Hands and feet and side reveal
  Wounds of love, High Priest-
  hood's seal!
Advocate, for us he pleads;
Heavenly Priest, he intercedes!

3 Christians, raise your eyes
  above!
He will come again in love,
  On that great and wondrous
  Day
When this world will pass away!

4 At his word new heavens and
      earth
Will in glory spring to birth!
Joy of angels, joy of men,
Come, Lord Jesus, come again!
                        JAMES QUINN

309   *For children*

O SON of Man, our Hero strong
      and tender,
   Whose servants are the brave
      in all the earth,
Our living sacrifice to thee we
      render,
   Who sharest all our sorrows,
      all our mirth.
O feet so strong to climb the
      path of duty,
   O lips divine that taught the
      words of truth,
Kind eyes that marked the
      lilies in their beauty,

And heart that kindled at the
      zeal of youth;

2 Lover of children, boyhood's
      inspiration,
   Of all mankind the Servant
      and the King;
O Lord of joy and hope and con-
      solation,
   To thee our fears and joys
      and hopes we bring.
Not in our failures only and our
      sadness
   We seek thy presence, Com-
      forter and Friend;
O rich man's Guest, be with us
      in our gladness,
   O poor man's Mate, our low-
      liest tasks attend.
                FRANK FLETCHER, 1870–1954

The following are also suitable
No.
158 Give the king thy judgments, O
      God
 36 The Lord is King! lift up thy voice

---

310   PSALM 50, verses 1–6, 14
            and 23

THE mighty God even the '
      Lord hath spoken : and
called the earth from the
rising of the sun unto the
going ' down thereof.

Out of Zion the per ' fection of
   beauty : — ' God hath shined.

Our God shall come and shall '
   not keep silence : a fire shall
   devour before him   and it
   shall be very tempestuous
   round ' about him.

He shall call to the ' heavens from
   above : and to the earth that
   he may ' judge his people.

Gather my saints to ' gether unto
   me : those that have made a
   covenant with me by ' sacrifice.

And the heavens shall de ' clare
   his righteousness : for God is '
   judge himself.

Offer unto ' God thanksgiving :
   and pay thy vows unto ' the
   most High.

Whoso offereth praise ' glori-fieth
   me : and to him that ordereth
   his conversation aright   will
   I show the salva ' tion of
   God.

*Glory be to the ' Father ' and
   to the Son : and to the ' Holy
   Ghost.*

*As it was in the beginning is
   now and ' ever shall · be : world
   without ' end Amen.*

311

PSALM 96, verses 9,
11–13

IN beauty of his holiness,
  O do the Lord adore;
Likewise let all the earth
    throughout
  Tremble his face before.
Let heavens be glad before the
    Lord,
  And let the earth rejoice;
Let seas and all their fullness
    roar,
  And make a mighty noise.

2 Let fields rejoice, and every-
    thing
  That springeth of the earth;
Then of the forest all the trees
  Shall shout aloud with mirth
Before the Lord; because he
    comes,
  To judge the earth comes he;
He'll judge the world with
    righteousness,
  The people faithfully.

3 All glory be to God on high,
  And to the earth be peace;
Goodwill is shown by heaven to
    men,
  And never more shall cease.
To Father, Son, and Holy Ghost,
  The God whom we adore,
Be glory, as it was, and is,
  And shall be evermore. Amen

The King who reigns in Salem's
    towers
  Shall all the world command.

4 Among the nations he shall
    judge;
  His judgments truth shall
    guide;
His sceptre shall protect the
    just,
  And quell the sinner's pride.

5 No strife shall rage, nor hostile
    feuds
  Disturb those peaceful years;
To ploughshares men shall beat
    their swords,
  To pruning-hooks their
    spears.

6 No longer hosts encountering
    hosts
  Shall crowds of slain deplore:
They hang the trumpet in the
    hall,
  And study war no more.

7 Come then, O house of Jacob! come
  To worship at his shrine;
And, walking in the light of
    God,
  With holy beauties shine.
      Scottish Paraphrases, 1781
        From Isaiah 2:2–5

312 PARAPHRASE 18

BEHOLD! the mountain of
  the Lord
  In latter days shall rise
On mountain tops above the
    hills,
  And draw the wondering
    eyes.

2 To this the joyful nations round,
  All tribes and tongues, shall
    flow;
Up to the hill of God, they'll
    say,
  And to his house we'll go.

3 The beam that shines from
    Zion hill
  Shall lighten every land;

313

CHRIST is coming! let crea-
  tion
  From her groans and travail
    cease;
Let the glorious proclamation
  Hope restore and faith in-
    crease:
Christ is coming! Christ is
    coming!
  Come, thou blessèd Prince of
    Peace.

2 Earth can now but tell the story
  Of thy bitter cross and pain;
She shall yet behold thy glory,
  When thou comest back to
    reign:

111

Christ is coming! Christ is
coming!
Let each heart repeat the
strain.

3 Long thine exiles have been
pining,
Far from rest, and home, and
thee:
But, in heavenly vestures shining,
They their loving Lord shall
see:
Christ is coming! Christ is
coming!
Haste the joyous jubilee.

4 With that blessèd hope before
us,
Let no harp remain unstrung;
Let the mighty advent chorus
Onward roll from tongue to
tongue:
'Christ is coming! Christ is
coming!
Come, Lord Jesus, quickly
come!'

JOHN ROSS MACDUFF, 1818–95

314

HARK what a sound, and too
divine for hearing,
Stirs on the earth and
trembles in the air!
Is it the thunder of the Lord's
appearing?
Is it the music of his people's
prayer?

2 Surely he cometh, and a thousand voices
Shout to the saints, and to
the deaf are dumb;
Surely he cometh, and the
earth rejoices,
Glad in his coming who hath
sworn, 'I come'.

3 This hath he done, and shall
we not adore him?
This shall he do, and can we
still despair?
Come, let us quickly fling ourselves before him,
Cast at his feet the burden of
our care.

4 Yea, through life, death,
through sorrow and
through sinning
He shall suffice me, for he
hath sufficed:
Christ is the end, for Christ
was the beginning,
Christ the beginning, for
the end is Christ.

FREDERIC WILLIAM HENRY MYERS
1843–1901

315

*Wachet auf! ruft uns die
Stimme*

'WAKE, awake! for night
is flying,'
The watchmen on the heights
are crying,
'Awake, Jerusalem, at
last!'
Midnight hears the welcome
voices,
And at the thrilling cry rejoices:
'Come forth, ye virgins,
night is past!
The Bridegroom comes;
awake,
Your lamps with glad-
ness take;
Alleluia!
And for his marriage feast
prepare,
For ye must go to meet
him there.'

2 Zion hears the watchmen
singing,
And all her heart with joy is
springing,
She wakes, she rises from
her gloom;
For her Lord comes down all-
glorious,
The strong in grace, in truth
victorious;
Her Star is risen, her Light
is come!
Ah come, thou blessèd
One,
God's own belovèd Son;
Alleluia!
We follow till the halls we
see
Where thou hast bid us sup
with thee.

3   Now let all the heavens adore
        thee,
And men and angels sing before
        thee,
    With harp and cymbal's
        clearest tone;
Of one pearl each shining
        portal,
Where we are with the choir
        immortal
    Of angels round thy dazzl-
        ing throne;
      Nor eye hath seen, nor
        ear
      Hath yet attained to
        hear
        What there is ours;
But we rejoice, and sing to
        thee
Our hymn of joy eternally.
        PHILIPP NICOLAI, 1556–1608
        Tr. CATHERINE WINKWORTH
        1827–78

316

L O! he comes, with clouds de-
    scending,
    Once for favoured sinners
        slain;
Thousand thousand saints at-
        tending
    Swell the triumph of his
        train;
Alleluia! Alleluia! Alleluia!
God appears on earth to
        reign.

2 Every eye shall now behold him,
    Robed in dreadful majesty;
Those who set at naught and
        sold him,
    Pierced, and nailed him to
        the tree,
    Deeply wailing, deeply wail-
        ing, deeply wailing,
    Shall the true Messiah see.

3 Those dear tokens of his Passion
    Still his dazzling body bears;
Cause of endless exaltation
    To his ransomed wor-
        shippers;
Alleluia! Alleluia! Alleluia!
See! the day of God appears!

4 Yea, Amen! let all adore thee,
    High on thine eternal throne;
Saviour, take the power and
        glory,
    Claim the kingdom for thine
        own:
    O come quickly; O come
        quickly; O come quickly;
Alleluia! come, Lord, come!
        CHARLES WESLEY, 1707–88
        altered
Based on a hymn by JOHN CENNICK
        1718–55

317

H AIL to the Lord's Anointed,
    Great David's greater
        Son!
Hail, in the time appointed,
    His reign on earth begun!
He comes to break oppression,
    To set the captive free,
To take away transgression,
    And rule in equity.

2 He comes with succour speedy
    To those who suffer wrong,
To help the poor and needy,
    And bid the weak be strong,
To give them songs for sighing,
    Their darkness turn to light
Whose souls, condemned and
        dying,
    Were precious in his sight.

3 He shall come down like
        showers
    Upon the fruitful earth,
And love, joy, hope, like flowers,
    Spring in his path to birth.
Before him, on the mountains,
    Shall peace, the herald, go;
And righteousness in fountains
    From hill to valley flow.

4 For him shall prayer unceasing
    And daily vows ascend,
His Kingdom still increasing,
    A Kingdom without end.
The mountain dews shall
        nourish
    A seed, in weakness sown,
Whose fruit shall spread and
        flourish
    And shake like Lebanon.

5 O'er every foe victorious,
   He on his throne shall rest,
From age to age more glorious,
   All blessing and all-blest.
The tide of time shall never
   His covenant remove;
His Name shall stand for ever;
   That Name to us is Love.

JAMES MONTGOMERY, 1771–1854
From Psalm 72

318(i)

Mine eyes have seen the glory of the coming of the Lord:
He is trampling out the vintage where the grapes of wrath are stored;
He hath loosed the fatal lightning of his terrible swift sword:
   His truth is marching on.

2 He hath sounded forth the trumpet that shall never call retreat;
He is sifting out the hearts of men before his judgment-seat:
O, be swift, my soul, to answer him; be jubilant, my feet!
   Our God is marching on.

3 In the beauty of the lilies Christ was born across the sea,
With a glory in his bosom that transfigures you and me:
As he died to make men holy, let us live to make men free,
   While God is marching on.

4 He is coming like the glory of the morning on the wave;
He is wisdom to the mighty; he is succour to the brave;
So the world shall be his footstool, and the soul of time his slave:
   Our God is marching on!

JULIA WARD HOWE, 1819–1910

318(ii)

Mine eyes have seen the glory of the coming of the Lord:
He is trampling out the vintage where the grapes of wrath are stored;
He hath loosed the fatal lightning of his terrible swift sword:
   His truth is marching on.
   Glory, glory, Alleluia!
   Glory, glory, Alleluia!
   Glory, glory, Alleluia!
   His truth is marching on.

2 He hath sounded forth the trumpet that shall never call retreat;
He is sifting out the hearts of men before his judgment-seat:
O, be swift, my soul, to answer him; be jubilant, my feet!
   Our God is marching on.
   Glory, glory, Alleluia!
   Glory, glory, Alleluia!
   Glory, glory, Alleluia!
   Our God is marching on.

3 In the beauty of the lilies Christ was born across the sea,
With a glory in his bosom that transfigures you and me:
As he died to make men holy, let us live to make men free,
   While God is marching on.
   Glory, glory, Alleluia!
   Glory, glory, Alleluia!
   Glory, glory, Alleluia!
   While God is marching on.

4 He is coming like the glory of the morning on the wave;
He is wisdom to the mighty; he is succour to the brave;
So the world shall be his footstool, and the soul of time his slave:
   Our God is marching on.
   Glory, glory, Alleluia!
   Glory, glory, Alleluia!
   Glory, glory, Alleluia!
   Our God is marching on.

JULIA WARD HOWE, 1819–1910
and others

319

YE servants of the Lord,
 Each in his office wait,
Observant of his heavenly word,
 And watchful at his gate.

2 Let all your lamps be bright,
 And trim the golden flame;
Gird up your loins, as in his
 sight,
 For awesome is his name.

3 Watch: 'tis your Lord's com-
 mand,
 And while we speak he's near;
Mark the first signal of his hand,
 And ready all appear.

4 O happy servant he,
 In such a posture found!
He shall his Lord with rapture
 see,
 And be with honour crowned.

5 Christ shall the banquet
 spread
 With his own royal hand,
And raise that faithful servant's
 head
 Amid the angelic band.

PHILIP DODDRIDGE, 1702–51

320

COME, thou long-expected
 Jesus,
 Born to set thy people free;
From our fears and sins release
 us;
 Let us find our rest in thee.

2 Israel's Strength and Consola-
 tion,
 Hope of all the earth thou art,
Dear Desire of every nation,
 Joy of every longing heart.

3 Born thy people to deliver,
 Born a Child and yet a King,
Born to reign in us for ever,
 Now thy gracious Kingdom
 bring.

4 By thine own eternal Spirit
 Rule in all our hearts alone;
By thine all-sufficient merit
 Raise us to thy glorious
 throne.

CHARLES WESLEY, 1707–88

321

THE Lord will come and not
 be slow,
 His footsteps cannot err;
Before him righteousness shall
 go,
 His royal harbinger.
Truth from the earth, like to a
 flower,
 Shall bud and blossom then;
And justice, from her heavenly
 bower,
 Look down on mortal men.

2 Surely to such as do him fear
 Salvation is at hand!
And glory shall ere long appear
 To dwell within our land.
Rise, God, judge thou the earth
 in might,
 This wicked earth redress;
For thou art he who shall by
 right
 The nations all possess.

3 The nations all whom thou hast
 made
 Shall come, and all shall
 frame
To bow them low before thee,
 Lord,
 And glorify thy Name.
For great thou art, and wonders
 great
 By thy strong hand are done:
Thou in thy everlasting seat
 Remainest God alone.

JOHN MILTON, 1608–74
From Psalms 85, 82, 86

322

THY Kingdom come, O God;
 Thy rule, O Christ, begin;
Break with thine iron rod
 The tyrannies of sin.

2 Where is thy reign of peace
    And purity and love?
  When shall all hatred cease,
    As in the realms above?

3 When comes the promised time
    That war shall be no more,
  And lust, oppression, crime,
    Shall flee thy face before?

4 We pray thee, Lord, arise,
    And come in thy great might:
  Revive our longing eyes,
    Which languish for thy sight.

5 Men scorn thy sacred Name,
    And wolves devour thy fold;
  By many deeds of shame
    We learn that love grows
      cold.

6 O'er lands both near and far
    Thick darkness broodeth yet;
  Arise, O Morning Star,
    Arise, and never set.

          LEWIS HENSLEY, 1824–1905
                          altered

323

'THY Kingdom come!'—on
    bended knee
  The passing ages pray;
And faithful souls have yearned
    to see
  On earth that Kingdom's
    day.

2 But the slow watches of the
    night
  Not less to God belong;
And for the everlasting right
  The silent stars are strong.

3 And lo! already on the hills
  The flags of dawn appear;
Gird up your loins, ye prophet
    souls,
  Proclaim the day is near:

4 The day in whose clear-shining
    light
  All wrong shall stand re-
    vealed,
When justice shall be throned
    with might,
  And every hurt be healed:

5 When knowledge, hand in hand
    with peace,
  Shall walk the earth
    abroad,—
The day of perfect righteous-
    ness,
  The promised day of God.

          FREDERICK LUCIAN HOSMER
                          1840–1929

324

BLEST is the man, O God,
    That stays himself on thee:
Who wait for thy salvation,
    Lord,
  Shall thy salvation see.

2 When we in darkness walk,
    Nor feel the heavenly flame,
Then is the time to trust our
    God,
  And rest upon his Name.

3 Soon shall our doubts and
    fears
  Subside at his control;
His loving-kindness shall break
    through
  The midnight of the soul.

4 Wait till the shadows flee;
    Wait thy appointed hour;
Wait till the Bridegroom of thy
    soul
  Reveals his love with power.

          AUGUSTUS MONTAGUE TOPLADY
                          1740–78

325   *Ἀπὸ δόξης εἰς δόξαν*
              πορευόμενοι

FROM glory to glory advanc-
    ing, we praise thee, O
    Lord;
Thy Name with the Father and
  Spirit be ever adored.

2 From strength unto strength
    we go forward on Zion's
    highway,
To appear before God in the
    city of infinite day.

3 Thanksgiving, and glory and
   worship, and blessing and
   love,
 One heart and one song have
   the saints upon earth and
   above.

4 O Lord, evermore to thy servants thy presence be nigh;
 Ever fit us by service on earth
   for thy service on high.
       From the *Liturgy of St. James*
   Tr. CHARLES WILLIAM HUMPHREYS
                   1840–1921

The following are also suitable

No.
 12 Lift up your heads, ye mighty gates
 505 Christ is the world's true light

PENTECOST

326 PSALM 104, verses 1–5,
                30–4

BLESS the Lord ' O my sŏul :
   O Lord my God thou art
very great thou art clothed
with honour and ' majesty.

Who coverest thyself with light
as ' with a garment : who
stretchest out the heavens '
like a curtain.

Who layeth the beams of his
chambers ' in the waters : who
maketh the clouds his chariot
who walketh upon the wings '
of the wind.

Who maketh his ' angels spirits : his ministers a ' flaming
fire.

Who laid the foun ' dations of
the earth : that it should not
be re ' moved for ever.

Thou sendest forth thy spirit
they ' are created : and thou
renewest the face ' of the
earth.

The glory of the Lord shall
en ' dure for ever : the Lord
shall rejoice in ' all his works.

He looketh on the earth ' and it
trembleth : he toucheth the
hills ' and they smoke.

I will sing unto the Lord as '
long as I live : I will sing
praise to my God while I '
have my being.

My meditation of ' him shall be
sweet : I will be glad ' in the
Lord.

*Glory be to the ' Father and to the
 Son : and to the ' Holy Ghost.*

*As it was in the beginning is
 now and ' ever shall be : world
 without ' end Amen.*

327

O DAY of joy and wonder!
  Christ's promise now ful-
   filled!
The coming of his Spirit
The Father's love has willed;
Our Lord in human body,
To mortal eye is lost,
Yet he returns for ever
At blessèd Pentecost!

2 The world in sheer amazement,
 The truth must now declare,
 That men who once were
   cowards,
 Are brave beyond compare,
 And tongues which could not
   utter
 Their faith in Jesus' name,
 Defy all persecution,
 His glory to proclaim!

3 So we too may know thy power,
 Thy courage makes us strong,
 Thy love, thy joy, thy patience,
 Can all to us belong,

If thou wilt dwell within us,
A Comforter divine;
Come to our hearts, we pray
thee,
And keep them ever thine.

VIOLET BUCHANAN

328 *Salve, festa dies, toto*
venerabilis aevo

* *HAIL thee, Festival Day! blest*
day that art hallowed for ever;
Day wherein God from heaven
shone on the world with his
grace.

2 Lo! in the likeness of fire, on
them that await his appearing,
He whom the Lord foretold,
suddenly, swiftly, descends.

3 Forth from the Father he comes
with his sevenfold mystical
dowry,
Pouring on human souls infinite
riches of God.

4 Hark! in a hundred tongues
Christ's own, his chosen
Apostles,
Preach to a hundred tribes
Christ and his wonderful
works.

5 Praise to the Spirit of life, all
praise to the Fount of our
being,
Light that dost lighten all,
Life that in all dost abide.

c. 14th century (York Processional)
Tr. GABRIEL GILLETT, 1873–1948

* *Verse 1 is also sung as a refrain*
after each verse.

329 *Beata nobis gaudia*

O JOY! because the circling
year
Hath brought our day of blessing here,
The day when first the light
divine
Upon the Church began to
shine.

2 Like unto quivering tongues of
flame
Upon each one the Spirit
came,—
Tongues, that the earth might
hear their call,
And fire, that love might burn
in all.

3 Thus wondrously were spread
abroad
To all the wondrous works of
God;
To each in his familiar tone
The glorious marvel was made
known.

4 While hardened scoffers vainly
jeered,
The listening strangers heard
and feared;
They knew the prophet's word
fulfilled,
And owned the work which God
had willed.

5 *Praise we the Father and the Son,*
And Holy Spirit with them One:
And may the Son on us bestow
The gifts that from the Spirit
flow.
Amen.

c. 4th century
Tr. JOHN ELLERTON, 1826–93
and Compilers of *Hymns Ancient*
and Modern
Based on Acts 2: 1–4.

330 *Beata nobis gaudia*

R EJOICE! the year upon its
way
Has brought again that blessèd
day,
When on the chosen of the Lord
The Holy Spirit was outpoured.

2 On each the fire, descending,
stood
In quivering tongues' simi-
litude—
Tongues, that their words might
ready prove,
And fire, to make them flame
with love.

3 And now, O holy God, this day
Regard us as we humbly pray,
And send us, from thy heavenly seat,
The blessings of the Paraclete.

4 *To God the Father, God the Son,*
And God the Spirit, praise be done;
May Christ the Lord upon us pour
The Spirit's gift for evermore.
                    Amen.

c. 4th century
Tr. RICHARD ELLIS ROBERTS
1879–1953
Based on Acts 2:1–4

5 So, when the Spirit of our God
Came down his flock to find,
A voice from heaven was heard abroad,
A rushing mighty wind.

6 It fills the Church of God; it fills
The sinful world around;
Only in stubborn hearts and wills
No place for it is found.

7 Come, Lord; come, Wisdom, Love, and Power;
Open our ears to hear;
Let us not miss the accepted hour;
Save, Lord, by love or fear.

JOHN KEBLE, 1792–1866
* *This verse may be omitted.*

331

WHEN God of old came down from heaven,
In power and wrath he came;
Before his feet the clouds were riven,
Half darkness and half flame.

2 But, when he came the second time,
He came in power and love;
Softer than gale at morning prime
Hovered his holy Dove.

*3 The fires that rushed on Sinai down
In sudden torrents dread,
Now gently light, a glorious crown,
On every sainted head.

4 And, as on Israel's awe-struck ear
The voice exceeding loud,
The trump that angels quake to hear,
Thrilled from the deep, dark cloud,

332

LORD God, the Holy Ghost,
In this accepted hour,
As on the day of Pentecost,
Descend in all thy power.

2 We meet with one accord
In our appointed place,
And wait the promise of our Lord,
The Spirit of all grace.

3 Like mighty rushing wind
Upon the waves beneath,
Move with one impulse every mind;
One soul, one feeling breathe.

4 The young, the old inspire
With wisdom from above;
And give us hearts and tongues of fire,
To pray and praise and love.

5 Spirit of light, explore
And chase our gloom away,
With lustre shining more and more
Unto the perfect day.

JAMES MONTGOMERY, 1771–1854

THE HOLY SPIRIT IN THE CHURCH

333 PSALM 102 (ii), verses
13–18

THOU shalt arise, and mercy
yet
Thou to mount Zion shalt extend:
The time is come for favour
set,
The time when thou shalt blessing send.

2 Thy saints take pleasure in her
stones,
Her very dust to them is dear.
All heathen lands and kingly
thrones
On earth thy glorious Name shall
fear.

3 God in his glory shall appear,
When Zion he builds and re-
pairs.
He shall regard and lend his ear
Unto the needy's humble
prayers:

4 The afflicted's prayer he will not
scorn.
All times this shall be on record:
And generations yet unborn
Shall praise and magnify the
Lord.

5 *To Father, Son, and Holy Ghost,*
The God whom earth and heaven
adore,
Be glory, as it was of old,
Is now, and shall be evermore.
Amen.

334

HOLY Spirit, ever living
As the Church's very life;
Holy Spirit, ever striving
Through her in a ceaseless
strife;
Holy Spirit, ever forming
In the Church the mind of
Christ;
Thee we praise with endless
worship
For thy fruit and gifts unpriced.

2 Holy Spirit, ever working
Through the Church's ministry;
Quick'ning, strength'ning, and
absolving,
Setting captive sinners free;
Holy Spirit, ever binding
Age to age, and soul to soul,
In a fellowship unending
Thee we worship and extol.

TIMOTHY REES, 1874–1939

335

LOVE of the Father, Love of
God the Son,
From whom all came, in whom
was all begun;
Who formest heavenly beauty
out of strife,
Creation's whole desire and
breath of life:

2 Thou the All-holy, thou
supreme in might,
Thou dost give peace, thy presence maketh right;
Thou with thy favour all things
dost enfold,
With thine all-kindness free
from harm wilt hold.

3 Purest and highest, wisest and
most just,
There is no truth save only in
thy trust;
Thou dost the mind from
earthly dreams recall,
And bring, through Christ, to
him for whom are all.

4 Eternal Glory, all men thee
adore,
Who art and shalt be wor-
shipped evermore:
Us whom thou madest, comfort
with thy might,
And lead us to enjoy thy
heavenly light.

ROBERT BRIDGES, 1844–1930
Based on *Amor Patris et Filii*
12th century

336

OUR blest Redeemer, ere he breathed
His tender last farewell,
A Guide, a Comforter bequeathed,
With us to dwell.

2 He came in tongues of living flame,
To teach, convince, subdue;
All-powerful as the wind he came,
As viewless too.

3 He came sweet influence to impart,
A gracious, willing Guest,
While he can find one humble heart
Wherein to rest.

4 And his that gentle voice we hear,
Soft as the breath of even,
That checks each fault, that calms each fear,
And speaks of heaven.

5 And every virtue we possess,
And every victory won,
And every thought of holiness,
Are his alone.

6 Spirit of purity and grace,
Our weakness, pitying, see;
O make our hearts thy dwelling-place,
And worthier thee.
HENRIETTE AUBER, 1773–1862

337

FOR thy gift of God the Spirit,
With us, in us, e'er to be,
Pledge of life and hope of glory,
Saviour, we would worship thee.

2 He who in creation's dawning
Brooded o'er the pathless deep,
Still across our nature's darkness
Moves to wake our souls from sleep.

3 He it is, the living Author,
Wakes to life the sacred Word;
Reads with us its holy pages,
And reveals our risen Lord.

4 He it is who works within us,
Teaching rebel hearts to pray;
He whose holy intercessions
Rise for us both night and day.

5 Fill us with thy holy fullness,
God the Father, Spirit, Son;
In us, through us, then, forever,
Shall thy perfect will be done.
EDITH MARGARET CLARKSON

338

SPIRIT of mercy, truth and love,
O shed thine influence from above,
And still from age to age convey
The wonders of this sacred day.

2 In every clime, by every tongue,
Be God's surpassing glory sung:
Let all the listening earth be taught
The acts our great Redeemer wrought.

3 Unfailing Comfort, heavenly Guide,
Still o'er thy Holy Church preside;
Still let mankind thy blessings prove;
Spirit of mercy, truth and love.
Anonymous. Foundling Hospital Collection, 1774

339

O BREATH of life, come sweeping through us,
Revive thy Church with life and power;
O Breath of life, come, cleanse, renew us,
And fit thy Church to meet this hour.

2 O Wind of God, come bend us,
    break us,
Till humbly we confess our
    need;
Then in thy tenderness remake
    us,
Revive, restore; for this we
    plead.

3 O Breath of love, come breathe
    within us,
Renewing thought and will and
    heart:
Come, Love of Christ, afresh to
    win us,
Revive thy Church in every
    part.

4 Revive us, Lord! is zeal abating
While harvest fields are vast
    and white?
Revive us, Lord, the world is
    waiting,
Equip thy Church to spread the
    light.
        BESSIE PORTER HEAD, 1850–1936

340

SPIRIT of Light—Holy,
  Shine in this world of thine;
Lighten thou our darkness,
    clear
Blindness from out our minds.
Guide thou our ways, so may
    we
Walk in the light of thy truth,
Come, Spirit, come.

2 Spirit of Love—Holy,
Fire thou this world of thine;
Chasten thou the pride of race
Marring our common life.
Kindle our love, that loving,
All may true brotherhood find,
Come, Spirit, come.

3 Spirit of Life—Holy,
Breathe o'er this world of
    thine;
Teach us all to know and do
All that will make men free.
Thy kingdom come, on earth as
In thy blest heaven above,
Come, Spirit, come.

4 Spirit of Power—Holy,
Mighty and infinite;
Work within this world of thine
Breaking the powers of sin.
Take thou thy throne, and
    reigning,
Claim the whole world for thine
    own.
Great Spirit, come.
        ARTHUR MORRIS JONES

341

HOW great the harvest is
    Of him who came to save
    us!
The hearts of men are his,
    Our law the love he gave us.
The world lay cruel, blind,
    Naught holding, naught
        divining;
He came to human kind,
    And now the light is shining,
    Is shining, is shining.

2 And though the news did seem
    Too good for man's believing,
'Tis not an empty dream
    Too high for our achieving.
He triumphed in the strife,
    O'er all his foes he towered;
They killed the Prince of Life,
    But he hath death o'er-
        powered, o'erpowered,
    O'erpowered, o'erpowered.

3 Then came the Father's call;
    His work on earth was
        ended;
That he might light on all,
    To heaven the Lord ascended.
To heaven so near to earth
    Our hearts we do surrender:
There all things find their worth
    And human life its splendour,
        its splendour,
    Its splendour, its splendour.

4 The power by which there came
    The Word of God among us
Was love's eternal flame,
    Whose light and heat are
        flung us;
That Spirit sent from God,
    Within our hearts abiding,

Hath brought us on our road
 And still the world is guiding,
  is guiding,
 Is guiding, is guiding.

5 In Three made manifest,
  Thou source of all our being,
 Thou loveliest, truest, best,
  Beyond our power of seeing;
 Thou power of light and love,
  Thou life that never diest—
 To thee in whom all move
  Be glory in the highest, the
   highest,
  The highest, the highest,
        PERCY DEARMER, 1867–1936

342 *Veni, Creator Spiritus*

COME, Holy Ghost, our souls
  inspire
And lighten with celestial fire;
Thou the anointing Spirit art,
Who dost thy sevenfold gifts
  impart.

2 Thy blessèd unction from above
Is comfort, life, and fire of love;
Enable with perpetual light
The dulness of our blinded
  sight:

3 Anoint and cheer our soilèd
  face
With the abundance of thy
  grace:
Keep far our foes; give peace at
  home:
Where thou art Guide no ill can
  come.

4 Teach us to know the Father,
  Son,
 And thee of Both, to be but
  One,

That through the ages all along
This may be our endless song,
 'Praise to thine eternal
  merit,
 Father, Son, and Holy Spirit.'
        Amen.
        9th century
    Tr. JOHN COSIN, 1594–1672
    The following are also suitable

No.
103 Breathe on me, Breath of God
104 Come, Holy Spirit, come
105 Come, thou Holy Paraclete
115 Come down, O Love Divine
See also hymns on the Holy Spirit in
Part I, Section 2 and Part I, Section 3

343(i)

Alleluia!

343(ii)

Alleluia, Alleluia, Alleluia!

343(iii)

Alleluia, Alleluia,
Praise God the Lord most high.
Alleluia, Alleluia,
His word doth last for aye.

344

GLORY be to the Father,
  and to the Son, and to the
   Holy Ghost:
As it was in the beginning, is
  now, and ever shall be,
  world without end. Amen.

III

RESPONSE TO THE WORD OF GOD

ADORATION AND THANKSGIVING

345   TE DEUM LAUDAMUS

Chant A

WE praise ' thee O ' God :
we ac- ' knowledge thee
to ' be the ' Lord :
All the ' earth doth ' worship
thee : the ' Father ' ever- '
lasting.

2 To thee all angels ' cry a- '
loud : the ' heavens and ' all
the ' powers therein :
To thee ' cherubim and '
seraphim : con- ' tinual- ' ly
do ' cry.

3 Holy holy holy Lord ' God of
Sa- ' baoth : heaven and
earth are full of the '
majesty ' of thy ' glory :
The glorious company of the
a- ' postles ' praise thee : the
goodly ' fellowship of the '
prophets ' praise thee.

4 The noble army of ' martyrs '
praise thee : the holy
Church throughout ' all the '
world doth ac- ' knowledge
thee :
The Father of an ' infinite '
majesty : thine honourable
true and only Son also
the ' Holy ' Ghost the ' Comforter.

Chant B

5 Thou art the King of ' Glory
O ' Christ : thou art the ever- '
lasting ' Son of the ' Father :
When thou tookest upon thee
to de- ' liver ' man : thou
didst not ab- ' hor the '
Virgin's ' womb.

6 When thou hadst overcome
the ' sharpness of ' death :
thou didst open the King-
dom of ' heaven to ' all
be- ' lievers :
Thou sittest at the ' right
hand of ' God : in the '
glory ' of the ' Father.

7 We believe that thou shalt
come to ' be our ' Judge :
we therefore pray thee help
thy servants whom thou
hast re- ' deemed with thy '
precious ' blood :
Make them to be ' numbered
with thy ' saints : in ' glory '
ever- ' lasting.

Chant C

8 O Lord save thy people and '
bless thine ' heritage :
govern them and ' lift them '
up for ' ever :
Day by day we ' magnify '
thee : and we worship
thy ' Name ever ' world
without ' end.

9 Vouchsafe O Lord to keep us
this ' day without ' sin :
O Lord have mercy up- ' on
us have ' mercy up- ' on us :
O Lord let thy mercy lighten
upon us as our ' trust is in '
thee : O Lord in thee have
I trusted let me ' never '
be con- ' founded.

346   PSALM 145 (ii), verses 1–6

O LORD, thou art my God
and King;
Thee will I magnify and praise:
I will thee bless, and gladly sing
Unto thy holy Name always.

2 Each day I rise I will thee bless,
 And praise thy Name time with-
  out end.
 Much to be praised, and great
  God is;
 His greatness none can compre-
  hend.

3 Race shall thy works praise
  unto race,
 The mighty acts show done by
  thee.
 I will speak of the glorious
  grace,
 And honour of thy majesty;

4 Thy wondrous works I will
  record.
 By men the might shall be ex-
  tolled
 Of all thy dreadful acts, O
  Lord:
 And I thy greatness will unfold.

5 *To Father, Son, and Holy Ghost,*
 The God whom earth and
  heaven adore,
 Be glory, as it was of old,
 Is now, and shall be evermore.
  Amen.

347 PSALM 150

PRAISE ye the Lord. God's
  praise within
 His sanctuary raise;
 And to him in the firmament
 Of his power give ye praise.

2 Because of all his mighty acts,
 With praise him magnify:
 O praise him, as he doth excel
 In glorious majesty.

3 Praise him with trumpet's
  sound; his praise
 With psaltery advance:
 With timbrel, harp, stringed
  instruments,
 And organs, in the dance.

4 Praise him on cymbals loud;
  him praise
 On cymbals sounding high.
 Let each thing breathing praise
  the Lord.
 Praise to the Lord give ye.

5 *To Father, Son, and Holy Ghost,*
 The God whom we adore,
 Be glory, as it was, and is,
 And shall be evermore. Amen.

348 PSALM 98, verses 1–3, 5–9

SING a new song to Jehovah,
  For he wondrous things
   hath wrought;
 His right hand and arm most
  holy
 Victory to him have brought.

2 Lo! the Lord his great salvation
  Openly hath now made
   known;
 In the sight of every nation
  He his righteousness hath
   shown.

3 Mindful of his truth and
   mercy
  He to Israel's house hath
   been;
 And the Lord our God's salvation
  All the ends of earth have
   seen.

4 Sound the trumpet and the
   cornet,
  Shout before the Lord the
   King;
 Sea, and all its fullness,
   thunder;
  Earth, and all its people,
   sing.

5 Let the rivers in their gladness
  Clap their hands with one
   accord;
 Let the mountains sing together
  Joyfully before the Lord.

6 For to judge the earth he
   cometh;
  And with righteousness shall
   he
 Judge the world, and all the
   nations
  With most perfect equity.

7 *Glory be to God, the Father;*
 Glory be to God, the Son;
 Glory be to God, the Spirit;
 While eternal ages run. Amen.

349 PSALM 98

O SING unto the Lord a
new song for he hath
done ' marvellous ' things :
his right hand and his holy '
arm hath ' gotten him the '
victory :
The Lord hath made ' known
his sal- ' vation : his righteousness hath he openly '
showed in the ' sight of the '
heathen.

2 He hath remembered his
mercy and his truth to-
ward the ' house of ' Israel :
all the ends of the earth
have seen the sal- ' vation '
of our ' God :
Make a joyful noise unto the
Lord ' all the ' earth : make
a loud ' noise and re- ' joice
and sing ' praise.

3 Sing unto the ' Lord with the '
harp : with the ' harp and
the ' voice of a ' psalm :
With trumpets and ' sound of '
cornet : make a joyful ' noise
before the ' Lord the ' King.

4 Let the sea roar, and the ' fullness there- ' of : the ' world
and ' they that ' dwell
therein :
Let the ' floods clap their '
hands : let the hills be joyful to- ' gether be- ' fore
the ' Lord.

5 For he cometh to ' judge the '
earth : with righteousness
shall he judge the ' world
and the ' people with '
equity.

*Glory ' be to the ' Father : and to
the Son ' and to the ' Holy '
Ghost :
As it ' was in the be- ' ginning :
is now and ever shall be '
world without ' end.*
A- ' men.

350 PSALM 136, Gelineau version

O give thanks to the Lord
for he is good,
*Great is his love, love without
end.*
Give thanks to the God of gods,
*Great is his love, love without
end.*
Give thanks to the Lord of
lords,
*Great is his love, love without
end.*

2 Who alone has wrought marvellous works,
*Great is his love, love without
end.*
Whose wisdom it was made the
skies,
*Great is his love, love without
end.*
Who spread the earth on the
seas,
*Great is his love, love without
end.*

3 It was he who made the great
lights,
*Great is his love, love without
end.*
The sun to rule in the day,
*Great is his love, love without
end.*
The moon and stars in the night,
*Great is his love, love without
end.*

4 The first-born of the Egyptians
he smote,
*Great is his love, love without
end.*
Brought Israel out from their
midst,
*Great is his love, love without
end.*
Arm outstretched with power
in his hand,
*Great is his love, love without
end.*

5 He let Israel inherit their land,
*Great is his love, love without
end.*

On his servant their land he
bestowed,
*Great is his love, love without
end.*

He remembered us in our distress.
*Great is his love, love without
end.*

6 And he snatched us away from
our foes,
*Great is his love, love without
end.*

He gives food to all living
things,
*Great is his love, love without
end.*

To the God of heaven give
thanks,
*Great is his love, love without
end.*

* A more literal translation of the
Refrain is: 'For his great love is without
end.' But this does not fit the musical
setting so well.

351 PSALM 103, verses 1–5

O THOU my soul, bless God
the Lord;
And all that in me is
Be stirred up his holy Name
To magnify and bless.

2 Bless, O my soul, the Lord thy
God,
And not forgetful be
Of all his gracious benefits
He hath bestowed on thee.

3 All thine iniquities who doth
Most graciously forgive:
Who thy diseases all and pains
Doth heal, and thee relieve.

4 Who doth redeem thy life, that
thou
To death mayest not go
down;

Who thee with loving-kindness
doth
And tender mercies crown:

5 Who with abundance of good
things
Doth satisfy thy mouth;
So that, even as the eagle's age,
Renewed is thy youth.

6 *To Father, Son, and Holy Ghost,
The God whom we adore,
Be glory, as it was, and is,
And shall be evermore. Amen.*

352

H OLY, holy, holy, Lord
God Almighty!
Early in the morning our song
shall rise to thee;
Holy, holy, holy, merciful and
mighty,
God in Three Persons, blessèd
Trinity!

2 Holy, holy, holy! all the saints
adore thee,
Casting down their golden
crowns around the glassy
sea,
Cherubim and seraphim falling
down before thee,
Which wert, and art, and
evermore shalt be.

3 Holy, holy, holy! though the
darkness·hide thee,
Though the eye of sinful man
thy glory may not see,
Only thou art holy; there is
none beside thee,
Perfect in power, in love, and
purity.

*Holy, holy, holy, Lord God
Almighty!
All thy works shall praise thy
Name in earth and sky and
sea;
Holy, holy, holy, merciful and
mighty,
God in Three Persons, blessèd
Trinity! Amen.*

REGINALD HEBER, 1783–1826

127

353

ROUND the Lord in glory
seated,
Cherubim and seraphim
Filled his temple, and repeated
Each to each the alternate
hymn:
'*Lord thy glory fills the
heaven;*
*Earth is with its fullness
stored;*
Unto thee be glory given,
Holy, holy, holy Lord.'

2 Heaven is still with glory ringing,
Earth takes up the angels'
cry,
'Holy, holy, holy,' singing,
'Lord of hosts, the Lord
most high.'

3 With his seraph train before
him,
With his holy Church below,
Thus conspire we to adore him,
Bid we thus our anthem flow:
RICHARD MANT, 1776–1848

354

GLORY be to God the Father,
Glory be to God the Son,
Glory be to God the Spirit,—
Great Jehovah, Three in
One!
Glory, glory, glory, glory
While eternal ages run!

2 Glory be to him who loved us,
Washed us from each spot
and stain!
Glory be to him who bought us,
Made us kings with him to
reign!
Glory, glory, glory, glory
To the Lamb that once was
slain!

3 Glory to the King of angels,
Glory to the Church's King,
Glory to the King of nations!
Heaven and earth, your
praises bring;
Glory, glory, glory, glory
To the King of Glory bring!

4 'Glory, blessing, praise eternal!'
Thus the choir of angels sings;
'Honour, riches, power, do-
minion!'
Thus its praise creation
brings;
Glory, glory, glory, glory,
Glory to the King of kings!
Amen.
HORATIUS BONAR, 1808–89

355
Gott ist gegenwärtig

GOD reveals his presence:
Let us now adore him,
And with awe appear before
him.
God is in his temple:
All within keep silence,
Prostrate lie with deepest re-
verence.
Him alone
God we own,
Him our God and Saviour:
Praise his Name for ever.

2 God reveals his presence:
Hear the harps resounding,
See the crowds the throne sur-
rounding;
Holy, holy, holy!
Hear the hymn ascending,
Angels, saints, their voices
blending.
Bow thine ear
To us here;
Hearken, O Lord Jesus,
To our meaner praises.

3 O thou Fount of blessing
Purify my spirit,
Trusting only in thy merit:
Like the holy angels
Who behold thy glory,
May I ceaselessly adore thee.
Let thy will
Ever still
Rule thy Church terrestrial,
As the hosts celestial.
GERHARD TERSTEEGEN, 1697–1769
Tr. FREDERICK WILLIAM FOSTER
1760–1835
and JOHN MILLER, 1756–90
revised WILLIAM MERCER 1811–73

356

MY God, how wonderful thou
   art,
  Thy majesty how bright!
How beautiful thy mercy-seat,
  In depths of burning light!

2 How dread are thine eternal
   years,
  O everlasting Lord,
By prostrate spirits day and
   night
  Incessantly adored!

3 O how I fear thee, living God,
  With deepest, tenderest fears,
And worship thee with trembl-
   ing hope
  And penitential tears!

4 Yet I may love thee too, O Lord,
  Almighty as thou art,
For thou hast stooped to ask of
   me
  The love of my poor heart.

5 No earthly father loves like
   thee;
  No mother, e'er so mild,
Bears and forbears as thou hast
   done
  With me, thy sinful child.

6 How beautiful, how beautiful
  The sight of thee must be,
Thine endless wisdom, bound-
   less power,
  And awesome purity!
       FREDERICK WILLIAM FABER
                1814–63

357

ETERNAL Light! eternal
  Light!
  How pure the soul must be,
When, placed within thy search-
   ing sight,
It shrinks not, but, with calm
   delight,
  Can live, and look on thee!

2 The spirits that surround thy
   throne
  May bear the burning bliss;
But that is surely theirs alone,
Since they have never, never
   known
  A fallen world like this.

3 O how shall I, whose native
   sphere
  Is dark, whose mind is dim,
Before the Ineffable appear,
And on my naked spirit bear
  The uncreated beam?

4 There is a way for man to rise
  To that sublime abode:
An offering and a sacrifice,
A Holy Spirit's energies,
  An Advocate with God.

5 These, these prepare us for the
   sight
  Of holiness above:
The sons of ignorance and night
May dwell in God's eternal
   Light,
  Through his eternal Love!
       THOMAS BINNEY, 1798–1874
                altered

358

THE God of Abraham
   praise,
  Who reigns enthroned above,
Ancient of everlasting days,
  And God of love.
Jehovah, Great I AM!
  By earth and heaven con-
   fessed,
I bow, and bless the sacred
   Name
  For ever blest.

2 The God of Abraham praise,
  At whose supreme command
From earth I rise, and seek the
   joys
  At his right hand.
I all on earth forsake—
  Its wisdom, fame, and
   power—
And him my only portion make,
  My shield and tower.

3 He by himself hath sworn,
  I on his oath depend:
I shall, on eagle's wings up-
   borne,
  To heaven ascend;
I shall behold his face,
  I shall his power adore,
And sing the wonders of his
   grace
  For evermore.

4   There dwells the Lord our
    King,
The Lord our Righteousness,
Triumphant o'er the world and
    sin,
  The Prince of Peace;
On Zion's sacred height
  His Kingdom he maintains,
And glorious with his saints in
    light
  For ever reigns.

5   *The whole triumphant host*
  Give thanks to God on high:
'*Hail, Father, Son, and Holy*
    Ghost!'
  They ever cry.
  Hail, Abraham's God, and
    mine!—
I join the heavenly lays,—
All might and majesty are thine,
  And endless praise. Amen.
        THOMAS OLIVERS, 1725–99
        Based on the Jewish *Yigdal*

359

PRAISE the Lord, his glories
  show,
  Alleluia!
Saints within his courts below,
  Alleluia!
Angels round his throne above,
  Alleluia!
All that see and share his love.
  Alleluia!

2 Earth to heaven, and heaven to
    earth,
Tell his wonders, sing his worth;
Age to age and shore to shore,
Praise him, praise him ever-
  more!

3 Praise the Lord, his mercies
  trace;
Praise his providence and grace,
All that he for man hath done,
All he sends us through his Son.

4 Strings and voices, hands and
    hearts,
In the concert bear your parts;
All that breathe, your Lord
  adore,
Praise him, praise him ever-
  more:
    HENRY FRANCIS LYTE, 1793–1847

360

PRAISE, my soul, the King of
  heaven;
  To his feet thy tribute bring;
Ransomed, healed, restored,
  forgiven,
Who like me his praise should
  sing?
  Praise him! Praise him!
  Praise him! Praise him!
Praise the everlasting King.

2 Praise him for his grace and
  favour
  To our fathers in distress;
Praise him, still the same for
  ever,
  Slow to chide and swift to
  bless:
  Praise him! Praise him!
  Praise him! Praise him!
Glorious in his faithfulness.

3 Father-like he tends and spares
  us;
  Well our feeble frame he
  knows;
In his hands he gently bears
  us,
  Rescues us from all our foes:
  Praise him! Praise him!
  Praise him! Praise him!
Widely as his mercy flows.

4 Frail as summer's flower we
  flourish;
  Blows the wind and it is
  gone;
But, while mortals rise and
  perish,
  God endures unchanging on:
  Praise him! Praise him!
  Praise him! Praise him!
Praise the high eternal One.

5 Angels, help us to adore him;
  Ye behold him face to face;
Sun and moon, bow down be-
  fore him;
  Dwellers all in time and space.
  Praise him! Praise him!
  Praise him! Praise him!
Praise with us the God of
  grace.
    HENRY FRANCIS LYTE, 1793–1847
         From Psalm 103

361

LET all the world in every
    corner sing,
  'My God and King!'
The heavens are not too
    high,
His praise may thither fly;
The earth is not too low,
His praises there may grow.
Let all the world in every
    corner sing,
  'My God and King!'

2 Let all the world in every corner
    sing,
  'My God and King!'
The Church with psalms must
    shout,
No door can keep them out;
But, above all, the heart
Must bear the longest part.
Let all the world in every corner
    sing,
  'My God and King!'
        GEORGE HERBERT, 1593–1633

When this hymn is sung to the tune
AUGUSTINE *the first two lines of v. 2 must*
be omitted.

362

FROM all that dwell below the
    skies
Let the Creator's praise arise:
    Alleluia! Alleluia!
Let the Redeemer's Name be
    sung
Through every land, in every
    tongue.
  Alleluia, Alleluia, Alleluia,
    Alleluia, Alleluia!

2 Eternal are thy mercies, Lord:
Eternal truth attends thy
    word:
Thy praise shall sound from
    shore to shore
Till suns shall rise and set no
    more:
        ISAAC WATTS, 1674–1748
        From Psalm 117

363

YE holy angels bright,
    Who wait at God's right
      hand,
Or through the realms of light
    Fly at your Lord's command,
    Assist our song,
      Or else the theme
      Too high doth seem
    For mortal tongue.

2 Ye blessèd souls at rest,
    Who ran this earthly race,
And now, from sin released,
    Behold the Saviour's face,
    His praises sound,
      As in his light
      With sweet delight
    Ye do abound.

3 Ye saints, who toil below,
    Adore your heavenly King,
And, onward as ye go,
    Some joyful anthem sing;
    Take what he gives,
      And praise him still
      Through good and ill,
    Who ever lives.

4 My soul, bear thou thy part,
    Triumph in God above,
And with a well-tuned heart
    Sing thou the songs of love.
    Let all thy days
      Till life shall end,
      Whate'er he send,
    Be filled with praise.
        RICHARD BAXTER, 1615–91
        and others

364

KING of glory, King of peace,
    I will love thee;
And, that love may never
    cease,
    I will move thee.
Thou hast granted my request,
    Thou hast heard me;
Thou didst note my working
    breast,
    Thou hast spared me.

2 Wherefore with my utmost art
  I will sing thee,
And the cream of all my heart
  I will bring thee.
Though my sins against me
  cried,
  Thou didst clear me,
And alone, when they replied,
  Thou didst hear me.

3 Seven whole days, not one in
  seven,
  I will praise thee;
In my heart, though not in
  heaven,
  I can raise thee.
Small it is, in this poor sort
  To enrol thee;
E'en eternity's too short
  To extol thee.

GEORGE HERBERT, 1593–1633

365

FOR the might of thine arm
  we bless thee, our God, our
  fathers' God.
Thou hast kept thy pilgrim
  people by the strength of thy
  staff and rod;
Thou hast called us to the
  journey which faithless feet
  ne'er trod;
*For the might of thine arm we
bless thee, our God, our
fathers' God.*

2 For the love of Christ con-
  straining, that bound their
  hearts as one;
For the faith in truth and
  freedom in which their work
  was done;
For the peace of God's evangel
  wherewith their feet were
  shod;

3 We are watchers of a beacon
  whose light must never die;
We are guardians of an altar
  that shows thee ever nigh;
We are children of thy freemen
  who sleep beneath the sod;

4 May the shadow of thy presence
  around our camp be spread;
Baptize us with the courage
  thou gavest to our dead;
O keep us in the pathway their
  saintly feet have trod:

CHARLES SILVESTER HORNE
1865–1914

366

SING to the Lord a joyful
  song,
  Lift up your hearts, your
  voices raise;
To us his gracious gifts belong,
  To him our songs of love and
  praise.

2 For life and love, for rest and
  food,
  For daily help and nightly
  care,
Sing to the Lord, for he is good,
  And praise his Name, for it is
  fair.

3 For strength to those who on
  him wait
  His truth to prove, his will
  to do,
Praise ye our God, for he is
  great,
  Trust in his Name, for it is
  true.

4 For joys untold, that from
  above
  Cheer those who love his
  sweet employ,
Sing to our God, for he is love,
  Exalt his Name, for it is joy.

5 *For he is Lord of heaven and
  earth,
  Whom angels serve and saints
  adore,
The Father, Son, and Holy
  Ghost,
  To whom be praise for ever-
  more. Amen.*

JOHN SAMUEL BEWLEY MONSELL
1811–75

367

FOR the beauty of the earth,
　For the beauty of the skies,
For the love which from our
　birth
　Over and around us lies,
Christ, our God, to thee we raise
This our sacrifice of praise.

2 For the beauty of each hour
　Of the day and of the night,
Hill and vale, and tree and
　flower,
　Sun and moon and stars of
　light,

3 For the joy of ear and eye,
　For the heart and mind's
　delight,
For the mystic harmony
　Linking sense to sound and
　sight,

4 For the joy of human love,
　Brother, sister, parent, child,
Friends on earth and friends
　above,
　For all gentle thoughts and
　mild,

5 For each perfect gift of thine
　To our race so freely given,
Graces human and divine,
　Flowers of earth and buds of
　heaven:

FOLLIOTT SANDFORD PIERPOINT
1835–1917

368　*Nun danket alle Gott*

NOW thank we all our God,
　With heart and hands
　and voices,
Who wondrous things hath
　done,
In whom his world rejoices,—
　Who, from our mothers'
　arms,
　Hath blessed us on our
　way
　With countless gifts of
　love,
And still is ours today.

2 O may this bounteous God
　Through all our life be near
　us,
With ever-joyful hearts
And blessèd peace to cheer us,
　And keep us in his grace,
　And guide us when per-
　plexed,
　And free us from all ills
　In this world and the
　next.

3 *All praise and thanks to God*
　The Father now be given,
The Son, and him who reigns
　With them in highest heaven,—
　The one, eternal God,
　Whom earth and heaven
　adore;
　For thus it was, is now,
　And shall be evermore.
　　　　　　　Amen.

MARTIN RINKART, 1586–1649
Tr. CATHERINE WINKWORTH
1827–78

369

GOD and Father, we adore
　thee
For the Son, thine image
　bright,
In whom all thy holy nature
　Dawned on our once hopeless
　night.

2 Far from thee our footsteps
　wandered,
　On dark paths of sin and
　shame;
But our midnight turned to
　morning,
　When the Lord of Glory
　came.

3 Word Incarnate, God revealing,
　Longed-for while dim ages
　ran,
Love Divine, we bow before
　thee,
　Son of God and Son of Man.

4 Let our life be new created,
　Ever-living Lord, in thee,
Till we wake with thy pure like-
　ness,
　When thy face in heaven we
　see;

5 Where the saints of all the ages,
  Where our fathers glorified,
  Clouds and darkness far be-
      neath them,
  In unending day abide.

6 God and Father, now we bless
      thee
    For the Son, thine image
      bright,
  In whom all thy holy nature
  Dawns on our adoring sight.

Verse 1 attributed to
JOHN NELSON DARBY, 1800–82
Verses 2–5 and adaptation of verse 6
HUGH FALCONER, 1859–1931

370 *Beim frühen Morgenlicht*

WHEN morning gilds the
      skies,
My heart awaking cries,
    'May Jesus Christ be praisèd'.
When evening shadows fall,
This rings my curfew-call,
    'May Jesus Christ be praisèd'.
When mirth for music longs,
This is my song of songs,
    'May Jesus Christ be praisèd'.
God's holy house of prayer
Hath none that can compare
    With   'Jesus   Christ   be
      praisèd'.

2 This greeting of great joy,
  I ne'er have found it cloy,
    'May Jesus Christ be praisèd'.
  When sorrow would molest,
  Then sing I undistrest,
    'May Jesus Christ be praisèd'.
  No lovelier antiphon
  In all high heav'n is known
    Than   'Jesus   Christ   be
      praisèd'.
  There to the Eternal Word
  The eternal psalm is heard,
    'O Jesus Christ be praisèd'.

3 Ye nations of mankind,
  In this your concord find,
    'May Jesus Christ be praisèd'.
  Let all the earth around
  Ring joyous with the sound
    'May Jesus Christ be praisèd'.

Sing, suns and stars of space,
Sing, ye that see his face,
    Sing 'Jesus Christ be praisèd'.
God's whole creation o'er,
For aye and evermore,
    Shall Jesus Christ be praisèd.

Anonymous German hymn,
early 19th century
Tr. ROBERT BRIDGES, 1844–1930

371

O FOR a thousand tongues, to
    sing
  My great Redeemer's praise,
The glories of my God and King,
  The triumphs of his grace!

2 Jesus! the Name that charms
      our fears,
    That bids our sorrows cease;
  'Tis music in the sinner's ears,
    'Tis life, and health, and
      peace.

3 He breaks the power of can-
      celled sin,
    He sets the prisoner free;
  His blood can make the foulest
      clean,
    His blood availed for me.

4 He speaks, and, listening to his
      voice,
    New life the dead receive,
  The mournful, broken hearts
      rejoice,
    The humble poor believe.

5 Hear him, ye deaf; his praise, ye
      dumb,
    Your loosened tongues em-
      ploy;
  Ye blind, behold your Saviour
      come;
    And leap, ye lame, for joy!

6 My gracious Master and my
      God,
    Assist me to proclaim,
  To spread through all the earth
      abroad
    The honours of thy Name.

CHARLES WESLEY, 1707–88

372

YE servants of God, your
Master proclaim,
And publish abroad his wonder-
ful Name;
The Name all-victorious of
Jesus extol;
His Kingdom is glorious, and
rules over all.

2 God ruleth on high, almighty to
save;
And still he is nigh, his presence
we have;
The great congregation his
triumph shall sing,
Ascribing salvation to Jesus our
King.

3 Salvation to God, who sits on
the throne!
Let all cry aloud, and honour
the Son:
The praises of Jesus the angels
proclaim,
Fall down on their faces, and
worship the Lamb.

4 Then let us adore, and give him
his right,
All glory and power, all wisdom
and might,
All honour and blessing, with
angels above,
And thanks never ceasing, and
infinite love.

CHARLES WESLEY, 1707–88

373 *Gloriosi Salvatoris*

TO the Name of our Salvation
Laud and honour let us pay,
Which for many a generation
Hid in God's foreknowledge
lay,
But with holy exultation
We may sing aloud today.

2 Jesus is the Name we treasure,
Name beyond what words
can tell,
Name of gladness, Name of
pleasure,
Ear and heart delighting well;
Name of sweetness passing
measure,
Saving us from sin and hell.

3 'Tis the Name that whoso
preacheth
Speaks like music to the ear;
Who in prayer this Name be-
seecheth
Sweetest comfort findeth
near;
Who its perfect wisdom
reacheth
Heav'nly joy possesseth here.

4 Jesus is the Name exalted
Over every other name;
In this Name, whene'er as-
saulted,
We can put our foes to
shame;
Strength to them who else had
halted,
Eyes to blind, and feet to
lame.

5 Therefore we, in love adoring,
This most blessèd Name
revere,
Holy Jesus, thee imploring
So to write it in us here
That hereafter, heavenward
soaring,
We may sing with angels
there.

15th century
Tr. Compilers of *Hymns Ancient
and Modern*, 1861
Based on the tr. by
JOHN MASON NEALE, 1818–66

374

TO God be the glory! great
things he hath done!
So loved he the world that he
gave us his Son,
Who yielded his life an atonement for sin,
And opened the life-gate that
all may go in.

2 O perfect redemption, the
purchase of blood!
To every believer the promise of
God;
The vilest offender who truly
believes,
That moment from Jesus a
pardon receives.

3 Great things he hath taught us,
    great things he hath done,
And great our rejoicing through
    Jesus the Son:
But purer and higher and
    greater will be
Our wonder, our transport,
    when Jesus we see.

FRANCES (CROSBY) VAN ALSTYNE
1820–1915

375 *Schönster Herr Jesu*

FAIREST Lord Jesus,
    Ruler of all nature,
O thou of God and Man the
    Son;
Thee will I cherish,
Thee will I honour,
Thou my soul's glory, joy and
    crown.

2   Fair are the meadows,
    Fairer still the woodlands,
Robed in the verdure and bloom
    of spring.
Jesus is fairer,
Jesus is purer,
He makes the saddest heart to
    sing.

3   Fair are the flowers,
    Fairer still the sons of men
In all the freshness of youth
    arrayed;
Yet is their beauty
Fading and fleeting;
Lord Jesus, thine will never
    fade.

4   Fair is the sunshine,
    Fairer still the moonlight,
And fair the twinkling starry
    host;
Jesus shines brighter,
Jesus shines purer
Than all the stars that heaven
    can boast.

Münster Gesangbuch, 1677
Tr. LILIAN STEVENSON, 1870–1960
and others

376

HOW sweet the Name of
    Jesus sounds
    In a believer's ear!
It soothes his sorrows, heals his
    wounds,
    And drives away his fear.

2 It makes the wounded spirit
    whole,
    And calms the troubled
    breast;
'Tis manna to the hungry soul,
    And to the weary rest.

3 Dear Name! the rock on which I
    build,
    My shield and hiding-place,
My never-failing treasury, filled
    With boundless stores of
    grace.

4 Jesus, my Shepherd, Husband,
    Friend,
    My Prophet, Priest, and
    King,
My Lord, my Life, my Way, my
    End,
    Accept the praise I bring.

5 Weak is the effort of my heart,
    And cold my warmest
    thought;
But, when I see thee as thou
    art,
    I'll praise thee as I ought.

6 Till then I would thy love pro-
    claim
    With every fleeting breath;
And may the music of thy
    Name
    Refresh my soul in death.

JOHN NEWTON, 1725–1807

377 *Jesu dulcis memoria*

JESUS, the very thought of
    thee
    With sweetness fills my
    breast;
But sweeter far thy face to see,
    And in thy presence rest.

2 Nor voice can sing, nor heart
    can frame,
  Nor can the memory find
A sweeter sound than thy blest
    Name,
  O Saviour of mankind!

3 O Hope of every contrite heart,
  O Joy of all the meek,
To those who fall how kind thou
    art!
  How good to those who seek!

4 But what to those who find?
    Ah, this
  Nor tongue nor pen can show;
The love of Jesus, what it is
  None but his loved ones
    know.

5 Jesus, our only joy be thou,
  As thou our prize wilt be;
Jesus, be thou our glory now,
  And through eternity.

Probably 12th century
Tr. EDWARD CASWALL, 1814–78
Lyra Catholica, 1849

378   *Jesu, Rex admirabilis*

O JESUS, King most wonder-
    ful,
  Thou Conqueror renowned,
Thou Sweetness most ineffable,
  In whom all joys are found!

2 When once thou visitest the
    heart,
  Then truth begins to shine,
Then earthly vanities depart,
  Then kindles love divine.

3 O Jesus, Light of all below,
  Thou Fount of life and fire,
Surpassing all the joys we
    know,
  And all we can desire,—

4 May every heart confess thy
    Name,
  And ever thee adore,
And, seeking thee, itself inflame
  To seek thee more and more.

5 Thee may our tongues for ever
    bless;
  Thee may we love alone,
And ever in our lives express
  The image of thine own.

Probably 12th century
Tr. EDWARD CASWALL, 1814–78
Lyra Catholica, 1849

379   *O Deus, ego amo te*

MY God, I love thee; not
    because
  I hope for heaven thereby,
Nor yet because who love thee
    not
  Are lost eternally.

2 Thou, O my Jesus, thou didst
    me
  Upon the cross embrace;
For me didst bear the nails and
    spear,
  And manifold disgrace,

3 And griefs and torments num-
    berless,
  And sweat of agony;
Even death itself; and all for
    one
  Who was thine enemy.

4 Then why, most loving Jesus
    Christ,
  Should I not love thee well,
Not for the sake of winning
    heaven,
  Or of escaping hell;

5 Not with the hope of gaining
    aught,
  Not seeking a reward;
But as thyself hast lovèd me,
  O ever-loving Lord?

6 Even so I love thee, and will
    love,
  And in thy praise will sing,
Solely because thou art my
    God,
  And my eternal King.

17th century Latin, based on a
Spanish sonnet
Tr. EDWARD CASWALL, 1814–78

380

MAN of Sorrows! wondrous Name
For the Son of God, who came
Ruined sinners to reclaim!
Alleluia! what a Saviour!

2 Bearing shame and scoffing rude,
In my place condemned he stood,
Sealed my pardon with his blood:

3 Guilty, vile, and helpless we;
Spotless Lamb of God was he:
Full atonement,—can it be?

4 Lifted up was he to die,
'It is finished' was his cry;
Now in heaven exalted high:

5 When he comes, our glorious King,
All his ransomed home to bring,
Then anew this song we'll sing:
PHILIPP BLISS, 1838–76

381

I WILL sing the wondrous story
Of the Christ who died for me,—
How he left the realms of glory
For the cross on Calvary:
Yes, I'll sing the wondrous story
Of the Christ who died for me,—
Sing it with his saints in glory,
Gathered by the crystal sea.

2 I was lost: but Jesus found me,
Found the sheep that went astray,
Raised me up and gently led me
Back into the narrow way:

3 Faint was I, and fears possessed me,
Bruised was I from many a fall;
Hope was gone, and shame distressed me:
But his love has pardoned all:

4 Days of darkness still may meet me,
Sorrow's paths I oft may tread;
But his presence still is with me,
By his guiding hand I'm led:

5 He will keep me till the river
Rolls its waters at my feet:
Then he'll bear me safely over,
Made by grace for glory meet:
FRANCIS HAROLD ROWLEY
1854–1952

382

ALL hail, the power of Jesus' Name!
Let angels prostrate fall;
Bring forth the royal diadem,
To *crown him Lord of all.

2 Crown him, ye martyrs of your God,
Who from his altar call;
Extol him in whose path ye trod,
And crown him Lord of all.

3 Ye seed of Israel's chosen race,
Ye ransomed of the fall,
Hail him who saves you by his grace,
And crown him Lord of all.

4 Let every tongue and every tribe,
Responsive to the call,
To him all majesty ascribe,
And crown him Lord of all.
EDWARD PERRONET, 1726–92

* *The words 'crown him' are sung four times in each verse.*

383 *For children*

COME, children, join to sing—
Alleluia! Amen!
Loud praise to Christ our King;
Alleluia! Amen!
Let all, with heart and voice,
Before his throne rejoice;
Praise is his gracious choice:
Alleluia! Amen!

2 Come, lift your hearts on high;
Alleluia! Amen!
Let praises fill the sky;
Alleluia! Amen!

He is our Guide and Friend;
To us he'll blessing send;
His love shall never end:
    Alleluia! Amen!

3 Praise yet the Lord again;
    Alleluia! Amen!
Life shall not end the strain;
    Alleluia! Amen!
On heaven's blissful shore
His goodness we'll adore,
Singing for evermore,
    Alleluia! Amen!
      CHRISTIAN HENRY BATEMAN
      1813–89

384   *For children*

COME, let us remember the
   joys of the town:
Gay vans and bright buses that
   roar up and down,
Shop-windows and playgrounds
   and swings in the park,
And street-lamps that twinkle
   in rows after dark.

2 Come, let us now lift up our
   voices in praise,
And to the Creator a thanksgiving raise,
For towns with their buildings
   of stone, steel and wood,
For people who love them and
   work for their good.

3 We thank thee, O God, for the
   numberless things
And friends and adventures
   which every day brings.
O may we not rest until all that
   we see
In towns and in cities is pleasing
   to thee.
      DORIS GILL
      Two verses omitted

385   *For children*

IT is a thing most wonderful,
   Almost too wonderful to be,
That God's own Son should
   come from heaven,
   And die to save a child like me.
2 And yet I know that it is true:
   He chose a poor and humble
     lot,

And wept, and toiled, and
   mourned, and died,
   For love of those who loved
    him not.

3 It is most wonderful to know
   His love for me so free and
    sure;
But 'tis more wonderful to see
   My love for him so faint and
    poor.

4 And yet I want to love thee,
   Lord;
   O light the flame within my
    heart,
And I will love thee more and
   more,
Until I see thee as thou art.
      WILLIAM WALSHAM HOW
      1823–97

386   *For younger children*

PRAISE him, praise him, all
   ye little children,
He is love, he is love;
Praise him, praise him, all ye
   little children,
He is love, he is love.

2 Thank him, thank him, all ye
   little children,
He is love, he is love;
Thank him, thank him, all ye
   little children,
He is love, he is love.

3 Love him, love him, all ye little
   children,
He is love, he is love;
Love him, love him, all ye little
   children,
He is love, he is love.

4 Crown him, crown him, all ye
   little children,
God is love, God is love;
Crown him, crown him, all ye
   little children,
God is love, God is love.
      Anonymous, c. 1890

The following are also suitable
Nos. 135–8. 145–6, 238, 640

F

AFFIRMATION

387 PSALM 23

THE Lord's my Shepherd, I'll not want.
He makes me down to lie
In pastures green: he leadeth me
The quiet waters by.

2 My soul he doth restore again;
And me to walk doth make
Within the paths of righteousness,
Even for his own Name's sake.

3 Yea, though I walk in death's dark vale,
Yet will I fear none ill:
For thou art with me; and thy rod
And staff me comfort still.

4 My table thou hast furnishèd
In presence of my foes;
My head thou dost with oil anoint,
And my cup overflows.

5 Goodness and mercy all my life
Shall surely follow me:
And in God's house for evermore
My dwelling-place shall be.

6 *To Father, Son, and Holy Ghost,*
The God whom we adore,
Be glory, as it was, and is,
And shall be evermore. Amen.

388

THE King of Love my Shepherd is,
Whose goodness faileth never;
I nothing lack if I am his
And he is mine for ever.

2 Where streams of living water flow
My ransomed soul he leadeth,
And where the verdant pastures grow
With food celestial feedeth.

3 Perverse and foolish oft I strayed,
But yet in love he sought me,
And on his shoulder gently laid,
And home rejoicing brought me.

4 In death's dark vale I fear no ill,
With thee, dear Lord, beside me;
Thy rod and staff my comfort still,
Thy cross before to guide me.

5 Thou spread'st a table in my sight;
Thy unction grace bestoweth;
And O what transport of delight
From thy pure chalice floweth!

6 And so through all the length of days
Thy goodness faileth never;
Good Shepherd, may I sing thy praise
Within thy house for ever!
HENRY WILLIAMS BAKER, 1821–77
From Psalm 23

389 PSALM 23, Gelineau version

THE Lórd is my Shépherd;
There is nóthing I shall wánt.
Frésh and gréen are the pástures
Where he gíves me repóse.
Near réstful wáters he leáds me,
To revíve my droóping spírit.

2 He gúides me alóng the right páth;
He is trúe to his Náme.
If I should wálk in the válley of dárkness
No evil would I féar.
You are thére with your croók and your stáff;
With thése you give me cómfort.

3 You have prepared a banquet
    for me,
In the sight of my foes.
My head you have anointed
    with oil;
My cup is overflowing.

4 Surely goodness and kindness
    shall follow me
All the days of my life.
In the Lord's own house shall
    I dwell
For ever and ever.

5 To the Father and Son give
    glory,
Give glory to the Spirit.
To God who is, who was, and
    who will be
For ever and ever.

Antiphon 1
My Shepherd is the Lord,
    nothing indeed shall I want.

Antiphon 2
His goodness shall follow me
    always, to the end of my
    days.

Antiphon 3
The Lord is my Shepherd,
    nothing shall I want; he
    leads me by safe paths,
    nothing shall I fear.

390   PSALM 89, verses
           15, 16, 18

O GREATLY blest the people
    are
The joyful sound that know;
In brightness of thy face, O
    Lord,
They ever on shall go.

2 They in thy Name shall all the
    day
Rejoice exceedingly;
And in thy righteousness shall
    they
Exalted be on high.

3 For God is our defence; and he
    To us doth safety bring:
The Holy One of Israel
    Is our almighty King.

4 *To Father, Son, and Holy Ghost,*
    The God whom we adore,
Be glory, as it was, and is,
    And shall be evermore. Amen.

391   PSALM 34, verses
         1, 2, 7–9, 11, 14, 15

G OD will I bless all times; his
    praise
My mouth shall still express.
My soul shall boast in God: the
    meek
Shall hear with joyfulness.

2 The angel of the Lord encamps,
    And round encompasseth
All those about that do him fear,
    And them delivereth.

3 O taste and see that God is
    good:
Who trusts in him is blest.
Fear God, his saints: none that
    him fear
Shall be with want oppressed.

4 O children, hither do ye come,
    And unto me give ear;
I shall you teach to understand
    How ye the Lord should fear.

5 Depart from ill, do good, seek
    peace,
Pursue it earnestly.
God's eyes are on the just; his
    ears
Are open to their cry.

6 *To Father, Son, and Holy Ghost,*
    The God whom we adore,
Be glory, as it was, and is,
    And shall be evermore. Amen.

392   PSALM 124 (ii)

N OW Israel may say, and that
    truly,
If that the Lord had not our
    cause maintained;
If that the Lord had not our
    right sustained,
When cruel men against us
    furiously
Rose up in wrath, to make of us
    their prey;

2 Then certainly they had de-
      voured us all,
  And swallowed quick, for aught
      that we could deem ;
  Such was their rage, as we might
      well esteem.
  And as fierce floods before them
      all things drown,
  So had they brought our soul to
      death quite down.

3 The raging streams, with their
      proud swelling waves,
  Had then our soul o'erwhelmèd
      in the deep.
  But blest be God, who doth us
      safely keep,
  And hath not given us for a
      living prey
  Unto their teeth, and bloody
      cruelty.

4 Even as a bird out of the
      fowler's snare
  Escapes away, so is our soul set
      free:
  Broke are their nets, and thus
      escapèd we.
  Therefore our help is in the
      Lord's great Name,
  Who heaven and earth by his
      great power did frame.

5 *Glory to God the Father, God the
      Son,*
  *And unto God the Spirit, Three
      in One.*
  *From age to age let saints his
      Name adore,*
  *His power and love proclaim from
      shore to shore,*
  *And spread his fame, till time
      shall be no more.*   *Amen.*

393   PSALM 126

WHEN Zion's bondage God
      turned back,
  As men that dreamed were
      we.
  Then filled with laughter was
      our mouth,
  Our tongue with melody:

2 They among the heathen said,
      'The Lord
  Great things for them hath
      wrought.'

The Lord hath done great things
      for us,
  Whence joy to us is brought.

3 As streams of water in the
      south,
  Our bondage, Lord, recall.
  Who sow in tears, a reaping
      time
  Of joy enjoy they shall.

4 That man who, bearing precious
      seed,
  In going forth doth mourn,
  He doubtless, bringing back his
      sheaves,
  Rejoicing shall return.

5 *To Father, Son, and Holy Ghost,*
  The God whom we adore,
  Be glory, as it was, and is,
      And shall be evermore. Amen.

394   PARAPHRASE 22, verses 3–8

ART thou afraid his power
      shall fail
  When comes thy evil day ?
  And can an all-creating arm
  Grow weary or decay ?

2 Supreme in wisdom as in power
      The Rock of ages stands ;
  Though him thou canst not see,
      nor trace
  The working of his hands.

3 He gives the conquest to the
      weak,
  Supports the fainting heart ;
  And courage in the evil hour
  His heavenly aids impart.

4 Mere human power shall fast
      decay,
  And youthful vigour cease ;
  But they who wait upon the
      Lord
  In strength shall still increase.

5 They with unwearied feet shall
      tread
  The path of life divine ;
  With growing ardour onward
      move,
  With growing brightness
      shine.

6 On eagles' wings they mount,
     they soar,
Their wings are faith and
     love,
Till, past the cloudy regions
     here,
They rise to heaven above.

Scottish Paraphrases, 1781
From Isaiah 40:28—end

395 PARAPHRASE 60

FATHER of peace, and God
     of love!
We own thy power to save,
That power by which our
     Shepherd rose
Victorious o'er the grave.

2 Him from the dead thou
     brought'st again,
When, by his sacred blood,
Confirmed and sealed for ever-
     more
The eternal covenant stood.

3 O may thy Spirit seal our souls,
And mould them to thy will,
That our weak hearts no more
     may stray,
But keep thy precepts still!

4 That to perfection's sacred
     height
We nearer still may rise,
And all we think, and all we do,
Be pleasing in thine eyes.

Scottish Paraphrases, 1781
From Hebrews 13:20, 21

396 PARAPHRASE 63

BEHOLD the amazing gift of
     love
The Father hath bestowed
On us, the sinful sons of men,
To call us sons of God!

2 Concealed as yet this honour
     lies,
By this dark world un-
     known,—
A world that knew not when he
     came,
Even God's eternal Son.

3 High is the rank we now pos-
     sess;
But higher we shall rise,
Though what we shall hereafter
     be
Is hid from mortal eyes.

4 Our souls, we know, when he
     appears,
Shall bear his image bright;
For all his glory, full disclosed,
Shall open to our sight.

5 A hope so great, and so divine,
May trials well endure;
And purge the soul from sense
     and sin,
As Christ himself is pure.

Scottish Paraphrases, 1781
From 1 John 3:1–3

397 *Deus Pater credentium*

O GOD, thou art the Father
     Of all that have believed:
From whom all hosts of angels
     Have life and power received.
O God, thou art the Maker
     Of all created things,
The righteous Judge of judges,
     The Almighty King of kings.

2 High in the heavenly Zion
     Thou reignest God adored;
And in the coming glory
     Thou shalt be Sovereign
          Lord.
Beyond our ken thou shinest,
     The everlasting Light;
Ineffable in loving,
     Unthinkable in might.

3 Thou to the meek and lowly
     Thy secrets dost unfold;
O God, thou doest all things,
     All things both new and old.
I walk secure and blessèd
     In every clime or coast,
In Name of God the Father,
     And Son, and Holy Ghost.

ST. COLUMBA, 521–97
Tr. DUNCAN MACGREGOR
1854–1923

398 ᵻm ᴀonᴀꝥᴀn ᴅom ᴍꝛ ᴀn ꝛᴌᴀᴅ

ALONE with none but thee,
　my God;
I journey on my way;
What need I fear, when thou
　art near,
O King of night and day?
More safe am I within thy hand,
Than if a host did round me
　stand.

2 My destined time is fixed by
　thee,
　And Death doth know his
　hour.
Did warriors strong around me
　throng,
　They could not stay his
　power;
No walls of stone can man de-
　fend
　When thou thy messenger
　dost send.

3 My life I yield to thy decree,
　And bow to thy control
In peaceful calm, for from thine
　arm
　No power can wrest my soul.
Could earthly omens e'er appal
　A man that heeds the
　heavenly call!

4 The child of God can fear no ill,
　His chosen dread no foe;
We leave our fate with thee, and
　wait
　Thy bidding when to go.
'Tis not from chance our com-
　fort springs,
Thou art our trust, O King of
　kings.

　　　　Attributed to St. COLUMBA
　　　　　　　　　　521–97
　　　　　　　　　Tr. anonymous

399

THOUGH in God's form he
　was,
Christ Jesus would not snatch
At parity with God;

2 Himself he sacrificed,
Taking a servant's form,
Being born like ev'ry man;

3 Revealed in human shape,
Obediently he stooped
To die upon a cross.

4 Him therefore God raised high,
Gave him the Name of Lord,
All other names above;

5 That at the Saviour's Name
No knee might be unbowed,
In heaven, or earth, or hell;

6 And ev'ry tongue confess,
To God the Father's praise,
That 'Jesus Christ is Lord'.

　　Tr. ARCHIBALD MacBRIDE HUNTER
　　　　　　　From Phil. 2:6–11

400

FIRMLY I believe and truly
　God is Three, and God is
　One;
And I next acknowledge duly
　Manhood taken by the Son.

2 And I trust and hope most fully
　In that Manhood crucified;
And each thought and deed un-
　ruly
　Do to death, as he has died.

3 Simply to his grace and wholly
　Light and life and strength
　belong,
And I love supremely, solely,
　Him the holy, him the strong.

4 And I hold in veneration
　For the love of him alone,
Holy Church as his creation,
　And her teachings as his own.

5 *Adoration aye be given,
　With and through the angelic
　host,
To the God of earth and heaven,
　Father, Son, and Holy Ghost.*
　　　　　　　　　Amen.

　　JOHN HENRY NEWMAN, 1801–90

401 ᴀᴅomꝛᴌᴜꝥ ᴍᴠoᴍᴜ ᴍᴜꝥᴄ ᴄꝛᴇn

TODAY I arise,
　Invoking the Blessèd
　Trinity,
Confessing the Blessèd Unity,
Creator of all the things
　that be.

AFFIRMATION

2 Today I arise,
  By strength of Christ and his
    mystic Birth,
  By his Passion, and
    Triumph's saving worth,
  By his coming again to judge
    the earth.
  *[Today I arise, today I arise.]

3 Today I arise,
  By seraphs serving the Lord
    above,
  By truths his ancient heralds
    prove,
  By saints in purity, labour,
    love.

4 Today I arise,
  By splendour of sun and
    flaming brand,
  By rushing wind, by lightning
    grand,
  By depth of sea, by strength
    of land.

5 Today I arise,
  With God my steersman, stay
    and guide,
  To guard, to counsel, to hear,
    to bide,
  His way before, his hosts
    beside—

6 Protecting me now
  From crafty wiles of demon
    crew,
  From foemen, be they many
    or few,
  From lusts that I can scarce
    subdue.

7 Lord Jesus the Christ,
  Today surround me with
    thy might;
  Before, behind, on left and
    right,
  Be thou in breadth, in length,
    in height.

8 Direct and control
  The minds of all who think
    on me,
  The lips of all who speak to
    me,
  The eyes of all who look on
    me.

9 Today I arise,
  Invoking the Blessèd Trinity,
  Confessing the Blessèd Unity:
  Saviour, on us salvation be!

St. PATRICK, 372–466
Tr. ROBERT ALEXANDER STEWART
MACALISTER, 1870–1950

* This refrain is to be omitted when the
Irish traditional tunes, RAMELTON and
CULRATHAIN are used.

402 Ꝺꝏᴍᴘɪᴜꝼ ɪᴍᴏɪᴜ ᴎɪᴜᴘᴛ ᴛᴘᴇᴎ

I BIND unto myself today
  The strong Name of the
    Trinity,
By invocation of the same,
  The Three in One, and One
    in Three.

2 I bind this day to me for ever,
  By power of faith, Christ's
    Incarnation;
His baptism in the Jordan
  river;
  His death on cross for my
    salvation;
  His bursting from the spicèd
    tomb;
  His riding up the heavenly
    way;
His coming at the day of doom:
  I bind unto myself today.

3 I bind unto myself today
  The virtues of the star-lit
    heaven,
The glorious sun's life-giving
  ray,
  The whiteness of the moon at
    even,
The flashing of the lightning
  free,
  The whirling wind's tem-
    pestuous shocks,
The stable earth, the deep salt
  sea
  Around the old eternal rocks.

4 I bind unto myself today
  The power of God to hold and
    lead,
His eye to watch, his might to
  stay,
  His ear to hearken to my
    need,

145

The wisdom of my God to
teach,
His hand to guide, his shield
to ward,
The word of God to give me
speech,
His heavenly host to be my
guard.

5 Christ be with me, Christ within
me,
Christ behind me, Christ before me,
Christ beside me, Christ to win
me,
Christ to comfort and restore
me,
Christ beneath me, Christ
above me,
Christ in quiet, Christ in
danger,
Christ in hearts of all that love
me,
Christ in mouth of friend and
stranger.

6 *I bind unto myself the Name,*
The strong Name of the
Trinity,
By invocation of the same,
The Three in One, and One in
Three,
Of whom all nature hath creation,
Eternal Father, Spirit, Word,
Praise to the Lord of my salva-
tion:
Salvation is of Christ the
Lord. Amen.

ST. PATRICK, 372–466
Version by CECIL FRANCES ALEXANDER
1818–95

Verses 1–4 and 6 are sung to ST. PATRICK.
Verse 5 is sung to CLONMACNOISE.

403

THEE will I love, my God and
King,
Thee will I sing, my strength
and tower:
For evermore thee will I trust,
O God most just of truth and
power;
Who all things hast in order
placed,
Yea, for thy pleasure hast
created;

And on thy throne, unseen, unknown,
Reignest alone in glory
seated.

2 Set in my heart thy love I find;
My wandering mind to thee
thou leadest:
My trembling hope, my strong
desire
With heavenly fire thou
kindly feedest.
Lo, all things fair thy path prepare,
Thy beauty to my spirit
calleth,
Thine to remain in joy or
pain,
And count it gain whate'er
befalleth.

3 O more and more thy love ex-
tend,
My life befriend with
heavenly pleasure;
That I may win thy paradise,
Thy pearl of price, thy count-
less treasure;
Since but in thee I can go free
From earthly care and vain
oppression,
This prayer I make for Jesus'
sake,
That thou me take in thy
possession.

ROBERT BRIDGES, 1844–1930
Yattendon Hymnal, 1899

404

GOD is my strong salvation;
What foe have I to fear?
In darkness and temptation
My light, my help is near.

2 Though hosts encamp around
me,
Firm to the fight I stand;
What terror can confound me,
With God at my right hand?

3 Place on the Lord reliance;
My soul, with courage wait;
His truth be thine affiance,
When faint and desolate.

4 His might thine heart shall
    strengthen,
  His love thy joy increase;
  Mercy thy days shall lengthen;
  The Lord will give thee peace.

JAMES MONTGOMERY, 1771–1854
From Psalm 27

---

405 *Meine Hoffnung stehet feste*

ALL my hope on God is
   founded;
  He doth still my trust renew.
Me through change and chance
   he guideth,
  Only good and only true.
    God unknown,
    He alone
  Calls my heart to be his
    own.

2 Pride of man and earthly
   glory,
  Sword and crown betray his
   trust;
What with care and toil he
   buildeth,
  Tower and temple, fall to
   dust.
    But God's power,
    Hour by hour,
  Is my temple and my tower.

3 God's great goodness aye endureth,
  Deep his wisdom passing
   thought:
Splendour, light, and life attend
   him,
  Beauty springeth out of
   naught.
    Evermore,
    From his store
  New-born worlds rise and
   adore.

*4 Daily doth the Almighty Giver
  Bounteous gifts on us be-
   stow;
His desire our soul delighteth,
  Pleasure leads us where we go.
    Love doth stand
    At his hand;
  Joy doth wait on his com-
   mand.

5 Still from man to God eternal
  Sacrifice of praise be done,
High above all praises praising
  For the gift of Christ his Son.
    Christ doth call
    One and all:
  Ye who follow shall not fall.

ROBERT BRIDGES, 1844–1930
Based on JOACHIM NEANDER
1650–80

* *This verse may be omitted.*

---

406 *Ein' feste Burg ist unser Gott*

A SAFE stronghold our God is
   still,
  A trusty shield and weapon;
He'll help us clear from all the
   ill
  That hath us now o'ertaken.
    The ancient prince of hell
    Hath risen with purpose
     fell;
    Strong mail of craft and
     power
    He weareth in this hour;
  On earth is not his fellow.

2 With force of arms we nothing
   can,
  Full soon were we down-
   ridden;
But for us fights the proper
   Man,
  Whom God himself hath
   bidden.
    Ask ye who is this same?
    Christ Jesus is his Name,
    The Lord Sabaoth's Son;
    He, and no other one,
  Shall conquer in the battle.

3 And were this world all devils
   o'er,
  And watching to devour us,
We lay it not to heart so sore;
  Not they can overpower us.
    And let the prince of ill
    Look grim as e'er he will,
    He harms us not a whit;
    For why—his doom is
     writ;
    A word shall quickly slay
     him.

4 God's word, for all their craft
    and force,
  One moment will not linger,
But, spite of hell, shall have its
    course;
  'Tis written by his finger.
    And, though they take our
      life,
    Goods, honour, children,
      wife,
    Yet is their profit small;
    These things shall vanish
      all:
The city of God remaineth.
        MARTIN LUTHER, 1483–1546
        Tr. THOMAS CARLYLE, 1795–1881

407   *Ein' feste Burg ist unser Gott*

A FORTRESS sure is God our
    King,
A shield that ne'er shall fail us;
His sword alone shall succour
    bring,
When evil doth assail us.
With craft and cruel hate
Doth Satan lie in wait,
And, armed with deadly power,
Seeks whom he may devour;
On earth where is his equal?

2 O who shall then our cham-
    pion be,
Lest we be lost for ever?
One sent by God—from sin 'tis
    he
The sinner shall deliver;
And dost thou ask his Name?
'Tis Jesus Christ—the same
Of Sabaoth the Lord,
The Everlasting Word;
'Tis he must win the battle.

3 God's word remaineth ever
    sure,
To us his goodness show'ng;
The Spirit's gifts, of sin the
    cure,
Each day he is bestowing.
Though naught we love be left,
Of all, e'en life, bereft,
Yet what shall Satan gain?
God's kingdom doth remain,
And shall be ours for ever.
        MARTIN LUTHER, 1483–1546
        Tr. GODFREY THRING, 1823–1903

408   *O quam iuvat fratres, Deus*

H APPY are they, they that
    love God,
  Whose hearts have Christ
    confessed,
Who by his cross have found
    their life,
  And 'neath his yoke their
    rest.

2 Glad is the praise, sweet are the
    songs,
  When they together sing;
And strong the prayers that
    bow the ear
  Of heaven's eternal King.

3 Christ to their homes giveth
    his peace,
  And makes their loves his
    own;
But ah, what tares the evil one
  Hath in his garden sown!

4 Sad were our lot, evil this
    earth,
  Did not its sorrows prove
The path whereby the sheep
    may find
  The fold of Jesus' love.

5 Then shall they know, they
    that love him,
  How all their pain was good;
And death itself cannot unbind
  Their happy brotherhood.
        ROBERT BRIDGES, 1844–1930
        Yattendon Hymnal, 1899
        Based on CHARLES COFFIN
        1676–1749

409

A ND can it be, that I should
    gain
  An interest in the Saviour's
    blood?
Died he for me, who caused his
    pain—
  For me, who him to death
    pursued?
Amazing love! how can it be
That thou, my God, shouldst
    die for me?

2 He left his Father's throne
  above,—
So free, so infinite his grace—
Emptied himself of all but love,
  And bled for Adam's helpless
  race:
'Tis mercy all, immense and free;
For, O my God, it found out me!

3 No condemnation now I dread;
  Jesus, and all in him, is
  mine!
Alive in him, my living Head,
  And clothed in righteousness
  divine,
Bold I approach the eternal
  throne,
And claim the crown, through
  Christ my own.
                    CHARLES WESLEY, 1707–88

410

NOT what these hands have
  done
Can save this guilty soul;
Not what this toiling flesh has
  borne
Can make my spirit whole.

2   Not what I feel or do
    Can give me peace with God;
Not all my prayers, and sighs,
    and tears
    Can bear my heavy load.

3   Thy work alone, O Christ,
    Can ease this weight of sin;
Thy blood alone, O Lamb of
    God,
    Can give me peace within.

4   Thy love to me, O God,
    Not mine, O Lord, to thee,
Can rid me of this dark unrest,
    And set my spirit free.

5   Thy grace alone, O God,
    To me can pardon speak;
Thy power alone, O Son of God,
    Can this sore bondage break.

6   I bless the Christ of God,
    I rest on life divine,
And with unfaltering lip and
    heart,
    I call this Saviour mine.
                    HORATIUS BONAR, 1808–89, altered

411

MY hope is built on nothing
  less
Than Jesus' blood and right-
  eousness;
I dare not trust my sweetest
  frame,
But wholly lean on Jesus'
  Name.
    On Christ, the solid rock, I
    stand;
    All other ground is sinking
    sand.

2 When darkness seems to veil
  his face,
I rest on his unchanging grace;
In every high and stormy gale,
My anchor holds within the veil:

3 His oath, his covenant, and
  blood,
Support me in the whelming
  flood;
When all around my soul gives
  way,
He then is all my hope and stay:
                    EDWARD MOTE, 1797–1874

412

WILL your anchor hold in
  the storms of life,
When the clouds unfold their
  wings of strife?
When the strong tides lift, and
  the cables strain,
Will your anchor drift, or firm
  remain?
    We have an anchor that keeps
    the soul
    Steadfast and sure while the
    billows roll;
    Fastened to the Rock which
    cannot move,
    Grounded firm and deep in the
    Saviour's love!

2 Will your anchor hold in the
  straits of fear,
When the breakers roar and the
  reef is near?
While the surges rave, and the
  wild winds blow,
Shall the angry waves then your
  bark o'erflow?

3 Will your anchor hold in the
    floods of death,
When the waters cold chill your
    latest breath?
On the rising tide you can never
    fail,
While your anchor holds within
    the veil:

4 Will your eyes behold through
    the morning light
The city of gold and the harbour
    bright?
Will you anchor safe by the
    heavenly shore,
When life's storms are past for
    evermore?
    PRISCILLA JANE OWENS, 1829–1907

413

JESUS shall reign where'er the
    sun
Does his successive journeys
    run;
His Kingdom stretch from shore
    to shore,
Till moons shall wax and wane
    no more.

2 People and realms of every
    tongue
Dwell on his love with sweetest
    song;
And infant voices shall pro-
    claim
Their early blessings on his
    Name.

3 Blessings abound where'er he
    reigns:
The prisoner leaps to lose his
    chains,
The weary find eternal rest,
And all the sons of want are
    blest.

4 Let every creature rise and
    bring
Peculiar honours to our King,
Angels descend with songs
    again,
And earth repeat the long
    Amen.
    ISAAC WATTS, 1674–1748

414
Wir glauben all' an einen Gott

WE believe in one true God,
    Father, Son, and Holy
    Ghost,
Ever present help in need,
Praised by all the heavenly
    host;

2 We believe in Jesus Christ,
Son of God and Mary's Son,
Who descended from his
    throne,
And for us salvation won;

3 We confess the Holy Ghost,
Who from both fore'er pro-
    ceeds;
Who upholds and comforts us
In all trials, fears, and needs.

4 *Blest and Holy Trinity,*
Praise forever be to thee!
By whose mighty power alone
All is made and wrought and
    done. Amen.
    TOBIAS CLAUSNITZER, 1619–84
    Tr. CATHERINE WINKWORTH
    1827–78, altered

415

THE great love of God is re-
    vealed in the Son,
Who came to this earth to re-
    deem every one.
That love, like a stream flowing
    clear to the sea,
Makes clean every heart that
    from sin would be free.

2 It binds the whole world, every
    barrier it breaks,
The hills it lays low, and the
    mountains it shakes.
It's yours, it is ours, O how
    lavishly given!
The pearl of great price, and the
    treasure of heaven!
    DANIEL THAMBYRAJAH NILES
    1908–70

416 *For children*

GOD is love: his the care,
Tending each, everywhere.
God is love—all is there!
Jesus came to show him,
That mankind might know
    him:
Sing aloud, loud, loud!
Sing aloud, loud, loud!
    God is good!
    God is truth!
God is beauty! Praise him!

2 None can see God above;
All have here man to love;
Thus may we Godward move,
Finding him in others,
Holding all men brothers:

3 Jesus lived here for men,
Strove and died, rose again,
Rules our hearts, now as
    then;
For he came to save us
By the truth he gave us:

4 To our Lord praise we sing—
Light and life, friend and
    king,
Coming down love to bring,
Pattern for our duty,
Showing God in beauty:
            PERCY DEARMER, 1867–1936

417 *For younger children*

GOD is always near me,
Hearing what I say,
Knowing all my thoughts and
    deeds,
All my work and play.

2 God is always near me;
In the darkest night
He can see me just the same
As by mid-day light.

3 God is always near me,
Though so young and small;
Not a look or word or thought,
But God knows it all.
            PHILIPP BLISS, 1838–76
            The Charm, 1871

418 *For younger children*

JESUS loves me! this I know
For the Bible tells me so;
Little ones to him belong;
They are weak, but he is strong.
    *Yes! Jesus loves me,
    Loves me, loves me!
    Yes! Jesus loves me;
    For the Bible tells me so!

2 Jesus loves me! he who died
Heaven's gate to open wide;
He will wash away my sin,
Let his little child come in:

3 Jesus loves me! he will stay
Close beside me all the way;
Then his little child will take
Up to heaven, for his dear sake:
            ANNA BARTLETT WARNER
            1820–1915

* *When Tune* (ii), JESUS LOVES ME, *is
sung, the Refrain reads:*
Yes! Jesus loves me!
Yes! Jesus loves me!
Yes! Jesus loves me!
The Bible tells me so.

419 *For younger children*

LORD, I would own thy ten-
    der care,
And all thy love to me;
The food I eat, the clothes I
    wear,
Are all bestowed by thee.

2 'Tis thou preservest me from
    death
And dangers every hour;
I cannot draw another breath
    Unless thou give me power.

3 Kind angels guard me every
    night,
As round my bed they stay;
Nor am I absent from thy sight
    In darkness or by day.

4 My health and friends and
    parents dear
To me by God are given;
I have not any blessing here
    But what is sent from heaven.

5 Such goodness, Lord, and con-
 stant care
 A child can ne'er repay;
But may it be my daily prayer
 To love thee and obey.

JANE TAYLOR, 1783–1824

420

THE Church's one foundation
 Is Jesus Christ her Lord:
She is his new creation
 By water and the word;
From heaven he came and
 sought her
 To be his holy bride;
With his own blood he bought
 her,
 And for her life he died.

2 Elect from every nation,
 Yet one o'er all the earth,
Her charter of salvation
 One faith, one birth:
One holy Name she blesses,
 Partakes one holy food,
And to one hope she presses,
 With every grace endued.

3 'Mid toil and tribulation,
 And tumult of her war,
She waits the consummation
 Of peace for evermore,
Till with the vision glorious
 Her longing eyes are blest,
And the great Church victorious
 Shall be the Church at rest.

4 Yet she on earth hath union
 With God the Three in One,
And mystic sweet communion
 With those whose rest is won.
O happy ones and holy!
 Lord, give us grace that we,
Like them, the meek and lowly,
 On high may dwell with thee.

SAMUEL JOHN STONE, 1839–1900

421

GLORIOUS things of thee
 are spoken,
 Zion, city of our God;
He whose word cannot be
 broken
 Formed thee for his own
  abode.

On the Rock of Ages founded,
 What can shake thy sure
  repose?
With salvation's walls surrounded,
 Thou may'st smile at all thy
  foes.

2 See! the streams of living
  waters,
 Springing from eternal love,
Well supply thy sons and
  daughters,
 And all fear of want remove.
Who can faint while such a
  river
 Ever flows their thirst to as-
  suage,—
Grace, which, like the Lord the
  Giver,
 Never fails from age to age?

3 Round each habitation hover-
  ing,
 See! the cloud and fire appear,
For a glory and a covering,
 Showing that the Lord is
  near.
Blest inhabitants of Zion,
 Washed in the Redeemer's
  blood,
Jesus, whom their souls rely on,
 Makes them kings and priests
  to God.

4 Saviour, if of Zion's city
 I, through grace, a member
  am,
Let the world deride or pity,
 I will glory in thy Name.
Fading is the worldling's
  pleasure,
 All his boasted pomp and
  show;
Solid joys and lasting treasure
 None but Zion's children
  know.

JOHN NEWTON, 1725–1807

422

CITY of God, how broad and
 far
 Outspread thy walls sublime!
The true thy chartered freemen
 are,
 Of every age and clime.

2 One holy Church, one army
strong,
One steadfast, high intent;
One working band, one harvest-
song,
One King omnipotent.

3 How purely hath thy speech
come down
From man's primeval youth!
How grandly hath thine empire
grown,
Of freedom, love and truth!

4 How gleam thy watch-fires
through the night
With never-fainting ray!
How rise thy towers, serene and
bright,
To meet the dawning day!

5 In vain the surge's angry shock,
In vain the drifting sands:
Unharmed upon the eternal
Rock
The eternal City stands.
SAMUEL JOHNSON, 1822–82

423 *Igjennem Nat og Trængsel*

THROUGH the night of doubt
and sorrow
Onward goes the pilgrim
band,
Singing songs of expectation,
Marching to the promised
land.

2 Clear before us, through the
darkness,
Gleams and burns the guiding light;
Brother clasps the hand of
brother,
Stepping fearless through the
night;

3 One the light of God's own
presence,
O'er his ransomed people
shed,
Chasing far the gloom and
terror,
Brightening all the path we
tread;

4 One the object of our journey,
One the faith which never
tires,
One the earnest looking forward,
One the hope our God in-
spires;

5 One the strain that lips of
thousands
Lift as from the heart of one;
One the conflict, one the peril,
One the march in God begun;

6 One the gladness of rejoicing
On the far eternal shore,
Where the one Almighty Father
Reigns in love for evermore.
BERNHARDT SEVERIN INGEMANN
1789–1862
Tr. SABINE BARING-GOULD
1834–1924

424

THY hand, O God, has guided
Thy flock, from age to age;
The wondrous tale is written,
Full clear, on every page;
Our fathers owned thy goodness,
And we their deeds record;
And both of this bear witness,
*One Church, one Faith, one
Lord.*

2 Thy heralds brought glad
tidings
To greatest, as to least;
They bade men rise, and hasten
To share the great King's
feast;
And this was all their teaching,
In every deed and word,
To all alike proclaiming,

3 Through many a day of dark-
ness,
Through many a scene of
strife,
The faithful few fought bravely
To guard the nation's life.
Their Gospel of redemption,
Sin pardoned, man restored,
Was all in this enfolded,

4 Thy mercy will not fail us,
 Nor leave thy work undone;
With thy right hand to help us,
 The victory shall be won;
And then, by men and angels,
 Thy Name shall be adored,
And this shall be their anthem:
　　　　EDWARD HAYES PLUMPTRE
　　　　　　　1821–91

425

IN Christ there is no East or
 West,
In him no South or North,
But one great fellowship of
 love
 Throughout the whole wide
 earth.

2 In him shall true hearts every-
 where
 Their high communion find,
His service is the golden cord
 Close-binding all mankind.

3 Join hands, then, brothers of
 the Faith,
Whate'er your race may be:
Who serves my Father as a son
 Is surely kin to me.

4 In Christ now meet both East
 and West,
 In him meet South and North,
All Christlike souls are one in
 him,
 Throughout the whole wide
 earth.

　　　　JOHN OXENHAM, 1852–1941

426　　　*For children*

A GLORIOUS company we
 sing,
The Master and his men,
He sent them forth to tell his
 love
By voice and hand and pen.

2 A loving company we sing,
When Jesus sent to save
All sick and blind and hungry
 folk,
The outcast and the slave.

3 We join this glorious company
Of Jesus and his friends,
To spread throughout this
 troubled world
His love that never ends.

　　　　ALBERT FREDERICK BAYLY
　　The following are also suitable
　　Nos. 139, 140, 151, 169, 324, 333

427　　*For younger children*

THE Church is wherever God's
 people are praising,
Singing their thanks for joy on
 this day.
The Church is wherever disciples
 of Jesus
Remember his story and walk
 in his way.

2 The Church is wherever God's
 people are helping,
Caring for neighbours in sickness and need.
The Church is wherever God's
 people are sharing
The words of the Bible in gift
 and in deed.
　　　　CAROL ROSE IKELER

DEDICATION AND DISCIPLESHIP

428

LORD of creation, to thee be
 all praise!
Most mighty thy working, most
 wondrous thy ways!
Who reignest in glory no tongue
 can e'er tell,
Yet deign'st in the heart of the
 humble to dwell.

2 Lord of all power, I give thee
 my will,
In joyful obedience thy tasks
 to fulfil.
Thy bondage is freedom; thy
 service is song;
And, held in thy keeping, my
 weakness is strong.

3 Lord of all wisdom, I give thee
     my mind,
     Rich truth that surpasseth
       man's knowledge to find.
   What eye hath not seen and
     what ear hath not heard
   Is taught by thy Spirit and
     shines from thy Word.

4 Lord of all bounty, I give thee
     my heart;
   I praise and adore thee for all
     that thou art;
   Thy love to inflame me, thy
     counsel to guide,
   Thy presence to shield me,
     whate'er may betide.

5·Lord of all being, I give thee
     my all;
   If e'er I disown thee, I stumble
     and fall;
   But, sworn in glad service thy
     word to obey,
   I walk in thy freedom to the
     end of the way.

            JACK COPLEY WINSLOW

429

MY God, accept my heart
  this day
And make it always thine,
That I from thee no more may
  stray,
No more from thee decline.

2 Before the cross of him who
  died,
  Behold, I prostrate fall;
Let every sin be crucified,
  And Christ be all in all.

3 Anoint me with thy heavenly
  grace,
  And seal me for thine own;
That I may see thy glorious
  face,
  And worship near thy throne.

4 Let every thought and work
  and word
  To thee be ever given;
Then life shall be thy service,
  Lord,
  And death the gate of heaven.

5 *All glory to the Father be,*
  All glory to the Son,
  All glory, Holy Ghost, to thee,
    While endless ages run. Amen.
        MATTHEW BRIDGES, 1800–94

430

'TAKE up thy cross,' the
    Saviour said,
  'If thou wouldst my disciple
    be;
Take up thy cross, with willing
  heart,
  And humbly follow after me.'

2 Take up thy cross; let not its
  weight
  Fill thy weak soul with vain
    alarm;
His strength shall bear thy
  spirit up,
  And brace thy heart, and
    nerve thine arm.

3 Take up thy cross, nor heed the
  shame,
  And let thy foolish pride be
    still;
Thy Lord refused not e'en to die
  Upon a cross, on Calvary's hill.

4 Take up thy cross, then, in his
  strength,
  And calmly every danger
    brave;
'Twill guide thee to a better
  home,
  And lead to victory o'er the
    grave.

5 Take up thy cross, and follow
  Christ,
  Nor think till death to lay
    it down;
For only he who bears the cross
  May hope to wear the glorious
    crown.

        CHARLES WILLIAM EVEREST
                1814–77

431

JESUS, Master, whose I am,
  Purchased, thine alone to be,
By thy blood, O spotless Lamb,
  Shed so willingly for me,
Let my heart be all thine own,
Let me live to thee alone.

2 Jesus, Master, I am thine:
  Keep me faithful, keep me
    near;
  Let thy presence in me shine,
    All my homeward way to
      cheer.
  Jesus, at thy feet I fall,
  O be thou my All in All.

3 Jesus, Master, whom I serve,
    Though so feebly and so ill,
  Strengthen hand and heart and
    nerve
    All thy bidding to fulfil;
  Open thou mine eyes to see
  All the work thou hast for me.

4 Jesus, Master, wilt thou use
    One who owes thee more than
      all?
  As thou wilt! I would not
    choose;
    Only let me hear thy call.
  Jesus, let me always be
  In thy service glad and free.

          FRANCES RIDLEY HAVERGAL
                  1836–79

432

MAY the mind of Christ my
    Saviour
  Live in me from day to day,
By his love and power controlling
  All I do or say.

2 May the word of God dwell
    richly
  In my heart from hour to
    hour,
So that all may see I triumph
  Only through his power.

3 May the peace of God my Father
  Rule my life in everything,
That I may be calm to comfort
  Sick and sorrowing.

4 May the love of Jesus fill me,
  As the waters fill the sea;
Him exalting, self abasing,
  This is victory.

5 May I run the race before me,
  Strong and brave to face the
    foe,
Looking unto Jesus
  As I onward go.

          KATE BARCLAY WILKINSON
                  1859–1928

433

GOD be in my head, and in
    my understanding;
God be in mine eyes, and in my
    looking;
God be in my mouth, and in my
    speaking;
God be in my heart, and in my
    thinking;
God be at mine end, and at my
    departing.

          Book of Hours (1514)

434

O JESUS, I have promised
    To serve thee to the end;
Be thou for ever near me,
  My Master and my Friend:
I shall not fear the battle
  If thou art by my side,
Nor wander from the pathway
  If thou wilt be my Guide.

2 O let me feel thee near me:
    The world is ever near;
I see the sights that dazzle,
  The tempting sounds I hear;
My foes are ever near me,
  Around me and within;
But, Jesus, draw thou nearer,
  And shield my soul from
    sin.

3 O let me hear thee speaking
    In accents clear and still,
Above the storms of passion,
  The murmurs of self-will;
O speak to reassure me,
  To hasten or control;
O speak, and make me listen,
  Thou Guardian of my soul.

4 O Jesus, thou hast promised,
    To all who follow thee,
That where thou art in glory
  There shall thy servant be;
And, Jesus, I have promised
  To serve thee to the end;
O give me grace to follow,
  My Master and my Friend.

          JOHN ERNEST BODE, 1816–74

435

LORD, in the fullness of my
 might,
 I would for thee be strong:
While runneth o'er each dear
 delight,
 To thee should soar my song.

2 I would not give the world my
 heart,
 And then profess thy love;
I would not feel my strength
 depart,
 And then thy service prove.

3 I would not with swift-wingèd
 zeal
 On the world's errands go,
And labour up the heavenly hill
 With weary feet and slow.

4 O not for thee my weak desires,
 My poorer, baser part!
O not for thee my fading fires,
 The ashes of my heart!

5 O choose me in my golden time:
 In my dear joys have part!
For thee the glory of my prime,
 The fullness of my heart!

THOMAS HORNBLOWER GILL
1819–1906

436

O MASTER, let me walk with
 thee
In lowly paths of service free;
Thy secret tell; help me to bear
The strain of toil, the fret of
 care.

2 Help me the slow of heart to
 move
By some clear winning word of
 love;
Teach me the wayward feet to
 stay,
And guide them in the homeward way.

3 Teach me thy patience; still
 with thee
In closer, dearer company,
In work that keeps faith sweet
 and strong,
In trust that triumphs over
 wrong,

4 In hope that sends a shining ray
Far down the future's broaden-
 ing way,
In peace that only thou canst
 give,
With thee, O Master, let me live.

WASHINGTON GLADDEN
1836–1918

437

LOVE Divine, all loves excell-
 ing,
 Joy of heaven, to earth come
 down,
Fix in us thy humble dwelling,
 All thy faithful mercies
 crown.
Jesus, thou art all compassion,
 Pure, unbounded love thou
 art;
Visit us with thy salvation,
 Enter every trembling heart.

2 Come, almighty to deliver;
 Let us all thy life receive;
Suddenly return, and never,
 Never more thy temples leave.
Thee we would be always
 blessing,
 Serve thee as thy hosts above,
Pray, and praise thee, without
 ceasing,
 Glory in thy perfect love.

3 Finish then thy new creation:
 Pure and spotless let us be;
Let us see thy great salvation,
 Perfectly restored in thee,
Changed from glory into glory,
 Till in heaven we take our
 place,
Till we cast our crowns before
 thee,
 Lost in wonder, love, and
 praise.

CHARLES WESLEY, 1707–88

438

GRACIOUS Spirit, Holy
 Ghost,
Taught by thee, we covet most,
Of thy gifts at Pentecost,
 Holy, heavenly love.

157

2 Faith that mountains could remove,
Tongues of earth or heaven
above,
Knowledge, all things, empty
prove
Without heavenly love.

3 Though I as a martyr bleed,
Give my goods the poor to feed,
All is vain if love I need;
Therefore give me love.

4 Love is kind, and suffers long;
Love is meek, and thinks no
wrong,
Love than death itself more
strong;
Therefore give us love.

5 Prophecy will fade away,
Melting in the light of day;
Love will ever with us stay;
Therefore give us love.

6 Faith and hope and love we see,
Joining hand in hand, agree;
But the greatest of the three,
And the best, is love.
CHRISTOPHER WORDSWORTH, 1807-85
From 1 Corinthians 13

439

O LORD and Master of us all,
Whate'er our name or sign,
We own thy sway, we hear thy
call,
We test our lives by thine.

2 Thou judgest us: thy purity
Doth all our lusts condemn;
The love that draws us nearer
thee
Is hot with wrath to them.

3 Our thoughts lie open to thy
sight;
And naked to thy glance
Our secret sins are, in the light
Of thy pure countenance.

4 Yet, weak and blinded though
we be,
Thou dost our service own;
We bring our varying gifts to
thee,
And thou rejectest none.

5 Apart from thee all gain is loss,
All labour vainly done;
The solemn shadow of thy cross
Is better than the sun.

6 Our Friend, our Brother, and
our Lord,
What may thy service be?
Nor name, nor form, nor ritual
word,
But simply following thee.

7 We faintly hear; we dimly see;
In differing phrase we pray;
But, dim or clear, we own in thee
The Light, the Truth, the
Way.
JOHN GREENLEAF WHITTIER
1807-92

440

'LIFT up your hearts!' We
lift them, Lord, to thee;
Here at thy feet none other may
we see:
'Lift up your hearts!' E'en so,
with one accord,
We lift them up, we lift them
to the Lord.

2 Above the level of the former
years,
The mire of sin, the slough of
guilty fears,
The mist of doubt, the blight of
love's decay,
O Lord of light, lift all our
hearts today!

3 Lift every gift that thou thyself
hast given;
Low lies the best till lifted up
to heaven:
Low lie the bounding heart, the
teeming brain,
Till, sent from God, they mount
to God again.

4 Then, as the trumpet-call, in
after years,
'Lift up your hearts!' rings
pealing in our ears,
Still shall those hearts respond
with full accord,
'We lift them up, we lift them
to the Lord!'
HENRY MONTAGU BUTLER
1833-1918

441

SOLDIERS of Christ! arise,
  And put your armour on,
Strong in the strength which
    God supplies
  Through his eternal Son;
Strong in the Lord of hosts,
  And in his mighty power;
Who in the strength of Jesus
    trusts
  Is more than conqueror.

2 Stand, then, in his great might,
  With all his strength endued;
And take, to arm you for the
    fight,
  The panoply of God.
To keep your armour bright
  Attend with constant care,
Still walking in your Captain's
    sight,
  And watching unto prayer.

3 From strength to strength go
    on;
  Wrestle, and fight, and pray;
Tread all the powers of darkness
    down,
  And win the well-fought
    day,—
That, having all things done,
  And all your conflicts passed,
Ye may o'ercome through Christ
    alone,
  And stand complete at last.
        CHARLES WESLEY, 1707–88

442

FIGHT the good fight with
    all thy might;
Christ is thy strength, and
    Christ thy right;
Lay hold on life, and it shall
    be
Thy joy and crown eternally.

2 Run the straight race through
    God's good grace,
Lift up thine eyes, and seek his
    face;
  Life with its path before us
    lies;
  Christ is the way, and Christ
    the prize.

3 Cast care aside; and on thy
    Guide
Lean, and his mercy will
    provide,—
  Lean, and the trusting soul
    shall prove
  Christ is its life, and Christ its
    love.

4 Faint not, nor fear; his arm is
    near;
He changeth not, and thou art
    dear;
  Only believe, and thou shalt
    see
  That Christ is all in all to thee.
    JOHN SAMUEL BEWLEY MONSELL
                1811–75

443

WHO would true valour see,
  Let him come hither;
One here will constant be,
    Come wind, come wea-
      ther;
There's no discouragement
Shall make him once relent
His first avowed intent
    To be a pilgrim.

2 Whoso beset him round
    With dismal stories,
Do but themselves confound;
    His strength the more is.
No lion can him fright,
He'll with a giant fight,
But he will have a right
    To be a pilgrim.

3 Hobgoblin nor foul fiend
    Can daunt his spirit;
He knows he at the end
    Shall life inherit.
Then fancies fly away;
He'll fear not what men say;
He'll labour night and day
    To be a pilgrim.
        JOHN BUNYAN, 1628–88

444

I FEEL the winds of God to-
    day;
  Today my sail I lift,
Though heavy oft with drench-
    ing spray,
  And torn with many a rift;

159

If hope but light the water's
    crest,
    And Christ my bark will use,
I'll seek the seas at his behest,
    And brave another cruise.

2 It is the wind of God that dries
    My vain regretful tears,
Until with braver thoughts shall
    rise
    The purer, brighter years;
If cast on shores of selfish ease
    Or pleasure I should be,
Lord, let me feel thy freshening
    breeze,
    And I'll put back to sea.

3 If ever I forget thy love
    And how that love was
    shown,
Lift high the blood-red flag
    above:
    It bears thy Name alone.
Great Pilot of my onward way,
    Thou wilt not let me drift;
I feel the winds of God today,
    Today my sail I lift.

JESSIE ADAMS, 1863–1954

445

Make me a captive, Lord,
    And then I shall be
    free;
Force me to render up my
    sword,
    And I shall conqueror be.
I sink in life's alarms
    When by myself I stand;
Imprison me within thine
    arms,
    And strong shall be my
    hand.

2 My heart is weak and poor
    Until it master find;
It has no spring of action sure—
    It varies with the wind.
It cannot freely move
    Till thou hast wrought its
    chain;
Enslave it with thy matchless
    love,
    And deathless it shall reign.

3 My power is faint and low
    Till I have learned to serve;
It wants the needed fire to glow,
    It wants the breeze to nerve;
    It cannot drive the world,
    Until itself be driven;
Its flag can only be unfurled
    When thou shalt breathe from
    heaven.

4 My will is not my own
    Till thou hast made it thine;
If it would reach a monarch's
    throne
    It must its crown resign;
    It only stands unbent,
    Amid the clashing strife,
When on thy bosom it has leant
    And found in thee its life.

GEORGE MATHESON, 1842–1906

446

*Land of our Birth, we
    pledge to thee
Our love and toil in the years
    to be;
When we are grown and take
    our place,
As men and women with our
    race.

2 Father in heaven, who lovest
    all,
O help thy children when they
    call;
That they may build from age
    to age
An undefilèd heritage.

3 Teach us to bear the yoke in
    youth,
With steadfastness and careful
    truth;
That, in our time, thy grace
    may give
The truth whereby the nations
    live.

4 Teach us to rule ourselves al-
    way,
Controlled and cleanly night
    and day;
That we may bring, if need arise,
No maimed or worthless sacri-
    fice.

5 Teach us to look, in all our ends,
  On thee for Judge, and not our friends;
  That we, with thee, may walk uncowed
  By fear or favour of the crowd.

6 Teach us the strength that cannot seek,
  By deed or thought, to hurt the weak;
  That, under thee, we may possess
  Man's strength to succour man's distress.

7 Teach us delight in simple things,
  And mirth that has no bitter springs;
  Forgiveness free of evil done,
  And love to all men 'neath the sun!

*8 Land of our Birth, our faith, our pride,
  For whose dear sake our fathers died;
  O Motherland, we pledge to thee,
  Head, heart, and hand through the years to be!
  RUDYARD KIPLING, 1865–1936

  The complete poem is given here, but verses 1 and 8 should be omitted unless the occasion warrants their use.

447

1 LORD and Master, who hast called us
  All our days to follow thee,
  We have heard thy clear commandment,
  'Bring the children unto Me.'

2 So we come to thee, the teacher,
  At thy feet we kneel to pray:
  We can only lead the children
  When thyself shalt show the way.

3 Teach us thy most wondrous method,
  As of old in Galilee
  Thou didst show thy chosen servants
  How to bring men unto thee.

4 Give us store of wit and wisdom,
  Give us love which never tires,
  Give us thine abiding patience,
  Give us hope which aye inspires.

5 Mighty Wisdom of the Godhead,
  Thou the One eternal Word,
  Thou the counsellor, the teacher,
  Fill us with thy fullness, Lord.
  FLORENCE MARGARET SMITH
  1886–1958

448 *For young people*

1 JUST as I am, thine own to be,
  Friend of the young, who lovest me;
  To consecrate myself to thee,
    O Jesus Christ, I come.

2 In the glad morning of my day,
  My life to give, my vows to pay,
  With no reserve and no delay,
    With all my heart I come.

3 I would live ever in the light,
  I would work ever for the right,
  I would serve thee with all my might,
    Therefore to thee I come.

4 Just as I am, young, strong and free,
  To be the best that I can be
  For truth, and righteousness, and thee,
    Lord of my life, I come.
  MARIANNE FARNINGHAM
  1834–1909

  The following are also suitable
  Nos. 211, 88

449 *For children*

1 LOOKING upward every day,
    Sunshine on our faces;
  Pressing onward every day
    Toward the heavenly places;
  Growing every day in awe,
    For thy Name is holy;
  Learning every day to love
    With a love more lowly;

2 Walking every day more close
   To our Elder Brother;
Growing every day more true
   Unto one another;
Leaving every day behind
   Something which might hin-
      der;
Running swifter every day;
   Growing purer, kinder,—

3 Lord, so pray we every day:
   Hear us in thy pity,
That we enter in at last
   To the holy city.
Looking upward every day,
   Sunshine on our faces;
Press we onward every day
   Toward the heavenly places.
                MARY BUTLER, 1841–1916

450   *For children*

SAVIOUR, teach me, day by
      day,
Love's sweet lesson to obey;

Sweeter lesson cannot be,
Loving him who first loved me.

2 With a child's glad heart of love
   At thy bidding may I move,
Prompt to serve and follow
      thee,
Loving him who first loved me.

3 Teach me thus thy steps to
      trace,
Strong to follow in thy grace,
Learning how to love from thee,
Loving him who first loved me.

4 Love in loving finds employ,
In obedience all her joy;
Ever new that joy will be,
Loving him who first loved me.

5 Thus may I rejoice to show
That I feel the love I owe;
Singing, till thy face I see,
Of his love who first loved me.
            JANE ELIZA LEESON, 1809–81

STEWARDSHIP AND SERVICE

451

ALMIGHTY Father of all
      things that be,
Our life, our work, we consecrate to thee,
Whose heavens declare thy
   glory from above,
Whose earth below is witness to
   thy love.

2 For well we know this weary,
      soilèd earth
Is yet thine own by right of its
   new birth,
Since that great cross upreared
   on Calvary
Redeemed it from its fault and
   shame to thee.

3 Thine still the changeful beauty
   of the hills,
The purple valleys flecked with
   silver rills,
The ocean glistening 'neath the
   golden rays;
They all are thine, and voiceless
   speak thy praise.

4 Thou dost the strength to work-
      man's arm impart;
From thee the skilled musician's
   mystic art,
The grace of poet's pen or
   painter's hand
To teach the loveliness of sea
   and land.

5 Then grant us, Lord, in all
   things thee to own,
To dwell within the shadow of
   thy throne,
To speak and work, to think,
   and live, and move,
Reflecting thine own nature,
   which is love;

6 That so, by Christ redeemed
   from sin and shame,
And hallowed by thy Spirit's
   cleansing flame,
Ourselves, our work, and all our
   powers may be
A sacrifice acceptable to thee.
            ERNEST EDWARD DUGMORE
                        1843–1925

452

GOD, who hast given us
power to sound
Depths hitherto unknown;
To probe earth's hidden mysteries,
And make their might our
own;

2 Great are thy gifts: yet greater
far
This gift, O God, bestow,
That as to knowledge we attain
We may in wisdom grow.

3 Let wisdom's godly fear dispel
All fears that hate impart;
Give understanding to the mind,
And with new mind new
heart.

4 So for thy glory and man's good
May we thy gifts employ,
Lest, maddened by the lust of
power,
Man shall himself destroy.

GEORGE WALLACE BRIGGS
1875–1959

453

BEHOLD us, Lord, a little
space
From daily tasks set free,
And met within thy holy place
To rest awhile with thee.
Yet these are not the only walls
Wherein thou mayst be
sought;
On homeliest work thy blessing
falls,
In truth and patience
wrought.

2 Thine is the loom, the forge, the
mart,
The wealth of land and sea,
The worlds of science and of art,
Revealed and ruled by thee.
Work shall be prayer, if all be
wrought
As thou wouldst have it done,
And prayer, by thee inspired
and taught,
Itself with work be one.

JOHN ELLERTON, 1826–93

454

SON of God, eternal Saviour,
Source of life and truth and
grace,
Son of Man, whose birth in-
carnate
Hallows all our human race;
Thou, our Head, who, throned
in glory,
For thine own dost ever plead,
Fill us with thy love and pity,
Heal our wrongs, and help
our need.

2 As thou, Lord, hast lived for
others,
So may we for others live;
Freely have thy gifts been
granted,
Freely may thy servants give.
Thine the gold and thine the
silver,
Thine the wealth of land and
sea,
We but stewards of thy bounty,
Held in solemn trust for thee.

3 Come, O Christ, and reign
among us,
King of Love, and Prince of
Peace;
Hush the storm of strife and
passion,
Bid its cruel discords cease.
Ah, the past is dark behind us,
Strewn with wrecks and
stained with blood;
But before us gleams the vision
Of the coming brotherhood.

4 See the Christlike host advanc-
ing,
High and lowly, great and
small,
Linked in bonds of common
service
For the common Lord of all.
Thou who prayedst, thou who
willest
That thy people should be
one,
Grant, O grant our hope's
fruition:
Here on earth thy will be
done.

SOMERSET CORRY LOWRY
1855–1932

455

ANGEL voices, ever singing
Round thy throne of light,
Angel harps, for ever ringing,
Rest not day nor night;
Thousands only live to bless
thee,
And confess thee
Lord of might.

2 Yea, we know that thou re-
joicest
O'er each work of thine;
Thou didst ears and hands and
voices
For thy praise design;
Craftsman's art and music's
measure
For thy pleasure
All combine.

3 In thy house, great God, we
offer
Of thine own to thee,
And for thine acceptance
proffer,
All unworthily,
Hearts and minds and hands
and voices,
In our choicest
Psalmody.

4 *Honour, glory, might, and merit*
Thine shall ever be,
Father, Son, and Holy Spirit,
Blessèd Trinity.
Of the best that thou hast given,
Earth and heaven
Render thee. Amen.
FRANCIS POTT, 1832–1909

456

WE give thee but thine
own,
Whate'er the gift may be;
All that we have is thine alone,
A trust, O Lord, from thee.

2 May we thy bounties thus
As stewards true receive,
And gladly, as thou blessest
us,
To thee our first-fruits give.

3 O hearts are bruised and dead,
And homes are bare and cold,
And lambs for whom the
Shepherd bled
Are straying from the fold.

4 To comfort and to bless,
To find a balm for woe,
To tend the lone and fatherless,
Is angels' work below.

5 The captive to release,
To God the lost to bring,
To teach the way of life and
peace,
It is a Christ-like thing.

6 And we believe thy word,
Though dim our faith may
be,—
Whate'er for thine we do, O
Lord,
We do it unto thee.
WILLIAM WALSHAM HOW, 1823–97

457

FILL thou our life, O Lord
our God,
In every part with praise,
That our whole being may
proclaim
Thy being and thy ways.

2 Not for the lip of praise alone,
Nor ev'n the praising heart
We ask, but for a life made up
Of praise in every part.

3 Praise in the common things of
life,
Its goings out and in;
Praise in each duty and each
deed,
However small and mean.

4 So shalt thou, gracious Lord,
receive
From us the glory due;
And so shall we begin on earth
The song for ever new.

5 So shall no part of day or night
From sacredness be free;
But all our life, in every step,
Be fellowship with thee.
HORATIUS BONAR, 1808–89
altered

164

458

LORD of all good, our gifts
we bring to thee,
Use them thy holy purpose to
fulfil;
Tokens of love and pledges they
shall be
That our whole life is offered
to thy will.

2 Father, whose bounty all creation shows,
Christ, by whose willing sacrifice we live,
Spirit, from whom all life in
fullness flows,
To thee with grateful hearts
ourselves we give.

ALBERT FREDERICK BAYLY

459

FOUNTAIN of good, to own
thy love
Our thankful hearts incline;
What can we render, Lord, to
thee,
When all the worlds are
thine?

2 But thou hast needy brethren
here,
Partakers of thy grace,
Whose names thou wilt thyself
confess
Before the Father's face.

3 And in their accents of distress
Thy pleading voice is heard;
In them thou mayst be clothed
and fed,
And visited and cheered.

4 Thy face, with reverence and
with love,
We in thy poor would see;
O may we minister to them,
And in them, Lord, to thee.

PHILIP DODDRIDGE, 1702–51

460

O BROTHER man, fold to
thy heart thy brother!
Where pity dwells, the peace
of God is there;

To worship rightly is to love
each other,
Each smile a hymn, each
kindly deed a prayer.

2 For he whom Jesus loved hath
truly spoken:
The holier worship which he
deigns to bless
Restores the lost, and binds the
spirit broken,
And feeds the widow and the
fatherless.

3 Follow with reverent steps the
great example
Of him whose holy work was
doing good;
So shall the wide earth seem our
Father's temple,
Each loving life a psalm of
gratitude.

4 Then shall all shackles fall; the
stormy clangour
Of wild war-music o'er the
earth shall cease;
Love shall tread out the baleful
fire of anger,
And in its ashes plant the
tree of peace.

JOHN GREENLEAF WHITTIER
1807–92

461

O GOD of mercy, God of
might,
In love and pity infinite,
Teach us, as ever in thy sight,
To live our life to thee.

2 And thou, who cam'st on earth
to die
That fallen man might live
thereby,
O hear us, for to thee we cry,—
In hope, O Lord, to thee.

3 Teach us the lesson thou hast
taught,
To feel for those thy blood hath
bought,
That every word and deed and
thought
May work a work for thee.

4 For all are brethren, far and wide,
Since, thou, O Lord, for all hast died;
Then teach us, whatsoe'er betide,
To love them all in thee.

5 In sickness, sorrow, want, or care;
Whate'er it be, 'tis ours to share;
May we, where help is needed, there
Give help as unto thee.

6 And may thy Holy Spirit move
All those who live, to live in love,
Till thou shalt greet in heaven above
All those who give to thee.

GODFREY THRING, 1823–1903

462

TAKE my life, and let it be
Consecrated, Lord, to thee.
Take my moments and my days;
Let them flow in ceaseless praise.

2 Take my hands, and let them move
At the impulse of thy love.
Take my feet, and let them be
Swift and beautiful for thee.

3 Take my voice, and let me sing
Always, only, for my King.
Take my intellect, and use
Every power as thou shalt choose.

4 Take my will, and make it thine;
It shall be no longer mine.
Take my heart—it is thine own;
It shall be thy royal throne.

5 Take my love; my Lord, I pour
At thy feet its treasure-store.
Take myself, and I will be
Ever, only, all for thee.

FRANCES RIDLEY HAVERGAL
1836–79, altered

463

FORTH in thy Name, O Lord, I go,
My daily labour to pursue,
Thee, only thee, resolved to know
In all I think, or speak, or do.

2 The task thy wisdom hath assigned
O let me cheerfully fulfil,
In all my works thy presence find,
And prove thy good and perfect will.

3 Thee may I set at my right hand,
Whose eyes mine inmost substance see,
And labour on at thy command,
And offer all my works to thee.

4 Give me to bear thy easy yoke,
And every moment watch and pray,
And still to things eternal look,
And hasten to thy glorious day;

5 For thee delightfully employ
Whate'er thy bounteous grace hath given,
And run my course with even joy,
And closely walk with thee to heaven.

CHARLES WESLEY, 1707–88
altered

464   *For children*

THE wise may bring their learning,
The rich may bring their wealth,
And some may bring their greatness,
And some their strength and health:
We too would bring our treasures
To offer to the King;
We have no wealth or learning,
What gifts then shall we bring?

2 We'll bring the many duties
    We have to do each day;
We'll try our best to please him,
    At home, at school, at play:
And better are these treasures
    To offer to our King
Than richest gifts without
    them;
    Yet these we all may bring.

3 We'll bring him hearts that love
    him,
    We'll bring him thankful
    praise,
And souls for ever striving
    To follow in his ways:
And these shall be the treasures
    We offer to the King,
And these are gifts that ever
    Our grateful hearts may
    bring.

Book of Praise for Children (1881)
and Compilers of
The BBC Hymn Book, 1951

465 *For younger children*

HANDS to work and feet to
    run—
    God's good gifts to me and
    you;
Hands and feet he gave to us
    To help each other the whole
    day through.

2 Eyes to see and ears to hear—
    God's good gifts to me and
    you;

Eyes and ears he gave to us
    To help each other the whole
    day through.

3 Minds to think and hearts to
    love—
    God's good gifts to me and
    you;
Minds and hearts he gave to us
    To help each other the whole
    day through.

HILDA MARGARET DODD

466 *For younger children*

OUR thoughts go round the
    world
To children everywhere;
So much of joy is ours, O God,
Help us to love and share.

JESSIE ELEANOR MOORE, 1887-1969

467 *For younger children*

TAKE our gifts, O loving
    Jesus,
Use them in some lovely way,
For the happiness and comfort
    Of the whole wide world
    today.

2 Let us be allowed to help you,
    In some plan of loving care,
In some venture for the king-
    dom,
    By our pence and by our
    prayer.

MARGARET CROPPER

WITNESS AND ENCOURAGEMENT

468

SPEAK forth thy word, O
    Father,
Men's hungry minds to feed:
The people starve and perish,
    Unconscious of their need;
For so, Lord, thou hast made us
That not alone by bread,
But by thy word of comfort
Our hunger must be fed.

2 The secrets of the atom,
    The universe of light,
All wonders of creation
    Proclaim thy boundless
    might:
But only through the witness
    From man to man passed on
Dost thou reveal in fullness
The Gospel of thy Son.

3 To each man in his language,
To each man in his home,
By many paths and channels
The faith of Christ may come:
How shall men hear its message
If there be none to preach ?
How shall they learn its lesson
If there be none to teach ?

4 Take us, then, Lord, and use us
Thy messengers to be:
Our prayers, our gifts, our ser-
vice
We offer here to thee,
That every man and nation
May learn what we have heard,
And all the minds of millions
Shall feed upon thy word.

CHARLES JEFFRIES

469 *Dieu, nous avons vu
ta gloire*

* *G*OD, your glory we have seen
in your Son,
• Full of truth, full of heavenly grace:
In Christ make us live, his love
shine on our face,
And the nations shall see in us the
triumph you have won.

In the fields of this world his
good news he has sown,
And sends us out to reap till the
harvest is done.

3 In his love like a fire that con-
sumes he passed by.
The flame has touched our lips ;
let us shout, 'Here am I'.

4 He was broken for us, God-for-
saken his cry,
And still the bread he breaks ;
to ourselves we must die.

5 He has trampled the grapes of
new life on his cross.
Now drink the cup and live ; he
has filled it for us.

6 He has founded a kingdom that
none shall destroy ;
The corner-stone is laid. Go to
work : build with joy!

DIDIER RIMAUD
Refrain tr. RONALD JOHNSON
Verses tr. BRIAN WREN

* *Verse 1 is repeated as a refrain after
each verse.*

470

*G*O ye, said Jesus, and preach
the word,
All through the world let its
voice be heard,
Publish the tidings o'er land
and sea,
Tell men the truth that shall
make them free
And carry the Gospel on!

2 Lo, I am with you the whole
way through,
Blessing and guiding in all that
you do,
Go ye wherever man's feet have
trod,
Bearing the gift of the word of
God
And carry the Gospel on!

3 Swiftly and surely the truth
shall spread,
Winning its way as the word is
read,
Lifting the nations till old and
young,
Hearing God's voice in their
native tongue,
Shall carry the Gospel on!

4 Saviour, obeying thy great
command,
Safe in the grasp of thy guiding
hand,
Strong in the faith of thy holy
word,
Gladly we answer our risen
Lord,
And carry the Gospel on!

GEORGE OSBORNE GREGORY

471

*L*IFT up your heads, ye gates
of brass,
Ye bars of iron, yield,
And let the King of Glory pass ;
The cross is in the field.

2 Ye armies of the living God,
His sacramental host,
Where hallowed footstep never
trod,
Take your appointed post.

3 Follow the cross; the ark of peace
　　Accompany your path,
　To slaves and rebels bring release
　　From bondage and from wrath.

4 Though few and small and weak your bands,
　　Strong in your Captain's strength,
　Go to the conquest of all lands;
　　All must be his at length.

5 O fear not, faint not, halt not now;
　　Quit you like men, be strong;
　To Christ shall every nation bow,
　　And sing with you this song:

6 'Uplifted are the gates of brass;
　　The bars of iron yield;
　Behold the King of Glory pass!
　　The cross hath won the field.'

JAMES MONTGOMERY, 1771–1854

472(i)　*Verzage nicht, du Häuflein klein*

FEAR not, thou faithful Christian flock;
God is thy shelter and thy rock;
Fear not for thy salvation.
Though fierce the foe and dark the night,
The Lord of hosts shall be thy might,
Christ thine illumination.
Arise! Arise! thy foe defy!
Call on the Name of God most high,
With heavenly succour arm you!
'Gainst world and flesh and powers of hell,
Now for his honour quit you well.
Lo! there is naught can harm you.

ROBERT BRIDGES, 1844–1930
Based on JOHANN MICHAEL
ALTENBURG, 1584–1640
Verse 2 omitted

472(ii)

FAITH of our fathers, taught of old
By faithful shepherds of the fold,
　The hallowing of our nation;
Thou wast through many a wealthy year,
Through many a darkened day of fear,
　The rock of our salvation.
Arise, arise, good Christian men,
Your glorious standard raise again,
　The cross of Christ who calls you;
Who bids you live and bids you die
For his great cause, and stands on high
　To witness what befalls you.

2 Our fathers held the faith received,
By saints declared, by saints believed,
　By saints in death defended;
Through pain of doubt and bitterness,
Through pain of treason and distress,
　They for the right contended.
Arise, arise, good Christian men,
Your glorious standard raise again,
　The cross of Christ who bought you;
Who leads you forth in this new age,
With long-enduring hearts to wage
　The warfare he has taught you.

THOMAS ALEXANDER LACEY
1853–1931
Verses 2, 4 omitted

473

LORD, who in thy perfect wisdom
Times and seasons dost arrange,
Working out thy changeless purpose
In a world of ceaseless change;

Thou didst form our ancient
  nation,
Guiding it through all the days,
To unfold in it thy purpose
To thy glory and thy praise.

2 To our shores remote, benighted,
Barrier of the western waves,
Tidings in thy love thou sentest,
Tidings of the cross that saves.
Saints and heroes strove and
  suffered
Here thy gospel to proclaim;
We, the heirs of their en-
  deavour,
Tell the honour of their name.

3 Still thine ancient purpose
  standeth
Every change and chance
  above;
Still thine ancient Church re-
  maineth,
Witness to thy changeless love.
Grant us vision, Lord, and
  courage
To fulfil thy work begun;
In the Church and in the nation,
Kings of kings, thy will be
  done.
TIMOTHY REES, 1874–1939, altered

474

CHRIST is the King! O
  friends rejoice;
Brothers and sisters, with one
  voice
Make all men know he is your
  choice.

2 O magnify the Lord, and raise
Anthems of joy and holy praise
For Christ's brave saints of
  ancient days,

3 Who with a faith for ever new
Followed the King, and round
  him drew
Thousands of faithful men and
  true.

4 Let Love's unconquerable might
Your scattered companies unite
In service to the Lord of light:

5 So shall God's will on earth be
  done,
New lamps be lit, new tasks
  begun,
And the whole Church at last
  be one.
GEORGE KENNEDY ALLEN BELL
1883–1958

475

WE have heard a joyful
  sound,—
    'Jesus saves!'
Spread the gladness all around:
    'Jesus saves!'
Bear the news to every land,
  Climb the steeps and cross
    the waves;
Onward!—'tis our Lord's com-
  mand.
    Jesus saves!

2 Waft it on the rolling tide:
    'Jesus saves!'
Tell to sinners far and wide,
    'Jesus saves!'
Sing, ye islands of the sea;
  Echo back, ye ocean caves;
Earth shall keep her jubilee:
    Jesus saves!

3 Sing above the battle's strife
    'Jesus saves!'
By his death and endless life
    'Jesus saves!'
Sing it softly through the
  gloom,
  When the heart for mercy
    craves;
Sing in triumph o'er the tomb,
    'Jesus saves!'

4 Give the winds a mighty voice,
    'Jesus saves!'
Let the nations now rejoice:
    Jesus saves!
Shout salvation full and free
  To every strand that ocean
    laves,—
This our song of victory,
    'Jesus saves!'
PRISCILLA JANE OWENS
1829–1907

476

'FOR my sake and the Gospel's, go
And tell redemption's story';
His heralds answer, 'Be it so,
And thine, Lord, all the glory!'
They preach his birth, his life, his cross,
The love of his atonement
For whom they count the world but loss,
His Easter, his enthronement.

2 Hark! hark! the trump of jubilee
Proclaims to every nation,
From pole to pole, by land and sea,
Glad tidings of salvation.
Still on and on the anthems spread,
Of alleluia voices;
In concert with the holy dead,
The warrior Church rejoices.

3 He comes whose advent-trumpet drowns
The last of time's evangels,
Immanuel, crowned with many crowns,
The Lord of saints, and angels.
O Life, Light, Love, the great I AM
Triune, who changest never,
The throne of God and of the Lamb
Is thine, and thine for ever.

EDWARD HENRY BICKERSTETH
1825–1906, altered

477

RISE up, O men of God!
Have done with lesser things;
Give heart and soul and mind and strength
To serve the King of kings.

2 Rise up, O men of God!
His Kingdom tarries long;
Bring in the day of brotherhood,
And end the night of wrong.

3 Rise up, O men of God!
The Church for you doth wait:
His strength shall make your spirit strong,
Her service make you great.

4 Lift high the cross of Christ!
Tread where his feet have trod;
As brothers of the Son of Man
Rise up, O men of God!

WILLIAM PIERSON MERRILL
1867–1954, altered

478

SOLDIERS of the cross, arise!
Gird you with your armour bright;
Mighty are your enemies,
Hard the battle ye must fight.

2 O'er a faithless fallen world
Raise your banner in the sky;
Let it float there wide unfurled;
Bear it onward; lift it high.

3 'Mid the homes of want and woe,
Strangers to the living word,
Let the Saviour's herald go,
Let the voice of hope be heard.

4 Where the shadows deepest lie,
Carry truth's unsullied ray;
Where are crimes of blackest dye,
There the saving sign display.

5 To the weary and the worn
Tell of realms where sorrows cease;
To the outcast and forlorn
Speak of mercy and of peace.

6 Guard the helpless; seek the strayed;
Comfort troubles; banish grief;
In the might of God arrayed,
Scatter sin and unbelief.

7 Be the banner still unfurled,
Still unsheathed the Spirit's sword,
Till the kingdoms of the world
Are the Kingdom of the Lord.

WILLIAM WALSHAM HOW, 1823–97

479

WHO is on the Lord's side?
Who will serve the King?
Who will be his helpers
Other lives to bring?
Who will leave the world's side?
Who will face the foe?
Who is on the Lord's side?
Who for him will go?
By thy call of mercy,
By thy grace divine,
We are on the Lord's side;
Saviour, we are thine.

2 Jesus, thou hast bought us,
Not with gold or gem,
But with thine own life-blood,
For thy diadem.
With thy blessing filling
Each who comes to thee,
Thou hast made us willing,
Thou hast made us free.
By thy grand redemption,
By thy grace divine,
We are on the Lord's side;
Saviour, we are thine.

3 Fierce may be the conflict,
Strong may be the foe,
But the King's own army
None can overthrow.
Round his standard ranging,
Victory is secure,
For his truth unchanging
Makes the triumph sure.
Joyfully enlisting,
By thy grace divine,
We are on the Lord's side;
Saviour, we are thine.

4 Chosen to be soldiers
In an alien land,
Chosen, called, and faithful,
For our Captain's band,
In the service royal
Let us not grow cold;
Let us be right loyal,
Noble, true, and bold.
Master, thou wilt keep us,
By thy grace divine,
Always on the Lord's side,
Saviour, always thine.

FRANCES RIDLEY HAVERGAL
1836–79

480

ONWARD! Christian soldiers,
Marching as to war,
With the cross of Jesus
Going on before.
Christ, the Royal Master,
Leads against the foe;
Forward into battle,
See! his banners go:
Onward! Christian soldiers,
Marching as to war,
With the cross of Jesus
Going on before.

2 At the sign of triumph
Satan's legions flee;
On then, Christian soldiers,
On to victory!
Hell's foundations quiver
At the shout of praise;
Brothers, lift your voices,
Loud your anthems raise:

3 Like a mighty army
Moves the Church of God;
Brothers, we are treading
Where the saints have trod.
We are not divided,
All one body we,
One in hope, in doctrine,
One in charity:

4 Crowns and thrones may
perish,
Kingdoms rise and wane,
But the Church of Jesus
Constant will remain;
Gates of hell can never
'Gainst that Church prevail;
We have Christ's own
promise,
And that cannot fail:

5 Onward, then, ye people!
Join our happy throng;
Blend with ours your voices
In the triumph song:
'Glory, laud, and honour
Unto Christ the King!'
This, through countless ages,
Men and angels sing:

SABINE BARING-GOULD
1834–1942

481

STAND up! stand up for Jesus,
  Ye soldiers of the cross!
Lift high his royal banner;
  It must not suffer loss.
From victory to victory
  His army he shall lead,
Till every foe is vanquished,
  And Christ is Lord indeed.

2 Stand up! stand up for Jesus!
    The trumpet-call obey;
  Forth to the mighty conflict
    In this his glorious day!
  Ye that are men, now serve him
    Against unnumbered foes;
  Your courage rise with danger,
    And strength to strength
      oppose.

3 Stand up! stand up for Jesus!
    Stand in his strength alone;
  The arm of flesh will fail you;
    Ye dare not trust your own.
  Put on the gospel armour,
    Each piece put on with prayer;
  Where duty calls, or danger,
    Be never wanting there.

4 Stand up! stand up for Jesus!
    The strife will not be long;
  This day the noise of battle,
    The next the victor's song.
  To him that overcometh
    A crown of life shall be;
  He with the King of Glory
    Shall reign eternally.
          GEORGE DUFFIELD, 1818–88

482

YIELD not to temptation, for
  yielding is sin;
Each victory will help you some
  other to win;
Fight manfully onward; dark
  passions subdue;
Look ever to Jesus, he will carry
  you through.
    Ask the Saviour to help you,
    Comfort, strengthen, and
      keep you;
    He is willing to aid you;
    He will carry you through.

2 Shun evil companions; bad
    language disdain;
  God's Name hold in reverence,
    nor take it in vain;
  Be thoughtful and earnest,
    kind-hearted and true;
  Look ever to Jesus, he will carry
    you through.

3 To him that o'ercometh God
    giveth a crown;
  Through faith we shall conquer,
    though often cast down;
  He who is our Saviour our
    strength will renew;
  Look ever to Jesus, he will carry
    you through.
          HORATIO RICHMOND PALMER
          1834–1907

483

GO, labour on: spend and be
  spent,
Thy joy to do the Father's
  will;
It is the way the Master went;
  Should not the servant tread
    it still?

2 Go, labour on while it is day:
    The world's dark night is
      hastening on;
  Speed, speed thy work; cast
      sloth away;
    It is not thus that souls are
      won.

3 Men die in darkness at thy
    side,
  Without a hope to cheer the
    tomb;
  Take up the torch and wave it
    wide,
    The torch that lights time's
      thickest gloom.

4 Toil on, faint not, keep watch,
    and pray;
  Be wise the erring soul to
    win;
  Go forth into the world's high-
    way,
    Compel the wanderer to come
      in.

5 Toil on, and in thy toil rejoice;
    For toil comes rest, for exile
        home;
Soon shalt thou hear the Bride-
    groom's voice,
    The midnight peal, 'Behold,
        I come!'

HORATIUS BONAR, 1808–89

484

COURAGE, brother! do not
    stumble,
    Though thy path be dark as
        night;
There's a star to guide the
    humble;
'Trust in God, and do the
    right'.
Let the road be rough and
    dreary,
    And its end far out of sight,
Foot it bravely; strong or
    weary,
    *Trust in God, and do the right.

2 Perish policy and cunning,
    Perish all that fears the light!
Whether losing, whether win-
    ning,
    Trust in God, and do the right.
Some will hate thee, some will
    love thee,
    Some will flatter, some will
        slight;
Cease from man, and look above
    thee,
    Trust in God, and do the right.

3 Simple rule, and safest guiding,
    Inward peace, and inward
        might,
Star upon our path abiding,—
    Trust in God, and do the right.
Courage, brother! do not
    stumble,
    Though thy path be dark as
        night;
There's a star to guide the
    humble:
    'Trust in God, and do the
        right.'

NORMAN MACLEOD, 1812–72

* When this hymn is sung to Tune (ii)
COURAGE, BROTHER, the words 'Trust in
God' must be sung three times in the last
line of each verse.

485

LORD, speak to me, that I
    may speak
    In living echoes of thy tone;
As thou hast sought, so let me
    seek
    Thy erring children lost and
        lone.

2 O lead me, Lord, that I may
    lead
    The wandering and the
        wavering feet;
O feed me, Lord, that I may
    feed
    Thy hungering ones with
        manna sweet.

3 O strengthen me, that, while I
    stand
    Firm on the rock, and strong
        in thee,
I may stretch out a loving hand
    To wrestlers with the troubled
        sea.

4 O teach me, Lord, that I may
    teach
    The precious things thou dost
        impart;
And wing my words, that they
    may reach
    The hidden depths of many a
        heart.

5 O give thine own sweet rest to
    me,
    That I may speak with sooth-
        ing power
A word in season, as from thee,
    To weary ones in needful
        hour.

6 O fill me with thy fullness, Lord,
    Until my very heart o'erflow
In kindling thought and glowing
    word,
    Thy love to tell, thy praise
        to show.

7 O use me, Lord, use even me,
    Just as thou wilt, and when,
        and where,
Until thy blessèd face I see,
    Thy rest, thy joy, thy glory
        share.

FRANCES RIDLEY HAVERGAL
1836–79

486

LOVER of souls and Lord of
all the living,
Whose service maketh free,
Hear us who once again our-
selves are giving
Thy servants sure to be.

2 Thou who dost bear the whole
world's tribulation
Upon thy heart alone,
Thou who hast bought us by
thy cross and passion,
And chosen us for thine own,

3 Show us thyself, that we may
know their sorrow
Who have not seen thy face;
Show us their darkness, and
the radiant morrow
Of thine eternal grace.

4 Show us the love wherewith
thy heart is burning,
The travail of thy soul:
Grant us to share thy heart's
desire and yearning
That thou mightest make them
whole.

*5 Make strong our hands, by
thine own great hand grasp-
ing,
Avail and guide our youth;
Grant to us now life that is
everlasting,
And then to know thy truth.

HELEN WADDELL, 1889–1965

* This verse may be omitted.

487

AND did those feet in ancient
time
Walk upon England's moun-
tains green?
And was the Holy Lamb of God
On England's pleasant pastures seen?

And did the countenance divine
Shine forth upon our clouded
hills?
And was Jerusalem builded here
Among these dark satanic
mills?

2 Bring me my bow of burning
gold!
Bring me my arrows of desire!
Bring me my spear! O clouds,
unfold!
Bring me my chariot of fire!
I will not cease from mental
fight,
Nor shall my sword sleep in
my hand,
Till we have built Jerusalem
In England's green and
pleasant land.

WILLIAM BLAKE, 1757–1827

488   *For younger children*

JESUS bids us shine, with a
pure, clear light,
Like a little candle burning in
the night.
In this world is darkness; so let
us shine,
You in your small corner, and I
in mine.

2 Jesus bids us shine, first of all
for him;
Well he sees and knows it, if our
light grows dim:
He looks down from heaven to
see us shine,
You in your small corner, and I
in mine.

3 Jesus bids us shine, then, for all
around;
Many kinds of darkness in the
world are found—
Sin, and want, and sorrow; so
we must shine,
You in your small corner, and I
in mine.

SUSAN WARNER, 1819–85

INTERCESSION: FOR THE CHURCH

489 Psalm 122, verses 1, 2, 6–9

I JOY'D when to the house
of God,
Go up, they said to me.
Jerusalem, within thy gates
Our feet shall standing be.

2 Pray that Jerusalem may have
Peace and felicity:
Let them that love thee and thy
peace
Have still prosperity.

3 Therefore I wish that peace may
still
Within thy walls remain,
And ever may thy palaces
Prosperity retain.

4 Now, for my friends' and
brethren's sakes,
Peace be in thee, I'll say.
And for the house of God our
Lord,
I'll seek thy good alway.

5 *To Father, Son, and Holy Ghost,*
The God whom we adore,
Be glory, as it was, and is,
And shall be evermore. Amen.

490

JESUS, with thy Church abide;
Be her Saviour, Lord, and
Guide,
While on earth her faith is tried:
We beseech thee, hear us.

2 Keep her life and doctrine pure;
Grant her patience to endure,
Trusting in thy promise sure:

3 May she one in doctrine be,
One in truth and charity,
Winning all to faith in thee:

4 May her scattered children be
From reproach of evil free,
Blameless witnesses for thee:

5 May she thus all glorious be,
Spotless and from wrinkle free,
Pure and bright, and worthy
thee:

Thomas Benson Pollock
1836–96

491 *Christe, du Beistand deiner*
Kreuzgemeine

LORD of our life, and God of
our salvation,
Star of our night, and Hope of
every nation,
Hear and receive thy Church's
supplication,
Lord God Almighty.

2 See round thine ark the hungry
billows curling;
See how thy foes their banners
are unfurling;
Lord, while their darts en-
venomed they are hurl-
ing,
Thou canst preserve us.

3 Lord, thou canst help when
earthly armour faileth;
Lord, thou canst save when
deadly sin assaileth;
Lord, o'er thy rock nor death
nor hell prevaileth;
Grant us thy peace, Lord.

4 Grant us thy help till foes are
backward driven;
Grant them thy truth that they
may be forgiven;
Grant peace on earth, and, after
we have striven,
Peace in thy heaven.

Philip Pusey, 1799–1855
Based on Matthäus Apelles von
Löwenstern, 1594–1648

492

O THOU, who at thy
Eucharist didst pray
That all thy Church might
be for ever one,

Grant us at every Eucharist to say,
With longing heart and soul,
'Thy will be done'.
O may we all one bread, one body be,
One through this sacrament of unity.

2 For all thy Church, O Lord, we intercede;
Make thou our sad divisions soon to cease;
Draw us the nearer each to each, we plead,
By drawing all to thee, O Prince of Peace;
Thus may we all one bread, one body be,
One through this sacrament of unity.

3 We pray thee too for wanderers from thy fold;
O bring them back, good Shepherd of the sheep,

Back to the faith which saints believed of old,
Back to the Church which still that faith doth keep;
Soon may we all one bread, one body be,
One through this sacrament of unity.

4 So, Lord, at length when sacraments shall cease,
May we be one with all thy Church above,
One with thy saints in one unbroken peace,
One with thy saints in one unbounded love:
More blessèd still, in peace and love to be
One with the Trinity in Unity.

WILLIAM HARRY TURTON
1856–1938
Based on St. John 17:11

INTERCESSION:
FOR THE CHURCH'S MISSION

493   PSALM 67

LORD, bless and pity us,
Shine on us with thy face:
That the earth thy way, and nations all
May know thy saving grace.

2 Let people praise thee, Lord;
Let people all thee praise.
O let the nations all be glad,
In songs their voices raise:

3 Thou wilt justly people judge,
On earth rule nations all.
Let people praise thee, Lord; let them
Praise thee, both great and small.

4 The earth her fruit shall yield,
Our God shall blessing send.
God shall us bless; men shall him fear
Unto earth's utmost end.

5 *To thee be glory, Lord,*
Whom heaven and earth adore,
To Father, Son, and Holy Ghost,
One God for evermore. Amen.

494

THOU whose almighty word
Chaos and darkness heard
And took their flight,
Hear us, we humbly pray,
And, where the gospel day
Sheds not its glorious ray,
Let there be light.

2 Thou who didst come to bring,
On thy redeeming wing,
Healing and sight,
Health to the sick in mind,
Sight to the inly blind,
O now to all mankind
Let there be light.

3 Spirit of truth and love,
Life-giving, holy Dove,
　　Speed forth thy flight;
Move o'er the waters' face,
Bearing the lamp of grace,
And in earth's darkest place
　　Let there be light.

4 Blessèd and holy Three,
Glorious Trinity,
　　Wisdom, Love, Might,
Boundless as ocean's tide
Rolling in fullest pride,
Through the world far and wide
　　Let there be light.

JOHN MARRIOTT, 1780–1825

495

O LORD our God, arise!
　　The cause of truth
maintain,
And wide o'er all the peopled
　　world
Extend her blessèd reign.

2 Thou Prince of Life, arise!
Nor let thy glory cease;
Far spread the conquests of thy
　　grace,
And bless the earth with
　　peace.

3 Thou Holy Ghost, arise!
Expand thy quickening wing,
And o'er a dark and ruined
　　world
Let light and order spring.

4 All on the earth, arise!
To God the Saviour sing;
From shore to shore, from earth
　　to heaven,
Let echoing anthems ring.

RALPH WARDLAW, 1779–1853

496

O SPIRIT of the living God,
　　In all thy plenitude of
grace,
Where'er the foot of man hath
　　trod,
Descend on our apostate race.

2 Give tongues of fire and hearts
　　of love,
　　To preach the reconciling
　　word;
Give power and unction from
　　above,
　　Whene'er the joyful sound is
　　heard.

3 Be darkness, at thy coming,
　　light;
　　Confusion order, in thy path;
Souls without strength inspire
　　with might;
　　Bid mercy triumph over
　　wrath.

4 O Spirit of the Lord, prepare
　　All the round earth her God
　　to meet;
Breathe thou abroad like morn-
　　ing air,
　　Till hearts of stone begin to
　　beat.

5 Baptize the nations; far and
　　nigh
　　The triumphs of the cross
　　record;
The Name of Jesus glorify,
　　Till every kindred call him
　　Lord.

JAMES MONTGOMERY, 1771–1854

497

G OD of mercy, God of grace,
　　Show the brightness of
thy face;
Shine upon us, Saviour, shine,
Fill thy Church with light divine,
And thy saving health extend
Unto earth's remotest end.

2 Let the people praise thee, Lord;
Be by all that live adored;
Let the nations shout and sing
Glory to their Saviour King,
At thy feet their tribute pay,
And thy holy will obey.

3 Let the people praise thee, Lord;
Earth shall then her fruits afford,
God to man his blessing give,
Man to God devoted live—
All below and all above,
One in joy and light and love.

HENRY FRANCIS LYTE, 1793–1847

498

ARM of the Lord, awake,
awake!
Put on thy strength, the nations
shake,
And let the world, adoring, see
Triumphs of mercy wrought by
thee.

2 Say to the heathen from thy
throne,
'I am Jehovah, God alone';
Thy voice their idols shall confound,
And cast their altars to the
ground.

3 Let Zion's time of favour come;
O bring the tribes of Israel
home;
And let our wondering eyes be-
hold
Gentiles and Jews in Jesus' fold.

4 Almighty God, thy grace proclaim
In every clime of every name;
Let adverse powers before thee
fall,
And crown the Saviour Lord
of all.

WILLIAM SHRUBSOLE, 1759–1829

499

ETERNAL God, whose power
upholds
Both flower and flaming star,
To whom there is no here nor
there,
No time, no near nor far,
No alien race, no foreign shore,
No child unsought, unknown,
O send us forth, thy prophets
true,
To make all lands thine own!

2 O God of love, whose spirit
wakes
In every human breast,
Whom love, and love alone, can
know,
In whom all hearts find rest,

Help us to spread thy gracious
reign,
Till greed and hate shall cease,
And kindness dwell in human
hearts,
And all the earth find peace!

3 O God of truth, whom science
seeks
And reverent souls adore,
Who lightest every earnest
mind
Of every clime and shore,
Dispel the gloom of error's
night,
Of ignorance and fear,
Until true wisdom from above
Shall make life's pathway
clear!

4 O God of beauty, oft revealed
In dreams of human art,
In speech that flows to melody,
In holiness of heart;
Teach us to ban all ugliness
That blinds our eyes to
thee,
Till all shall know the loveliness
Of lives made fair and free.

5 O God of righteousness and
grace,
Seen in the Christ, thy Son,
Whose life and death reveal thy
face,
By whom thy will was done,
Inspire thy heralds of good
news
To live thy life divine,
Till Christ is formed in all man-
kind,
And every land is thine!

HENRY HALLAM TWEEDY
1868–1953

500

CHRIST for the world we
sing!
The world to Christ we bring
With fervent prayer;
The wayward and the lost,
By restless passions tossed,
Redeemed at countless cost
From dark despair.

2 Christ for the world we sing!
   The world to Christ we bring
     With one accord;
   With us the work to share,
   With us reproach to dare,
   With us the cross to bear,
     For Christ our Lord.

3 Christ for the world we sing!
   The world to Christ we bring
     With joyful song;
   The new-born souls, whose days,
   Reclaimed from error's ways,
   Inspired with hope and praise,
     To Christ belong.

SAMUEL WOLCOTT, 1813–86

501
For children

FAR round the world thy
   children sing their song:
From East and West their
   voices sweetly blend,
Praising the Lord in whom
   young lives are strong,
Jesus our Guide, our Hero, and
   our Friend.

2 Where thy wide ocean, wave on
   rolling wave,
Beats through the ages, on each
   island shore,
They praise their Lord, whose
   hand alone can save,
Whose sea of love surrounds
   them evermore.

3 Still there are lands where none
   have seen thy face,
Children whose hearts have
   never shared thy joy;

Yet thou wouldst pour on these
   thy radiant grace,
Give thy glad strength to every
   girl and boy.

4 All round the world let children
   sing thy song:
From East and West their
   voices sweetly blend,
Praising the Lord in whom
   young lives are strong,
Jesus our Guide, our Hero, and
   our Friend.

BASIL JOSEPH MATHEWS
1879–1951

502
For children

GOD of heaven, hear our
   singing;
   Only little ones are we,
Yet, a great petition bringing,
   Father, now we come to thee.

2 Let thy Kingdom come, we
   pray thee;
   Let the world in thee find rest;
Let all know thee, and obey thee,
   Loving, praising, blessing,
   blest.

3 Let the sweet and joyful story
   Of the Saviour's wondrous
   love,
Wake on earth a song of glory,
   Like the angels' song above.

4 Father, send the glorious hour,
   Every heart be thine alone,
For the Kingdom, and the
   power,
   And the glory are thine own.

FRANCES RIDLEY HAVERGAL
1836–79

INTERCESSION: FOR THE WORLD

503

THY love, O God, has all mankind created,
   And led thy people to this
   present hour:
In Christ we see love's glory
   consummated;
   Thy Spirit manifests his
   living power.

2 We bring thee, Lord, in fervent
   intercession
   The children of thy world-
   wide family:
With contrite hearts we offer
   our confession,
   For we have sinned against
   thy charity.

3 From out the darkness of our
hope's frustration;
From all the broken idols of
our pride;
We turn to seek thy truth's
illumination;
And find thy mercy waiting
at our side.

4 In pity look upon thy children's
striving
For life and freedom, peace
and brotherhood;
Till, at the fullness of thy truth
arriving,
We find in Christ the crown
of every good.

5 Inspire thy Church, mid earth's
discordant voices,
To preach the gospel of her
Lord above;
Until the day this warring world
rejoices
To hear the mighty harmonies
of love,

6 Until the tidings men have long
awaited,
From north to south, from
east to west shall ring;
And all mankind, by Jesus
liberated,
Proclaims in jubilation, Christ
is King!

ALBERT FREDERICK BAYLY

504

O GOD of love, O King of
peace,
Make wars throughout the
world to cease;
The wrath of sinful man restrain:
Give peace, O God, give peace
again.

2 Remember, Lord, thy works of
old,
The wonders that our fathers
told;
Remember not our sin's dark
stain:
Give peace, O God, give peace
again.

3 Whom shall we trust but thee,
O Lord?
Where rest but on thy faithful
word?
None ever called on thee in vain:
Give peace, O God, give peace
again.

4 Where saints and angels dwell
above,
All hearts are knit in holy love;
O bind us in that heavenly
chain:
Give peace, O God, give peace
again.

HENRY WILLIAMS BAKER, 1821–77

505

CHRIST is the world's true
light,
Its captain of salvation,
The daystar clear and bright
Of every man and nation;
New life, new hope awakes,
Where'er men own his sway:
Freedom her bondage breaks,
And night is turned to day.

2 In Christ all races meet,
Their ancient feuds forgetting,
The whole round world com-
plete,
From sunrise to its setting:
When Christ is throned as Lord,
Men shall forsake their fear,
To ploughshare beat the sword,
To pruning-hook the spear.

3 One Lord, in one great name
Unite us all who own thee;
Cast out our pride and shame
That hinder to enthrone thee;
The world has waited long,
Has travailed long in pain;
To heal its ancient wrong,
Come, Prince of Peace, and
reign.

GEORGE WALLACE BRIGGS
1875–1959

506

O GOD of our divided world,
Light up thy way where
our ways part.
Restore the kinship of our birth,
Revive in us a single heart—

2 A heart that sees in Christ its
    goal
  And cares with Christ for every
    man,
  That seeks beyond all outward
    forms
  The brotherhood of God's own
    plan.

3 Where we have failed to under-
    stand
  Our brother's heart, O Lord
    forgive.
  Grant us the confidence to share
  The lights whereby our brothers
    live.

4 Then shall we know a richer
    world
  Where all divisions are dis-
    owned,
  Where heart joins heart and
    hand joins hand,
  Where man is loved and Christ
    enthroned.

    ALAN NORMAN PHILLIPS

507

FATHER Eternal, Ruler of
    Creation,
  Spirit of Life, which moved
    ere form was made,
Through the thick darkness
    covering every nation,
  Light to man's blindness, O
    be thou our aid!
    Thy Kingdom come, O Lord,
    thy will be done.

2 Races and peoples, lo! we stand
    divided,
  And, sharing not our griefs,
    no joy can share;
  By wars and tumults Love is
    mocked, derided,
  His conquering cross no king-
    dom wills to bear;

3 Envious of heart, blind-eyed,
    with tongues confounded,
  Nation by nation still goes
    unforgiven;
  In wrath and fear, by jealousies
    surrounded,
  Building proud towers which
    shall not reach to heaven.

4 Lust of possession worketh
    desolations;
  There is no meekness in the
    sons of earth.
  Led by no star, the rulers of
    the nations
  Still fail to bring us to the
    blissful birth.

5 How shall we love thee, holy,
    hidden Being,
  If we love not the world
    which thou hast made?
  O, give us brother-love, for
    better seeing
  Thy Word made flesh and in
    a manger laid.
    LAURENCE HOUSMAN, 1865–1959

508

ALMIGHTY Father, who dost
    give
The gift of life to all who live,
Look down on all earth's sin and
    strife,
And lift us to a nobler life.

2 Lift up our hearts, O King of
    kings,
To brighter hopes and kindlier
    things,
To visions of a larger good,
And holier dreams of brother-
    hood.

3 Thy world is weary of its
    pain,
Of selfish greed and fruitless
    gain,
Of tarnished honour, falsely
    strong,
And all its ancient deeds of
    wrong.

4 Hear thou the prayer thy ser-
    vants pray,
Uprising from all lands today,
And o'er the vanquished powers
    of sin
O bring thy great salvation in.
    JOHN HOWARD BERTRAM
    MASTERMAN, 1867–1933

509

O HOLY City, seen of John,
   Where Christ, the Lamb,
doth reign,
Within whose four-square walls
   shall come
No night, nor need, nor pain,
And where the tears are wiped
   from eyes
That shall not weep again!

2 O shame to us who rest content
   While lust and greed for gain
In street and shop and tenement
   Wring gold from human pain,
And bitter lips in blind despair
   Cry, 'Christ hath died in
   vain!'

3 Give us, O God, the strength to
   build
   The City that hath stood
Too long a dream, whose laws
   are love,
   Whose ways are brotherhood,
And where the sun that shineth
   is
   God's grace for human good.

4 Already in the mind of God
   That City riseth fair:
Lo, how its splendour challenges
   The souls that greatly dare—
Yea, bids us seize the whole of
   life
   And build its glory there.

WALTER RUSSELL BOWIE
1882–1969
(suggested by St. John's vision
in Revelation 21)

510

L ORD of light, whose Name
   out-shineth
   All the stars and suns of
   space,
Deign to make us thy co-
   workers
   In the Kingdom of thy grace;
Use us to fulfil thy purpose
   In the gift of Christ thy Son:
Father, as in highest heaven,
   So on earth thy will be done.

2 By the toil of lowly workers
   In some far outlying field;
By the courage where the
   radiance
   Of the cross is still revealed;
By the victories of meekness,
   Through reproach and suffer-
   ing won,—

3 Grant that knowledge, still in-
   creasing,
   At thy feet may lowly kneel;
With thy grace our triumphs
   hallow,
   With thy charity our zeal;
Lift the nations from the sha-
   dows
   To the gladness of the sun:

4 By the prayers of faithful watch-
   men,
   Never silent day or night;
By the cross of Jesus bringing
   Peace to men, and healing
   light;
By the love that passeth know-
   ledge,
   Making all thy children one:

HOWELL ELVET LEWIS, 1860–1953

511

O DAY of God, draw nigh
   In beauty and in power,
Come with thy timeless judg-
   ment now
To match our present hour.

2   Bring to our troubled minds,
   Uncertain and afraid,
The quiet of a steadfast faith,
   Calm of a call obeyed.

3   Bring justice to our land,
   That all may dwell secure,
And finely build for days to
   come
   Foundations that endure.

4   Bring to our world of strife
   Thy sovereign word of peace,
That war may haunt the earth
   no more
   And desolation cease.

5   O Day of God, draw nigh
As at creation's birth;
Let there be light again, and set
    Thy judgments in the earth.
ROBERT BALGARNIE YOUNG SCOTT

512

WHERE cross the crowded
    ways of life,
Where sound the cries of race
    and clan,
Above the noise of selfish strife,
We hear thy voice, O Son of
    Man.

2 In haunts of wretchedness and
    need,
    On shadowed thresholds dark
      with fears,
From paths where hide the lures
    of greed,
    We catch the vision of thy
      tears.

3 From tender childhood's help-
    lessness,
    From woman's grief, man's
      burdened toil,
From famished souls, from
    sorrow's stress,
    Thy heart has never known
      recoil.

4 The cup of water given for thee
    Still holds the freshness of thy
      grace;
Yet long these multitudes to see
    The sweet compassion of thy
      face.

5 O Master, from the mountain
    side
    Make haste, to heal these
      hearts of pain;
Among these restless throngs
    abide,
    O tread the city's streets
      again:

6 Till sons of men shall learn thy
    love,
    And follow where thy feet
      have trod;
Till glorious from thy heaven
    above,
    Shall come the City of our
      God.
FRANK MASON NORTH, 1850–1935

513

GOD of the pastures, hear our
    prayer,
Lord of the growing seed,
Bless thou the fields, for to thy
    care
We look in all our need.

2 God of the rivers in their course,
    Lord of the swelling sea,
Where man must strive with
    nature's force,
    Do thou his guardian be.

3 God of the dark and sombre
    mine,
    Lord of its hard-won store,
In toil and peril all be thine;
    Thy help and strength are sure.

4 God of the city's throbbing
    heart,
    Lord of its industry,
Bid greed and base deceit de-
    part,
    Give true prosperity.

5 God of authority and right,
    Lord of all earthly power,
To those who rule us grant thy
    light,
    Thy wisdom be their dower.

6 God of the nations, King of men,
    Lord of each humble soul,
We seek thy gracious aid again,
    Come down and make us whole.
THOMAS CHARLES HUNTER CLARE

514

ETERNAL Ruler of the
    ceaseless round
    Of circling planets singing on
      their way,
Guide of the nations from the
    night profound
    Into the glory of the perfect
      day:
Rule in our hearts, that we may
    ever be
Guided and strengthened and
    upheld by thee.

2 We are of thee, the children of
    thy love,
    The brothers of thy well-
      belovèd Son;
Descend, O Holy Spirit, like a
    dove,
    Into our hearts, that we may
      be as one;
As one with thee, to whom we
    ever tend;
As one with him, our Brother
    and our Friend.

3 We would be one in hatred of
    all wrong,
    One in our love of all things
      sweet and fair,
One with the joy that breaketh
    into song,
    One with the grief that
      trembleth into prayer,
One in the power that makes thy
    children free
To follow truth, and thus to
    follow thee.

4 O clothe us with thy heavenly
    armour, Lord,
Thy trusty shield, thy sword
    of love divine;
    Our inspiration be thy constant
    word;
    We ask no victories that are
      not thine;
Give or withhold, let pain or
    pleasure be;
Enough to know that we are
    serving thee.

JOHN WHITE CHADWICK
1840–1904

515

FATHER, who on man dost
    shower
Gifts of plenty from thy dower,
To thy people give the power
    All thy gifts to use aright.

2 Give pure happiness in leisure,
Temperance in every pleasure,
Holy use of earthly treasure,
    Bodies clear and spirits
    bright.

3 Lift from this and every nation
All that brings us degradation;
Quell the forces of temptation;
    Put thine enemies to flight.

4 Be with us, thy strength supply-
    ing,
That with energy undying,
Every foe of man defying,
    We may rally to the fight.

5 Thou who art our Captain ever,
Lead us on to great endeavour;
May thy Church the world
    deliver:
    Give us wisdom, courage,
    might.

6 Father, who hast sought and
    found us,
Son of God, whose love has
    bound us,
Holy Ghost, within us, round
    us—
    Hear us, Godhead infinite.

PERCY DEARMER, 1867–1936
The following are also suitable
Nos. 340, 211, 322

INTERCESSION: FOR THE NATION

516

GOD the Omnipotent! King,
    who ordainest
    Great winds thy clarions,
    lightnings thy sword;
Show forth thy pity on high
    where thou reignest;
    Give to us peace in our time,
    O Lord.

2 God the All-merciful! earth
    hath forsaken
    Meekness and mercy, and
    slighted thy word;
Bid not thy wrath in its terrors
    awaken;
    Give to us peace in our time,
    O Lord.

3 God the All-righteous One! man
hath defied thee;
Yet to eternity standeth thy
word;
Falsehood and wrong shall not
tarry beside thee;
Give to us peace in our time,
O Lord.

4 God the All-wise! by the fire of
thy chastening,
Earth shall to freedom and
truth be restored;
Through the thick darkness thy
Kingdom is hastening;
Thou wilt give peace in thy
time, O Lord.

5 So shall thy children, with
thankful devotion,
Praise him who saved them
from peril and sword,
Singing in chorus, from ocean
to ocean,
Peace to the nations, and
praise to the Lord.

HENRY FOTHERGILL CHORLEY
1808–72
and JOHN ELLERTON, 1826–93

517

GOD of Eternity, Lord of
the Ages,
Father and Spirit and Saviour
of men!
Thine is the glory of time's
numbered pages;
Thine is the power to revive
us again.

2 Thankful, we come to thee,
Lord of the nations,
Praising thy faithfulness,
mercy, and grace
Shown to our fathers in past
generations,
Pledge of thy love to our
people and race.

*3 Far from our ancient home,
sundered by oceans,
Zion is builded, and God is
adored:
Lift we our hearts in united
devotions!
Ends of the earth, join in
praise to the Lord!

*4 Beauteous this land of ours,
bountiful Giver!
Brightly the heavens thy glory
declare;
Streameth the sunlight on hill,
plain, and river,
Shineth thy cross over fields
rich and fair.

5 Pardon our sinfulness, God of
all pity,
Call to remembrance thy
mercies of old;
Strengthen thy Church to
abide as a city
Set on a hill for a light to thy
fold.

6 Head of the Church on earth,
risen, ascended!
Thine is the honour that dwells
in this place:
As thou hast blessed us
through years that have
ended,
Still lift upon us the light of
thy face.

ERNEST NORTHCROFT MERRINGTON
1876–1953

* Verse 3 for use overseas. Verse 4 for
use in the Southern Hemisphere, the refer-
ence being to the Southern Cross.

518

LORD, while for all mankind
we pray,
Of every clime and coast,
O hear us for our native land,
The land we love the most.

2 Our fathers' sepulchres are
here,
And here our kindred dwell,
Our children too; how should
we love
Another land so well?

3 O guard our shores from every
foe;
With peace our borders bless;
With prosperous times our cities
crown,
Our fields with plenteousness.

4 Unite us in the sacred love
    Of knowledge, truth, and
        thee;
And let our hills and valleys
        shout
    The songs of liberty.

5 Lord of the nations, thus to
        thee
    Our country we commend;
Be thou her refuge and her
        trust,
    Her everlasting Friend.

          JOHN REYNELL WREFORD
                   1800–81

519

JUDGE Eternal, throned in
   splendour,
    Lord of lords and King of
        kings,
With thy living fire of judgment
    Purge this land of bitter
        things;
Solace all its wide dominion
    With the healing of thy
        wings.

2 Still the weary folk are pining
    For the hour that brings
        release;
And the city's crowded clangour
    Cries aloud for sin to cease;
And the homesteads and the
        woodlands
    Plead in silence for their
        peace.

3 Crown, O God, thine own
        endeavour;
    Cleave our darkness with thy
        sword;
Feed the faithless and the
        hungry
    With the richness of thy
        word;
Cleanse the body of this Nation
    Through the glory of the
        Lord.

          HENRY SCOTT HOLLAND
           1847–1918, altered

520

O GOD of earth and altar,
   Bow down and hear our
        cry;
Our earthly rulers falter,
    Our people drift and die;
The walls of gold entomb us,
    The swords of scorn divide,
Take not thy thunder from
        us,
    But take away our pride.

2 From all that terror teaches,
    From lies of tongue and pen,
From all the easy speeches
    That comfort cruel men,
From sale and profanation
    Of honour and the sword,
From sleep and from damnation,
    Deliver us, good Lord!

3 Tie in a living tether
    The prince and priest and
        thrall;
Bind all our lives together,
    Smite us and save us all;
In ire and exultation,
    Aflame with faith, and free,
Lift up a living nation,
    A single sword to thee.

         GILBERT KEITH CHESTERTON
              1874–1936

521

GOD save our gracious Queen,
   Long live our noble Queen;
    God save the Queen!
Send her victorious,
Happy and glorious,
Long to reign over us:
    God save the Queen!

2 Thy choicest gifts in store
On her be pleased to pour;
    Long may she reign;
May she defend our laws,
And ever give us cause
To sing with heart and voice,
    'God save the Queen!'

          From the version of 1745

INTERCESSION: FOR THE FAMILY

522

OUR Father, by whose Name
All fatherhood is known,
Who dost in love proclaim
Each family thine own,
Bless thou all parents, guarding well,
With constant love as sentinel,
The homes in which thy people dwell.

2 O Christ, thyself a child
Within an earthly home,
With heart still undefiled,
Thou didst to manhood come;
Our children bless, in ev'ry place,
That they may all behold thy face,
And knowing thee may grow in grace.

3 O Spirit, who dost bind
Our hearts in unity,
Who teachest us to find
The love from self set free,
In all our hearts such love increase,
That ev'ry home by this release,
May be the dwelling place of peace.

FRANCIS BLAND TUCKER

523   *O selig Haus, wo man
dich aufgenommen*

O HAPPY home, where thou
art loved the dearest,
Thou loving Friend, and
Saviour of our race,
And where among the guests
there never cometh
One who can hold such high
and honoured place!

2 O happy home, where two in
heart united
In holy faith and blessèd hope
are one,
Whom death a little while alone
divideth,
And cannot end the union
here begun!

3 O happy home, whose little
ones are given
Early to thee, in humble faith
and prayer,—
To thee, their Friend, who from
the heights of heaven
Dost guide and guard with
more than mother's care!

4 O happy home, where each one
serves thee, lowly,
Whatever his appointed work
may be,
Till every common task seems
great and holy,
When it is done, O Lord, as
unto thee!

5 O happy home, where thou art
not forgotten
When joy is overflowing, full
and free:
O happy home, where every
wounded spirit
Is brought, Physician, Comforter, to thee:

6 Until at last, when earth's
day's work is ended,
All meet thee in the blessèd
home above,
From whence thou camest,
where thou hast ascended,
Thy everlasting home of
peace and love!

KARL JOHANN PHILIPP SPITTA
1801–59
Tr. SARAH LAURIE FINDLATER
1823–1907

524

THY Kingdom come; yea,
bid it come,
But, when thy Kingdom first
began
On earth, thy Kingdom was a
home,
A child, a woman, and a man.

2 The child was in the midst
thereof,
O blessèd Jesus, holiest one!
The centre and the fount of love,
Mary and Joseph's little Son.

Wherever on this earth shall be
A child, a woman, and a man,
The image of that trinity
Wherewith thy Kingdom first began,

4 Establish there thy Kingdom!
   Yea,
And o'er that trinity of love
Send down, as in thy appointed day,
The brooding spirit of thy Dove.

KATHARINE TYNAN-HINKSON
1861–1931

INTERCESSION:
FOR THE MINISTRY OF HEALING

525

FROM thee all skill and science flow,
All pity, care, and love,
All calm and courage, faith and hope;
O pour them from above.

2 And part them, Lord, to each and all,
As each and all shall need,
To rise like incense, each to thee,
In noble thought and deed.

3 And hasten, Lord, that perfect day
When pain and death shall cease,
And thy just rule shall fill the earth
With health, and light, and peace;

4 When ever blue the sky shall gleam,
And ever green the sod;
And man's rude work deface no more
The Paradise of God.

CHARLES KINGSLEY, 1819–75

526

FATHER, whose will is life and good
For all of mortal breath,
Bind strong the bond of brotherhood
Of those who fight with death.

2 Empower the hands and hearts and wills
Of friends in lands afar,
Who battle with the body's ills,
And wage thy holy war.

3 Where'er they heal the maimed and blind,
Let love of Christ attend:
Proclaim the good Physician's mind,
And prove the Saviour friend.

4 For still his love works wondrous charms,
And, as in days of old,
He takes the wounded to his arms,
And bears them to the fold.

5 O Father, look from heaven and bless,
Where'er thy servants be,
Their works of pure unselfishness,
Made consecrate to thee!

HARDWICKE DRUMMOND RAWNSLEY
1851–1920

INTERCESSION:
FOR TRAVELLERS AND THE ABSENT

527

ETERNAL Father, strong to save,
Whose arm hath bound the restless wave,
Who bidd'st the mighty ocean deep
Its own appointed limits keep:
O hear us when we cry to thee
For those in peril on the sea.

2 O Christ, whose voice the waters heard,
And hushed their raging at thy word,
Who walkedst on the foaming deep,
And calm amid the storm didst sleep:
O hear us when we cry to thee
For those in peril on the sea.

3 O Holy Spirit, who didst brood
Upon the waters dark and rude,
And bid their angry tumult cease,
And give, for wild confusion, peace:
O hear us when we cry to thee
For those in peril on the sea.

4 O Trinity of love and power,
Our brethren shield in danger's hour;
From rock and tempest, fire and foe,
Protect them wheresoe'er they go:
Thus evermore shall rise to thee
Glad hymns of praise from land and sea.

WILLIAM WHITING, 1825–78

528

THOU who dost rule on high,
Our Father and our Friend,
All those who ride the sky
We now to thee commend.
For though among the stars they move,
They cannot rise beyond thy love.

2 Alone in boundless space,
May they be still with thee;
The glory of thy face
Among the heavens see;
For thou, by land and sea and air,
Art with thy children everywhere.

3 When tempests loose their power
And dangers gather round,
In thee, in that dread hour,
May their defence be found;
O may that peace possess their mind
Which all thy trusting children find.

4 And soon from pole to pole,
Thy Kingdom, Lord, arise;
And peace alone control
The commerce of the skies;
Till all the gifts thou givest men,
We to thy glory give again.

ROBERT WESLEY LITTLEWOOD

529

HOLY Father, in thy mercy,
Hear our anxious prayer;
Keep our loved ones, now far distant,
'Neath thy care.

2 Jesus, Saviour, let thy presence
  Be their light and guide;
Keep, O keep them, in their
   weakness,
  At thy side.

3 When in sorrow, when in
   danger,
  When in loneliness,
In thy love look down and
   comfort
  Their distress.

4 May the joy of thy salvation
  Be their strength and
   stay;

May they love and may they
   praise thee
  Day by day.

5 Holy Spirit, let thy teaching
  Sanctify their life;
Send thy grace that they may
   conquer
  In the strife.

6 Father, Son, and Holy Spirit,
  God the One in Three,
Bless them, guide them, save
   them, keep them
  Near to thee.

ISABEL STEPHANA STEVENSON
1843–90

THE CHURCH TRIUMPHANT

530 PARAPHRASE 61

BLEST be the everlasting God,
 The Father of our Lord!
Be his abounding mercy praised,
 His majesty adored!

2 When from the dead he raised
  his Son,
 And called him to the sky,
He gave our souls a lively hope
 That they should never die.

3 To an inheritance divine
 He taught our hearts to rise;
'Tis uncorrupted, undefiled,
 Unfading in the skies.

4 Saints by the power of God are
  kept,
 Till the salvation come:
We walk by faith as strangers
  here
 But Christ shall call us home.

Scottish Paraphrases, 1781
From 1 Peter 1:3–5

531 PARAPHRASE 59, verses
      1–4, 13

BEHOLD what witnesses un-
  seen
 Encompass us around;
Men, once like us, with suffer-
  ing tried,
 But now with glory crowned.

2 Let us, with zeal like theirs
  inspired,
 Begin the Christian race,
And, freed from each encumber-
  ing weight,
 Their holy footsteps trace.

3 Behold a witness nobler still,
 Who trod affliction's path,
Jesus, at once the finisher
 And author of our faith.

4 He for the joy before him set,
 So generous was his love,
Endured the cross, despised the
  shame,
 And now he reigns above.

5 Then let our hearts no more
  despond,
 Our hands be weak no more;
Still let us trust our Father's love,
 His wisdom still adore.

Scottish Paraphrases, 1781
From Hebrews Ch. 12

532 PARAPHRASE 65,
    verses 5, 6, 8, 9, 11

HARK how the adoring hosts
  above
 With songs surround the
   throne!
Ten thousand thousand are
  their tongues;
 But all their hearts are one.

2 Worthy the Lamb that died,
      they cry,
   To be exalted thus;
Worthy the Lamb, let us reply;
   For he was slain for us.

3 Thou hast redeemed us with thy
      blood,
   And set the prisoners free;
Thou mad'st us kings and
      priests to God,
   And we shall reign with thee.

4 From every kindred, every
      tongue,
   Thou brought'st thy chosen
      race;
And distant lands and isles
      have shared
   The riches of thy grace.

5 *To him who sits upon the throne,*
   The God whom we adore,
And to the Lamb that once was
      slain,
   Be glory evermore. Amen.

                    Scottish Paraphrases, 1781
                    From Revelation 5:11–14

---

533   PARAPHRASE 66

HOW bright these glorious
      spirits shine!
   Whence all their white array?
How came they to the blissful
      seats
   Of everlasting day?
Lo! these are they, from suffer-
      ings great
   Who came to realms of light,
And in the blood of Christ have
      washed
   Those robes which shine so
      bright.

2 Now, with triumphal palms
      they stand
   Before the throne on high,
And serve the God they love,
      amidst
   The glories of the sky.
His presence fills each heart
      with joy,
   Tunes every mouth to sing:
By day, by night, the sacred
      courts
   With glad hosannas ring.

3 Hunger and thirst are felt no
      more,
   Nor suns with scorching ray;
God is their sun, whose cheering
      beams
   Diffuse eternal day.
The Lamb who dwells amidst
      the throne
   Shall o'er them still preside,
Feed them with nourishment
      divine,
   And all their footsteps guide.

*4 'Mong pastures green he'll lead
      his flock,
   Where living streams appear;
And God the Lord from every
      eye
   Shall wipe off every tear.

                    Scottish Paraphrases, 1781
                    From Revelation 7:13–end

   * *Verse* 4 *is sung to the second half*
of the tune.

534

FOR all the saints who from
      their labours rest,
Who thee by faith before the
      world confessed,
Thy Name, O Jesus, be for ever
   blest.

         Alleluia! Alleluia!

2 Thou wast their Rock, their
      Fortress, and their Might;
Thou, Lord, their Captain in the
      well-fought fight;
Thou, in the darkness drear
      their one true Light:

3 O may thy soldiers, faithful,
      true, and bold,
Fight as the saints who nobly
      fought of old,
And win, with them, the victor's
      crown of gold:

4 O blest communion, fellowship
      divine!
We feebly struggle, they in
      glory shine;
Yet all are one in thee, for all
      are thine:

5 And when the strife is fierce,
    the warfare long,
  Steals on the ear the distant
    triumph song,
And hearts are brave again, and
    arms are strong:

6 The golden evening brightens
    in the west;
Soon, soon to faithful warriors
    cometh rest;
Sweet is the calm of Paradise
    the blest:

7 But, lo! there breaks a yet more
    glorious day;
The saints triumphant rise in
    bright array;
The King of Glory passes on his
    way:

8 From earth's wide bounds, from
    ocean's farthest coast,
Through gates of pearl streams
    in the countless host,
Singing to Father, Son, and
    Holy Ghost:
        WILLIAM WALSHAM HOW, 1823–97

535   *O quanta, qualia sunt*
          illa sabbata

O WHAT their joy and their
   glory must be,
Those endless Sabbaths the
    blessèd ones see!
Crown for the valiant; to weary
    ones rest;
God shall be all, and in all ever
    blest.

2 What are the Monarch, his
    court, and his throne?
What are the peace and the joy
    that they own?
Tell us, ye blest ones, that in it
    have share,
If what ye feel ye can fully de-
    clare.

3 Truly Jerusalem name we that
    shore,
'Vision of peace', that brings
    joy evermore!
Wish and fulfilment can severed
    be ne'er,
Nor the thing prayed for come
    short of the prayer.

4 We, where no trouble distrac-
    tion can bring,
Safely the anthems of Zion shall
    sing;
While for thy grace, Lord, their
    voices of praise
Thy blessèd people shall ever-
    more raise.

5 *Low before him with our praises
   we fall,
Of whom, and in whom, and
    through whom are all;
Of whom, the Father; and
    through whom, the Son;
In whom, the Spirit, with these
   ever One.*   Amen.
        PETER ABELARD, 1079–1142
    Tr. JOHN MASON NEALE, 1818–66

536

THERE is a land of pure
   delight,
  Where saints immortal reign;
Infinite day excludes the night,
  And pleasures banish pain;

2 There everlasting spring abides,
  And never-withering flowers:
Death, like a narrow sea, divides
  This heavenly land from ours.

3 Sweet fields beyond the swell-
   ing flood
  Stand dressed in living green;
So to the Jews old Canaan stood,
  While Jordan rolled between.

4 But timorous mortals start and
   shrink
  To cross this narrow sea,
And linger, shivering on the
   brink,
  And fear to launch away.

5 O could we make our doubts
   remove—
  Those gloomy doubts that
   rise—
And see the Canaan that we
   love,
  With unbenclouded eyes;

6 Could we but climb where
     Moses stood,
   And view the landscape o'er,
Not Jordan's stream, nor
     death's cold flood,
   Should fright us from the
     shore.

ISAAC WATTS, 1674–1748

537 *Urbs Sion aurea, patria
          lactea*

JERUSALEM the golden,
   With milk and honey blest,
Beneath thy contemplation
   Sink   heart   and   voice
     oppressed:
I know not, O I know not
   What social joys are there,
What radiancy of glory,
   What light beyond compare.

2 They stand, those halls of Zion,
   Conjubilant with song,
And bright with many an angel,
   And all the martyr throng:
The Prince is ever in them;
   The daylight is serene;
The pastures of the blessèd
   Are decked in glorious sheen.

3 There is the throne of David,
   And there, from care re-
     leased,
The   shout   of   them   that
     triumph,
   The song of them that feast;
And they who, with their
     Leader,
   Have conquered in the fight,
For ever and for ever
   Are clad in robes of white.

4 O sweet and blessèd country,
   The home of God's elect!
O sweet and blessèd country,
   That eager hearts expect!
*Jesus, in mercy bring us
   To that dear land of rest,
Who art, with God the Father
   And Spirit, ever blest. Amen.*

Verses 1–3 BERNARD OF CLUNY
     12th century
Tr. JOHN MASON NEALE, 1818–66
     Verse 4 Compilers of
Hymns Ancient and Modern, 1861

538

FOR those we love within the
     veil,
   Who once were comrades of
     our way,
We thank thee, Lord; for they
     have won
   To cloudless day;

2 And life for them is life indeed,
   The splendid goal of earth's
     strait race;
And where no shadows inter-
     vene
   They see thy face.

3 Not as we knew them any more,
   Toilworn, and sad with
     burdened care,—
Erect, clear-eyed, upon their
     brows
   Thy Name they bear.

4 Free from the fret of mortal
     years,
   And knowing now thy perfect
     will,
With quickened sense and
     heightened joy
   They serve thee still.

5 O fuller, sweeter is that life,
   And larger, ampler is the air:
Eye cannot see nor heart con-
     ceive
   The glory there;

6 Nor know to what high purpose
     thou
   Dost yet employ their ripened
     powers,
Nor how at thy behest they
     touch
   This life of ours.

7 There are no tears within their
     eyes;
   With love they keep per-
     petual tryst;
And praise and work and rest
     are one,
   With thee, O Christ.

WILLIAM CHARTER PIGOTT
     1872–1943

539 *Caelestis aulae principes*

CAPTAINS of the saintly band,
Lights who lighten ev'ry land,
Princes who with Jesus dwell,
Judges of his Israel.

2 On the nations sunk in night
Ye have shed the Gospel light;
Sin and error flee away,
Truth reveals the promised day.

3 Not by warrior's spear and sword,
Not by art of human word,
Preaching but the cross of shame,
Rebel hearts for Christ ye tame.

4 Earth, that long in sin and pain
Groaned in Satan's deadly chain,
Now to serve its God is free
In the law of liberty.

5 Distant lands with one acclaim
Tell the honour of your name,
Who, wherever man has trod,
Teach the mysteries of God.

6 *Glory to the Three in One*
While eternal ages run,
Who from deepest shades of night
Called us to his glorious light.
Amen.

JEAN-BAPTISTE DE SANTEÜIL
1630-97
Tr. HENRY WILLIAMS BAKER
1821-77

540 *Aeterna Christi munera*

THE eternal gifts of Christ the King,
The apostles' glorious deeds, we sing;
And while due hymns of praise we pay,
Our thankful hearts cast grief away.

2 The Church in these her princes boasts,
These victor chiefs of warrior hosts;
The soldiers of the heavenly hall,
The lights that rose on earth for all.

3 'Twas thus the yearning faith of saints,
The unconquered hope that never faints,
The love of Christ that knows not shame,
The prince of this world overcame.

4 In these the Father's glory shone;
In these the will of God the Son;
In these exults the Holy Ghost;
Through these rejoice the heavenly host.

5 Redeemer, hear us of thy love,
That, with this glorious band above,
Hereafter, of thine endless grace,
Thy servants also may have place.

Attributed to ST. AMBROSE
c. 340-97
Tr. JOHN MASON NEALE, 1818-66
and others

541

THE Son of God goes forth to war,
A kingly crown to gain;
His blood-red banner streams afar:
Who follows in his train?
Who best can drink his cup of woe,
Triumphant over pain,
Who patient bears his cross below,
He follows in his train.

2 The martyr first, whose eagle
    eye
  Could pierce beyond the
    grave,
Who saw his Master in the
    sky,
  And called on him to save;
Like him, with pardon on his
    tongue
  In midst of mortal pain,
He prayed for them that did the
    wrong:
  Who follows in his train?

3 A glorious band, the chosen
    few
  On whom the Spirit came,
Twelve valiant saints, their
    hope they knew,
  And mocked the cross and
    flame;
They climbed the steep ascent
    of heaven,
  Through peril, toil, and pain:
O God, to us may grace be given
  To follow in their train.

REGINALD HEBER, 1783–1826

542 *Alleluia piis edite laudibus*

SING Alleluia forth in duteous
    praise,
Ye citizens of heaven; O
    sweetly raise
  An endless Alleluia.

2 Ye powers, who stand before
    the eternal Light,
In hymning choirs re-echo to
    the height:

3 Ye who have gained at length
    your palms in bliss,
Victorious ones, your chant
    shall still be this:

4 There, in one grand acclaim,
    for ever ring
The strains which tell the
    honour of your King:

While thee, by whom were all
    things made, we praise
For ever, and tell out in sweetest
    lays:

6 Almighty Christ, to thee our
    voices sing
  Glory for evermore; to thee we
    bring:

Mozarabic Breviary, 5th–8th century
Tr. JOHN ELLERTON, 1826–93

543

LET saints on earth in concert
    sing
  With those whose work is
    done;
For all the servants of our King
  In earth and heaven are one.

2 One family, we dwell in him,
    One Church, above, beneath;
Though now divided by the
    stream,
    The narrow stream of death.

3 One army of the living God,
    To his command we bow;
Part of his host hath crossed
    the flood,
    And part is crossing now.

4 Even now to their eternal home
    There pass some spirits blest,
While others to the margin
    come,
    Waiting their call to rest.

5 Jesus, be thou our constant
    Guide;
    Then, when the word is given,
Bid Jordan's narrow stream
    divide,
    And bring us safe to heaven.

CHARLES WESLEY, 1707–88

544 *O fryniau Caersalem ceir
        gweled*

FROM heavenly Jerusalem's
    towers,
    The path through the desert
    they trace;
And every affliction they suf-
    fered
    Redounds to the glory of
    grace;

196

Their look they cast back on
the tempests,
On fears, on grim death and
the grave,
Rejoicing that now they're in
safety,
Through him that is mighty
to save.

2 And we, from the wilds of the
desert,
Shall flee to the land of the
blest;
Life's tears shall be changed to
rejoicing,
Its labours and toil into rest:
There we shall find refuge
eternal,
From sin, from affliction,
from pain,
And in the sweet love of the
Saviour,
A joy without end shall
attain.

DAVID CHARLES, 1762–1834
Tr. LEWIS EDWARDS, 1809–87

545

FAR off I see the goal—
O Saviour, guide me;
I feel my strength is small—
Be thou beside me;
With vision ever clear,
With love that conquers fear,
And grace to persevere,
O Lord, provide me.

2 Whene'er thy way seem
strange,
Go thou before me;
And, lest my heart should
change,
O Lord, watch o'er me;
But, should my faith prove
frail,
And I through blindness fail,
O let thy grace prevail,
And still restore me.

3 Should earthly pleasures wane,
And joy forsake me,
And lonely hours of pain
At length o'ertake me,—
My hand in thine hold fast
Till sorrow be o'er-past,
And gentle death at last
For heaven awake me.

4 There, with the ransomed
throng
Who praise for ever
The love that made them
strong
To serve for ever,
I, too, would see thy face,
Thy finished work re-trace,
And magnify thy grace,
Redeemed for ever.

ROBERT ROWLAND ROBERTS
1865–1945

The following are also suitable
No.
14 We come unto our fathers' God
473 Lord, who in thy perfect wisdom

IV

THE SACRAMENTS

HOLY BAPTISM

546 THE APOSTLES'
CREED

I believe in
GOD THE FATHER ALMIGHTY,
MAKER OF HEAVEN AND
EARTH
and in
JESUS CHRIST HIS ONLY SON OUR
LORD
who was conceived by the
Holy Ghost,
born of the Virgin Mary,
suffered under Pontius Pilate,
was crucified, dead, and
buried;
he descended into hell.
The third day he rose again
from the dead,
he ascended into heaven, and
sitteth on the right hand
of God the Father Al-
mighty;
from thence he shall come to
judge the quick and the
dead.
I believe in
the HOLY GHOST;
the HOLY CATHOLIC CHURCH;
the COMMUNION OF SAINTS;
the FORGIVENESS OF SINS;
the RESURRECTION OF THE
BODY;
and the LIFE EVERLASTING.
Amen.

547 PSALM 78, verses 4(b)–7

THE praises of the Lord our
God,
And his almighty strength,
The wondrous works that he
hath done,
We will show forth at length.

2 His testimony and his law
In Israel he did place,
And charged our fathers it to
show
To their succeeding race;

3 That so the race which was to
come
Might well them learn and
know;
And sons unborn, who should
arise,
Might to their sons them
show:

4 That they might set their hope
in God,
And suffer not to fall
His mighty works out of their
mind,
But keep his precepts all.

5 *To Father, Son, and Holy Ghost,*
The God whom we adore,
Be glory, as it was, and is,
And shall be evermore. Amen.

548 PARAPHRASE 47,
verses 2–4

WHEN to the sacred font we
came,
Did not the rite proclaim,
That, washed from sin, and all
its stains,
New creatures we became?

2 With Christ the Lord we died
to sin;
With him to life we rise,
To life which, now begun on
earth,
Is perfect in the skies.

3 Too long enthralled to Satan's
    sway,
  We now are slaves no more;
For Christ hath vanquished
    death and sin,
  Our freedom to restore.

4 *To Father, Son, and Holy Ghost,*
  The God whom we adore,
Be glory, as it was, and is,
  And shall be evermore. Amen.

          Scottish Paraphrases, 1781
          From Romans 6:3–7

549

O UR children, Lord, in faith
    and prayer,
  We now devote to thee;
Let them thy covenant mercies
    share,
  And thy salvation see.

2 Such helpless babes thou didst
    embrace,
  While dwelling here below;
To us and ours, O God of grace,
  The same compassion show.

3 O thou whose infant feet were
    found
  Within thy Father's shrine,
Whose years, with changeless
    virtue crowned,
  Were all alike divine,

4 Dependent on thy bounteous
    breath,
  We seek thy grace alone,
In childhood, manhood, age,
    and death,
  To keep us still thine own.

    vv. 1, 2 THOMAS HAWEIS, 1734–1820
    vv. 3, 4 REGINALD HEBER, 1783–1826

550

* *L IFT high the cross, the love of*
    Christ proclaim
Till all the world adore his sacred
  name.

2 Come, brethren, follow where
    our Captain trod,
  Our King victorious, Christ the
    Son of God:

3 Led on their way by this
    triumphant sign,
  The hosts of God in conquering
    ranks combine:

4 Each new-born soldier of the
    Crucified
  Bears on his brow the seal of
    him who died:

5 This is the sign which Satan's
    legions fear
  And angels veil their faces to
    revere:

6 O Lord, once lifted on the
    glorious tree,
  As thou hast promised, draw
    men unto thee:

7 From farthest regions let them
    homage bring,
  And on his cross adore their
    Saviour King:

      MICHAEL ROBERT NEWBOLT
               1874–1956
      Based on GEORGE WILLIAM
        KITCHIN, 1827–1912

* *Verse 1 is repeated as a refrain after*
each verse.

551

A LITTLE child the Saviour
    came,
  The Mighty God was still his
    Name,
And angels worshipped as he
    lay
The seeming infant of a day.

2 He who, a little child, began
  The life divine to show to man,
Proclaims from heaven the
    message free,
'Let little children come to me.'

3 We bring them, Lord, and with
    the sign
  Of sprinkled water name them
    thine:
Their souls with saving grace
    endow;
Baptize them with thy Spirit
    now.

4 O give thine angels charge, good
 Lord,
 Them safely in thy way to
  guard;
 Thy blessing on their lives com-
  mand,
 And write their names upon thy
  hand.

5 O thou who by an infant's
 tongue
 Dost hear thy perfect glory
  sung,
 May these, with all the heavenly
  host,
 Praise Father, Son, and Holy
  Ghost.

    WILLIAM ROBERTSON, 1820–64

552 *Liebster Jesu, wir sind hier*

BLESSÈD Jesus, here we
 stand,
 Met to do as thou hast
  spoken;
 And this child, at thy com-
  mand,
 Now we bring to thee in token
 That to Christ it here is given,
 For of such shall be his
  heaven.

2 Therefore hasten we to thee;
 Take the pledge we bring, O
  take it;
 Let us here thy glory see,
 And in tender pity make it
 Now thy child, and leave it
  never—
 Thine on earth, and thine for
  ever.

3 Make it, Head, thy member
 now;
 Shepherd, take thy lamb and
  feed it;
 Prince of Peace, its peace be
  thou;
 Way of life, to heaven O lead
  it;
 Vine, this branch may nothing sever,
 Grafted firm in thee for ever.

4 Now upon thy heart it lies,
 What our hearts so dearly
  treasure;
 Heavenward lead our burdened
  sighs;
 Pour thy blessing without
  measure;
 Write the name we now have
  given,
 Write it in the book of
  heaven.

   BENJAMIN SCHMOLK, 1672–1737
   Tr. CATHERINE WINKWORTH
         1827–78

553

O FATHER, in thy father-
 heart
We know our children have
 their part;
We sign them in thy threefold
 Name,
And by the sprinkled water
 claim
Thy covenant in Christ revealed,
To us and to our children
 sealed:

2 Name of the Father, pledge that
 we
 Our inmost being draw from
  thee;
 Name of the Son, whereby we
  know
 The Father's love to men below;
 Name of the Spirit, blessèd sign
 That now we share the life
  divine.

   ELLA SOPHIA ARMITAGE
      1841–1931

554

O GOD, thy life-creating love
 This sacred trust to
parents gave.
In Christ thou camest from
 above
Thy children's souls to claim
 and save.

2 Help us who now our pledges give
  The young to train and guard and guide,
To learn of Christ, and so to live
That they may in thy love abide.

3 Grant, Lord, as strength and wisdom grow,
  That every child thy truth may learn.
Impart thy light, that each may know
Thy will and life's true way discern.

4 Then home and child, kept in thy peace,
  And guarded, Father, by thy care,
Will in the grace of Christ increase,
And all thy Kingdom's blessings share.

ALBERT FREDERICK BAYLY

555

After baptism

O LOVING Father, to thy care
  We give again this child of thine,
Baptized and blessed with faithful prayer
And sealed with Love's victorious sign.

2 As Christ, thy Son, did not refuse
  The homage of the children's cry,
So teach *him* childhood's gifts to use
Thy Name to praise and magnify.

3 Through youth and age, through shine and shade,
  Grant *him* to run *his* earthly race,
Forgetting not that man was made
  To show thy glory and thy grace:

4 Till, at the last, before thy throne
  He lays *his* earthly armour down,
His task of loving service done,
And, in thy mercy, takes *his* crown.

CYRIL ARGENTINE ALINGTON
1872-1955
The following are also suitable Nos. 402
(vv. 1, 2, 4, 6); 420 (vv. 1, 2); 421
(vv. 1–3); 429.

556

THE Lord bless you, and keep you: the Lord make his face to shine upon you, and be gracious unto you: the Lord lift up his countenance upon you, and give you peace.

557

Cradle Roll

FATHER, hear us as we pray
  For these little ones today:
Good and gentle may they be;
Early may they come to thee.

2 Bless, we pray thee, Saviour dear,
  All whose names are written here;
Guard and keep them safe from harm;
Hold them with thy loving arm.

EDITH FLORENCE BOYLE
MACALISTER, 1873-1950

HOLY COMMUNION

558

THE NICENE CREED

WE believe in
  ONE GOD THE FATHER ALMIGHTY, Maker of heaven and earth, and of all things visible and invisible:
and in
  ONE LORD JESUS CHRIST, the only begotten Son of God, begotten of his Father before all worlds, GOD OF GOD, LIGHT OF

LIGHT, VERY GOD OF VERY GOD, begotten, not made, being of one substance with the Father, by whom all things were made:

WHO, for us men, and for our salvation, came down from heaven, and was incarnate by the Holy Ghost of the Virgin Mary, AND WAS MADE MAN, and was crucified also for us under Pontius Pilate.

HE suffered and was buried; and the third day he rose again according to the Scriptures, and ascended into heaven, and sitteth on the right hand of the Father. And he shall come again with glory to judge both the quick and the dead, whose Kingdom shall have no end.

And we believe in
THE HOLY GHOST, the Lord and Giver of Life, who proceedeth from the Father and the Son; who with the Father and the Son together is worshipped and glorified; who spake by the prophets.

And we believe
ONE HOLY CATHOLIC AND APOSTOLIC CHURCH.

We acknowledge
ONE BAPTISM for the remission of sins.

And we look for
THE RESURRECTION OF THE DEAD, and the LIFE OF THE WORLD TO COME. Amen.

559

SALUTATION

Minister The Lord be with you;
People   *And with thy spirit.*

SURSUM CORDA

Minister Lift up your hearts;
People   *We lift them up unto the Lord.*
Minister Let us give thanks unto our Lord God;
People   *It is meet and right so to do.*

560

SANCTUS

Holy, Holy, Holy, Lord God of Hosts,
Heaven and earth are full of thy glory.
Glory be to thee, O Lord Most High. Amen.

561

BENEDICTUS QUI VENIT

Blessèd is he that cometh in the Name of the Lord:
*Hosanna in the highest.

  * *The word* Hosanna *is sung three times.*

562

THE LORD'S PRAYER

First form

OUR Father which art in heaven,
Hallowed be thy Name.
Thy Kingdom come.
Thy will be done in earth, as it is in heaven.
Give us this day our daily bread.
And forgive us our debts, as we forgive our debtors.
And lead us not into temptation, but deliver us from evil:
For thine is the Kingdom, and the power, and the glory, for ever. Amen.

Second form

OUR Father, who art in heaven,
Hallowed be thy Name.
Thy Kingdom come.
Thy will be done, on earth as it is in heaven.
Give us this day our daily bread.
And forgive us our trespasses, as we forgive those who trespass against us.

And lead us not into temptation, but deliver us from evil:
For thine, is the Kingdom, the power, and the glory, for ever and ever. Amen.

St Matthew 6:9–13

563 AGNUS DEI

O LAMB of God, that takest away the sins of the world, have mercy upon us.
O Lamb of God, that takest away the sins of the world, have mercy upon us.
O Lamb of God, that takest away the sins of the world, grant us thy peace.

564 PSALM 26, verses 6–8

MINE hands in innocence, O Lord,
I'll wash and purify;
So to thine holy altar go,
And compass it will I:

2 That I, with voice of thanksgiving,
May publish and declare,
And tell of all thy mighty works,
That great and wondrous are.

3 The habitation of thy house,
Lord, I have lovèd well;
Yea, in that place I do delight
Where doth thine honour dwell.

4 *To Father, Son, and Holy Ghost,*
The God whom we adore,
Be glory, as it was, and is,
And shall be evermore. Amen.

565 PSALM 116, verses 13, 14, 17–19

I'LL of salvation take the cup,
On God's name will I call:
I'll pay my vows now to the Lord
Before his people all.

2 Thank-offerings I to thee will give,
And on God's name will call.
I'll pay my vows now to the Lord
Before his people all;

3 Within the courts of God's own house,
Within the midst of thee,
O city of Jerusalem.
Praise to the Lord give ye.

4 *To Father, Son, and Holy Ghost,*
The God whom we adore,
Be glory, as it was, and is,
And shall be evermore. Amen.

566 PSALM 24

THE earth belongs unto the Lord,
And all that it contains;
The world that is inhabited,
And all that there remains.
For the foundations of the same
He on the seas did lay,
And he hath it establishèd
Upon the floods to stay.

2 Who is the man that shall ascend
Into the hill of God?
Or who within his holy place
Shall have a firm abode?
Whose hands are clean, whose heart is pure.
And unto vanity
Who hath not lifted up his soul,
Nor sworn deceitfully.

3 This is the man who shall receive
The blessing from the Lord;
The God of his salvation shall
Him righteousness accord.
This is the generation who
Do after him inquire;
They Jacob are, who seek thy face
With their whole hearts' desire.

4 Ye gates, lift up your heads on high;
Ye doors that last for aye,
Be lifted up, that so the King
Of glory enter may.

But who of glory is the King?
The mighty Lord is this;
*Even that same Lord that great
in might
And strong in battle is.

5 Ye gates, lift up your heads; ye
doors,
Doors that do last for aye,
Be lifted up, that so the King
Of glory enter may.
But who is he that is the King,
The King of glory? who is
this?
*The Lord of hosts, and none but
he,
The King of glory is.
†(Alleluia! Amen).

Metrical Psalter, 1650 (Irish)
* These two lines are repeated.
† The Alleluia is sung five times and
the Amen three times.

567 *Schmücke dich, o liebe Seele*

DECK thyself, my soul, with
gladness,
Leave the gloomy haunts of
sadness,
Come into the daylight's splendour,
There with joy thy praises
render
Unto him whose grace un-
bounded
Hath this wondrous banquet
founded;
High o'er all the heavens he
reigneth,
Yet to dwell with thee he
deigneth.

2 Hasten as a bride to meet him,
And with loving reverence greet
him,
For with words of life im-
mortal
Now he knocketh at thy portal;
Haste to ope the gates before
him,
Saying, while thou dost adore
him,
'Suffer, Lord, that I receive
thee,
And I never more will leave
thee.'

3 Sun, who all my life dost
brighten;
Light, who dost my soul en-
lighten;
Joy, the sweetest man e'er
knoweth;
Fount, whence all my being
floweth:
At thy feet I cry, my Maker,
Let me be a fit partaker
Of this blessèd food from
heaven,
For our good, thy glory, given.

4 Jesus, Bread of Life, I pray
thee,
Let me gladly here obey thee;
Never to my hurt invited,
Be thy love with love requited:
From this banquet let me
measure,
Lord, how vast and deep its
treasure;
Through the gifts thou here
dost give me,
As thy guest in heaven receive
me.

JOHANN FRANCK, 1618–77
Tr. CATHERINE WINKWORTH
1827–78

568

FATHER most loving, listen
to thy children
Who as thy family joyfully
foregather,
Singing the praises of thy Son,
our Brother,
Jesus beloved!

2 We stand attentive, listening to
God's Gospel,
Welcoming Jesus as he speaks
among us,
Mind and heart open, ready to
receive him,
Lips to proclaim him!

3 Father in heaven, bless the gifts
we offer,
Signs of our true love, hearts in
homage given!
Make them the one gift that is
wholly worthy,
Christ, spotless victim!

4 Father, we thank thee for thy
   Son's dear presence,
Coming to feed us as the Bread
   of heaven,
Making us one with him in
   sweet communion,
One with each other!

5 *Praised be our Father, lovingly*
   inviting
Guests to this banquet, praised
   the Son who feeds us,
Praised too the Spirit, sent by
   Son and Father,
Making us Christ-like! Amen.

JAMES QUINN

569
救世之身爲
眾生擘

THE bread of life, for all men
   broken!
  He drank the cup on Golgotha.
His grace we trust, and spread
   with reverence
  This holy feast, and thus remember.

2 With godly fear we seek thy
   presence;
  Our hearts are sad, people
   distressed.
Thy holy face is stained with
   bitter tears,
  Our human pain still bearest
   thou with us.

3 O Lord, we pray, come thou
   among us,
  Lighten our eyes, brightly
   appear!
Immanuel, heav'n's joy unending,
  Our life with thine for ever
   blending.

TIMOTHY TINGFANG LEW
1891–1947
Tr. WALTER REGINALD OXENHAM
TAYLOR

570

I AM not worthy, holy Lord,
  That thou shouldst come to
   me;
Speak but the word; one
   gracious word
  Can set the sinner free.

2 I am not worthy; cold and bare
   The lodging of my soul;
How canst thou deign to enter
   there?
  Lord, speak, and make me
   whole.

3 I am not worthy; yet, my God,
   How can I say thee nay,—
Thee, who didst give thy flesh
   and blood
  My ransom price to pay?

4 O come, in this sweet morning*
   hour,
Feed me with food divine;
And fill with all thy love and
   power
  This worthless heart of mine.

HENRY WILLIAMS BAKER, 1821–77

* Or evening.

571   *Jesu, dulcedo cordium*

JESUS, thou Joy of loving
   hearts,
  Thou Fount of life, thou
   Light of men,
From the best bliss that earth
   imparts
  We turn unfilled to thee
   again.

2 Thy truth unchanged hath ever
   stood;
  Thou savest those that on
   thee call:
To them that seek thee thou
   art good,
  To them that find thee, all in
   all.

3 We taste thee, O thou living
   Bread,
  And long to feast upon thee
   still;
We drink of thee, the Fountain-
   head,
  And thirst our souls from
   thee to fill.

4 Our restless spirits yearn for
   thee,
  Where'er our changeful lot is
   cast,—
Glad when thy gracious smile
   we see,
  Blest when our faith can
   hold thee fast.

5 O Jesus, ever with us stay;
  Make all our moments calm
    and bright;
  Chase the dark night of sin away;
  Shed o'er the world thy holy
    light.

12th century
Tr. RAY PALMER, 1808–87

572

COME, risen Lord, and deign
  to be our guest;
Nay, let us be thy guests;
  the feast is thine;
Thyself at thine own board
  make manifest,
In thine own sacrament of
  bread and wine.

2 We meet, as in that upper room
    they met;
  Thou at the table, blessing,
    yet dost stand;
  'This is my body': so thou
    givest yet;
  Faith still receives the cup as
    from thy hand.

3 One body we, one body who
    partake,
  One Church united in com-
    munion blest;
  One name we bear, one bread of
    life we break,
  With all thy saints on earth
    and saints at rest.

4 One with each other, Lord, for
    one in thee,
  Who art one Saviour and one
    living Head;
  Then open thou our eyes, that
    we may see;
  Be known to us in breaking
    of the bread.

GEORGE WALLACE BRIGGS
1875-1959
altered

573   *Before Communion*

HERE, O my Lord, I see
  thee face to face;
Here would I touch and
  handle things unseen,
Here grasp with firmer hand
  the eternal grace,
And all my weariness upon
  thee lean.

2 Mine is the sin, but thine the
    righteousness;
  Mine is the guilt, but thine
    the cleansing blood;
  Here is my robe, my refuge, and
    my peace—
  Thy blood, thy righteousness,
  O Lord my God.

3 Here would I feed upon the
    bread of God,
  Here drink with thee the
    royal wine of heaven;
  Here would I lay aside each
    earthly load,
  Here taste afresh the calm of
    sin forgiven.

4 This is the hour of banquet and
    of song;
  This is the heavenly table
    spread for me;
  Here let me feast, and, feasting,
    still prolong
  The hallowed hour of fellow-
    ship with thee.

After Communion

5 Too soon we rise; the symbols
    disappear;
  The feast, though not the
    love, is past and gone;
  The bread and wine remove,
    but thou art here,
  Nearer than ever, still my
    Shield and Sun.

6 I have no help but thine; nor
    do I need
  Another arm save thine to
    lean upon;
  It is enough, my Lord, enough
    indeed;
  My strength is in thy might,
    thy might alone.

7 Feast after feast thus comes
    and passes by,
  Yet, passing, points to the
    glad feast above,
  Giving sweet foretaste of the
    festal joy,
  The Lamb's great bridal
    feast of bliss and love.

HORATIUS BONAR, 1808–89
Order of verses altered

574

BREAD of the world, in
mercy broken,
Wine of the soul, in mercy shed,
By whom the words of life were
spoken,
And in whose death our sins
are dead:
Look on the heart by sorrow
broken,
Look on the tears by sinners
shed;
And be thy feast to us the token
That by thy grace our souls
are fed.

REGINALD HEBER, 1783–1826

575

THOU standest at the altar,
Thou   offerest   every
prayer;
In faith's unclouded vision
We see thee ever there.

2 Out of thy hand the incense
Ascends before the throne,
Where thou art interceding,
Lord Jesus, for thine own.

3 And, through thy blood ac-
cepted,
With thee we keep the feast:
Thou art the one Oblation;
Thou only art the Priest.

4 We come, O only Saviour;
On thee, the Lamb, we feed:
Thy flesh is bread from heaven;
Thy blood is drink indeed.

5 To thee, Almighty Father;
Incarnate Son, to thee;
To thee, Anointing Spirit,—
All praise and glory be. Amen.

EDWARD WILTON EDDIS
1825–1905, altered

576

O CHRIST, who sinless art
alone,
Our frailty and our sin who
knowest,
We stand in thee before the
throne
And plead the death thou
showest.

2 O Christ, our Sacrifice and
Priest,
Who in the glory intercedest,
We in the shadow keep the feast
And show the death thou
pleadest.

3 To thee in endless life enthroned,
O Christ, eternal praise be
given,
With Holy Ghost and Father
owned
One God in earth and heaven.
Amen.

ARTHUR WELLESLEY WOTHERSPOON
1853–1936

577

Σιγησάτω πᾶσα σὰρξ
βροτεία

LET all mortal flesh keep
silence,
And with fear and trembling
stand;
Ponder nothing earthly-minded,
For with blessing in his hand
Christ our God to earth de-
scendeth,
Our full homage to demand.

2 King of kings, yet born of
Mary,
As of old on earth he stood,
Lord of lords, in human ves-
ture—
In the body and the blood—
He will give to all the faithful
His own self for heavenly food.

3 Rank on rank the host of
heaven
Spreads its vanguard on the
way,
As the Light of light descendeth
From the realms of endless
day,
That the powers of hell may
vanish
As the darkness clears away.

4 At his feet the six-winged
Seraph;
Cherubim with sleepless eye,
Veil their faces to the Presence,
As with ceaseless voice they
cry,
'Alleluia, Alleluia,
Alleluia, Lord most high'.

Liturgy of St. James
Tr. GERARD MOULTRIE, 1829–85

578 *Pange, lingua, gloriosi*
Corporis mysterium

†NOW, my tongue, the mys-
tery telling
Of the glorious Body sing,
And the Blood, all price ex-
celling,
Which the Gentiles' Lord and
King,
In a Virgin's womb once
dwelling,
Shed for this world's ransom-
ing.

2 That last night, at supper
lying,
'Mid the Twelve, his chosen
band,
Jesus, with the law complying
Keeps the feast its rites demand;
Then, more precious food
supplying,
Gives himself with his own
hand.

3 Word-made-flesh, true bread
he maketh
By his word his Flesh to be,
Wine his Blood; which whoso
taketh
Must from carnal thoughts be
free;
Faith alone, though sight for-
saketh,
Shows true hearts the mystery.

---

*4 Therefore we, before him bend-
ing,
This great sacrament revere;
Types and shadows have their
ending,
For the newer rite is here;
Faith, our outward sense be-
friending,
Makes our inward vision
clear.

5 Unto God be praise and honour:
*To the Father, to the Son,
To the mighty Spirit, glory—*
Ever Three and ever One:
Power and glory in the highest
While eternal ages run. Amen.

ST. THOMAS AQUINAS
1227–74
Tr. EDWARD CASWALL, 1814–78
and Compilers of
Hymns Ancient and Modern, 1861

† *The pointing is for use with tune (i)*
PANGE LINGUA *only.*
* *Verses 4, 5 may be sung to* TANTUM
ERGO SACRAMENTUM, *no. 373.*

579

ALMIGHTY Father, Lord
most high,
Who madest all, who fillest all,
Thy Name we praise and
magnify,
For all our needs on thee we call.

2 We offer to thee of thine own,
Ourselves and all that we can
bring,
In bread and cup before thee
shown,
Our universal offering.

3 All that we have we bring to
thee,
Yet all is naught when all is
done,
Save that in it thy love can see
The sacrifice of thy dear Son.

4 By his command in bread and
cup
His body and his blood we
plead;
What on the cross he offered up
Is here our sacrifice indeed.

5 For all thy gifts of life and
grace,
Here we thy servants humbly
pray
That thou wouldst look upon
the face
Of thine anointed Son today.

VINCENT STUCKEY STRATTON
COLES, 1845–1929

580

AND now, O Father, mindful of the love
That bought us, once for all, on Calvary's Tree,
And having with us him that pleads above,
We here present, we here spread forth to thee
That only offering perfect in thine eyes,
The one true, pure, immortal sacrifice.

2 Look, Father, look on his anointed face,
And only look on us as found in him;
Look not on our misusings of thy grace,
Our prayer so languid, and our faith so dim:
For lo! between our sins and their reward
We set the Passion of thy Son our Lord.

3 And then for those, our dearest and our best,
By this their prevailing presence we appeal;
O fold them closer to thy mercy's breast,
O do thine utmost for their souls' true weal;
From tainting mischief keep them white and clear,
And crown thy gifts with strength to persevere.

4 And so we come: O draw us to thy feet,
Most patient Saviour, who canst love us still;
And by this food, so awesome and so sweet,
Deliver us from every touch of ill:
In thine own service make us glad and free,
And grant us never more to part with thee.

WILLIAM BRIGHT, 1824–1901
Based on *Unde et memores, Domine, nos servi tui*

581   *Verbum supernum prodiens, nec Patris*

FORTH from on high the Father sends
His Son, who yet stays by his side.
The Word made man for man then spends
His life till life's last eventide.

2 While Judas plans the traitor's sign,
The mocking kiss that Love betrays,
Jesus in form of bread and wine
His loving sacrifice displays.

3 He gives himself that faith may see
The heavenly Food on which men feed,
That flesh and blood of man may be
Fed by his flesh and blood indeed.

4 By birth he makes himself man's kin;
As Food before his guests he lies;
To death he bears man's cross of sin;
In heaven he reigns as man's blest prize.

5 O Priest and Victim, Lord of Life,
Throw wide the gates of Paradise!
We face our foes in mortal strife;
Thou art our strength! O heed our cries!

6 *To Father, Son, and Spirit blest,*
One only God, be ceaseless praise!
May he in goodness grant us rest
In heaven, our home, for endless days! Amen.

JAMES QUINN
From the Latin of
ST. THOMAS AQUINAS, 1227–74

582

IN love, from love, thou camest forth, O Lord,
Sent from the Father, his incarnate Word;

That in that perfect Name, by
thee confessed,
Our hearts with thine might
find their perfect rest.

2 Within the veil, thy mortal
travail o'er,
Thou livest unto God to die no
more;
And now, made sons of God,
with thee we stand,
Girt with the grace of thy confirming hand.

3 Thou art our Royal Priest before the throne;
Our priesthood is in thee, from
thee alone;
In thee we offer at our Father's
feet
The offering pure, with holy
incense sweet.

4 The sacred rite its ordered
course hath run,
All that thy Love ordained our
love hath done,
Still showing forth before our
Father's eyes
The one, pure, perfect, filial
sacrifice.

5 And now, O Lord, from out thy
chosen place
Thy voice proclaims anew the
feast of grace.
Cleanse thou us, Lord, in this
most holy hour
By thine own breath of resurrection power.

6 Lord of the living and the tran-
quil dead,
Reveal thyself, our one all-
glorious Head;
And through these hallowed
gifts of bread and wine
Feed thy one Body with the
Life divine.

7 O perfect Brother, and true
Son of God,
Impart to us thy Body and thy
Blood,
That through communion of
one mind, one heart,
We may advance to see thee
as thou art.

8 *Jesus, Immanuel, evermore
adored,
At thy great Name we bow, we
own thee Lord:
Glory be thine, O Father, thine,
O Son,
And thine, O Holy Spirit, ever
One.* Amen.
JOHN MacLEOD, 1840–98

583

LORD, enthroned in heavenly
splendour,
First-begotten from the dead,
Thou alone, our strong defender,
Liftest up thy people's head.
Alleluia! Alleluia!
Jesus, true and living Bread.

2 Here our humblest homage pay
we;
Here in loving reverence
bow;
Here for faith's discernment
pray we,
Lest we fail to know thee
now.
Alleluia! Alleluia!
Thou art here, we ask not
how.

3 Though the lowliest form doth
veil thee,
As of old in Bethlehem,
Here as there thine angels hail
thee,
Branch and Flower of Jesse's
stem.
Alleluia! Alleluia!
We in worship join with
them.

4 Paschal Lamb, thine offering,
finished
Once for all when thou wast
slain,
In its fullness undiminished
Shall for evermore remain,
Alleluia! Alleluia!
Cleansing souls from every
stain.

5 Life-imparting, heavenly
Manna,
Stricken Rock with stream-
ing side,

Heaven and earth with loud
   hosanna
Worship thee, the Lamb who
   died,
    Alleluia! Alleluia!
   Risen, ascended, glorified.

GEORGE HUGH BOURNE, 1840-1925

584 *Adoro te devote, latens*
Deitas

THEE we adore, O hidden
   Saviour, thee,
Who in thy sacrament dost
   deign to be:
Both flesh and spirit at thy
   presence fail,
Yet here thy presence we de-
   voutly hail.

2 O blest memorial of our dying
   Lord!
Thou living Bread, who life dost
   here afford,
O may our souls for ever live
   by thee,
And thou to us for ever precious
   be.

3 Fountain of goodness, Jesus,
   Lord, and God,
Cleanse us, unclean, with thy
   most cleansing blood;
Make us in thee devoutly to
   believe,
In thee to hope, to thee in love
   to cleave.

4 O Christ, whom now beneath a
   veil we see,
May what we thirst for soon our
   portion be,
There in the glory of thy dwelling-place
To gaze on thee unveiled, and
   see thy face.

ST. THOMAS AQUINAS, 1227-74
Tr. JAMES RUSSELL WOODFORD
1820-85, altered

585

ACCORDING to thy gracious
   word,
In meek humility,
This will I do, my dying Lord,
   I will remember thee.

2 Thy body, broken for my sake,
   My bread from heaven shall
   be;
Thy testamental cup I take,
   And thus remember thee.

3 Gethsemane can I forget?
   Or there thy conflict see,
Thine agony and bloody sweat,
   And not remember thee?

4 When to the cross I turn mine
   eyes,
   And rest on Calvary,
O Lamb of God, my sacrifice,
   I must remember thee,—

5 Remember thee, and all thy
   pains,
   And all thy love to me;
Yea, while a breath, a pulse re-
   mains,
   Will I remember thee.

6 And when these failing lips
   grow dumb,
   And mind and memory flee,
When thou shalt in thy King-
   dom come,
   Jesus, remember me.

JAMES MONTGOMERY, 1771-1854

586

FATHER, we thank thee who
   hast planted
Thy holy name within our
   hearts,
Knowledge and faith and life
   immortal
Jesus thy Son to us imparts.

2 Thou, Lord, didst make all for
   thy pleasure,
Didst give man food for all
   his days,
Giving in Christ the bread
   eternal;
Thine is the power, be thine
   the praise.

3 Watch o'er thy Church, O Lord,
 in mercy,
 Save it from evil, guard it
  still,
Perfect it in thy love, unite it,
 Cleansed and conformed unto
  thy will.

4 As grain, once scattered on the
 hillsides,
 Was in the bread we break
  made one,
So may thy world-wide Church
 be gathered
 Into thy Kingdom by thy
  Son.

From prayers in the *Didache*, probably
second century. Tr. and versified by
FRANCIS BLAND TUCKER
altered

587

AUTHOR of life divine,
 Who hast a table spread,
Furnished with mystic wine
 And everlasting bread,
Preserve the life thyself hast
 given,
And feed and train us up for
 heaven.

2 Our needy souls sustain
 With fresh supplies of love,
Till all thy life we gain,
 And all thy fullness prove,
And, strengthened by thy per-
 fect grace,
Behold without a veil thy face.

CHARLES WESLEY, 1707–88

588

ܢܒܝܠܐ ܦܢܝ ܐܬܘܐ ܘܦܚܝܬܐ

STRENGTHEN for service,
 Lord, the hands
That holy things have taken;
Let ears that now have heard
 thy songs
To clamour never waken.

2 Lord, may the tongues which
 'Holy' sang
Keep free from all deceiving;
The eyes which saw thy love be
 bright,
Thy blessèd hope perceiving.

3 The feet that tread thy holy
 courts
 From light do thou not
  banish;
The bodies by thy body fed
 With thy new life replenish.

Liturgy of Malabar
Tr. CHARLES WILLIAM HUMPHREYS
1840–1921
PERCY DEARMER, 1867–1936
and others

589

FORTH in the peace of Christ
 we go;
Christ to the world with joy we
 bring;
Christ in our minds, Christ on
 our lips,
Christ in our hearts, the world's
 true King.

2 King of our hearts, Christ
 makes us kings;
Kingship with him his servants
 gain;
With Christ, the Servant-Lord
 of all,
Christ's world we serve to
 share Christ's reign.

3 Priests of the world, Christ
 sends us forth
The world of time to consecrate,
The world of sin by grace to
 heal,
Christ's world in Christ to re-
 create.

4 Christ's are our lips, his word
 we speak;
Prophets are we whose deeds
 proclaim
Christ's truth in love that we
 may be
Christ in the world, to spread
 Christ's name.

5 We are the Church; Christ bids
 us show
That in his Church all nations
 find
Their hearth and home where
 Christ restores
True peace, true love, to all
 mankind.

JAMES QUINN

590 PARAPHRASE 38, verses 8, 10, 11

NOW, Lord! according to thy word,
Let me in peace depart;
Mine eyes have thy salvation seen,
And gladness fills my heart.

2 This great salvation, long prepared,
And now disclosed to view,
Hath proved thy love was constant still,
And promises were true.

3 That Sun I now behold, whose light
Shall heathen darkness chase,
And rays of brightest glory pour
Around thy chosen race.

4 *To Father, Son, and Holy Ghost,*
The God whom we adore,
Be glory, as it was, and is,
And shall be evermore. Amen.

Scottish Paraphrases, 1781
From St. Luke 2:29–32

The following are also suitable

V

OTHER ORDINANCES

CONFIRMATION

591   PARAPHRASE 54

I'M not ashamed to own my
   Lord,
  Or to defend his cause,
Maintain the glory of his cross,
  And honour all his laws.

2 Jesus, my Lord! I know his
   Name,
  His Name is all my boast;
Nor will he put my soul to
   shame,
  Nor let my hope be lost.

3 I know that safe with him re-
   mains,
  Protected by his power,
What I've committed to his
   trust,
  Till the decisive hour.

4 Then will he own his servant's
   name
  Before his Father's face,
And in the New Jerusalem
  Appoint my soul a place.

Scottish Paraphrases, 1781
From 2 Timothy 1:12

592

WE come, O Christ, to thee,
   True Son of God and man,
By whom all things consist,
  In whom all life began:
In thee alone we live and move,
And have our being in thy love.

2 Thou art the way to God,
  Thy blood our ransom paid;
In thee we face our Judge
  And Maker unafraid.
Before the throne absolved we
   stand:
Thy love has met thy law's
  demand.

3 Thou art the living truth!
  All wisdom dwells in thee,
Thou source of every skill,
  Eternal verity!
Thou great I AM! In thee we
   rest,
True answer to our every quest.

4 Thou only art true life,
  To know thee is to live
The more abundant life
  That earth can never give:
O risen Lord! We live in thee
And thou in us eternally!

5 We worship thee, Lord Christ,
  Our Saviour and our King,
To thee our youth and strength
  Adoringly we bring:
So fill our hearts that men may
   see
Thy life in us and turn to thee!

EDITH MARGARET CLARKSON

593

YE that know the Lord is
   gracious,
  Ye for whom a Corner-stone
Stands, of God elect and pre-
   cious,
    Laid that ye may build
     thereon,
See that on that sure founda-
   tion
  Ye a living temple raise,
Towers that may tell forth
   salvation,
    Walls that may re-echo
     praise.

2 Living stones, by God ap-
   pointed
  Each to his allotted place,
Kings and priests, by God
   anointed,
  Shall ye not declare his grace?

Ye, a royal generation,
　Tell the tidings of your birth,
Tidings of a new creation
　To an old and weary earth.

3 Tell the praise of him who
　　called you
　Out of darkness into light,
Broke the fetters that en-
　　thralled you,
　Gave you freedom, peace
　　and sight:
Tell the tale of sins forgiven,
　Strength renewed and hope
　　restored,
Till the earth, in tune with
　　heaven,
　Praise and magnify the Lord!

CYRIL ARGENTINE ALINGTON
1872–1955
From 1 Peter 2:3–10

594

WITNESS, ye men and
　angels, now,
Before the Lord we speak;
To him we make our solemn
　vow,
A vow we dare not break;

2 That, long as life itself shall last,
　Ourselves to Christ we yield;
Nor from his cause will we de-
　part,
　Or ever quit the field.

3 We trust not in our native
　strength,
　But on his grace rely,
That, with returning wants,
　the Lord
　Will all our need supply.

4 O guide our doubtful feet aright,
　And keep us in thy ways;
And while we turn our vows to
　prayers,
　Turn thou our prayers to
　praise.

BENJAMIN BEDDOME, 1717–95

595

WE magnify thy Name, O
　God,
That to thy people thou hast
　given
A covenant sign eternal.
Baptized into the Triune Name
Of Father, Son, and Holy
　Ghost
Thou didst them seal for ever.

2 Nurtured within thy family,
　Thy servants now proclaim to
　all
　Their faith in Christ their
　Saviour.
Confirm and strengthen them,
　O God,
Increase in them the Spirit's
　grace;
Grant them thy benediction.

3 May they, at Christ's own Table,
　be
Partakers of his flesh and blood
With grateful adoration.
May they in all things live like
　Christ,
And thereby witness to all men
That he is Lord eternal.

JOHN MONTEITH BARKLEY

The following are also suitable
Nos. 629, 342, 550 and hymns from section III, nos. 387–488.

ORDINATION

596　PSALM 103, verses 19–22

THE Lord prepared hath his
　throne
　In heavens firm to stand;
And every thing that being
　hath
　His kingdom doth command.

2 O ye his angels, that excel
　In strength, bless ye the
　Lord;
Ye who obey what he com-
　mands,
　And hearken to his word.

3 O bless and magnify the Lord,
   Ye glorious hosts of his:
Ye ministers, that do fulfil
Whate'er his pleasure is.

4 O bless the Lord, all ye his
      works,
   Wherewith the world is
      stored
In his dominions everywhere.
   My soul, bless thou the Lord.

5 *To Father, Son, and Holy Ghost,*
   The God whom we adore,
Be glory, as it was, and is,
   And shall be evermore. Amen.

597

POUR out thy Spirit from
      on high;
   Lord, thine ordainèd servants
      bless;
Graces and gifts to each supply,
   And clothe thy priests with
      righteousness.

2 Within thy temple when they
      stand,
   To teach the truth, as taught
      by thee,

Saviour, like stars in thy right
      hand
   The angels of the churches
      be!

3 Wisdom and zeal and faith im-
      part,
   Firmness with meekness,
      from above,
To bear thy people on their
      heart,
   And love the souls whom
      thou dost love.

4 To watch and pray, and never
      faint;
   By day and night strict
      guard to keep;
To warn the sinner, cheer
      the saint,
   Nourish thy lambs, and feed
      thy sheep;

5 Then, when their work is
      finished here,
   In humble hope their charge
      resign.
When the Chief Shepherd shall
      appear,
   O God, may they and we be
      thine.

JAMES MONTGOMERY, 1771–1854
The following is also suitable
No. 342 Come, Holy Ghost, our souls
inspire

MARRIAGE

598

PSALM 67

GOD be merciful unto ' us
   and ' bless us : and cause
his ' face to ' shine up- ' on
   us :
That thy way may be ' known
   upon ' earth : thy ' saving '
   health a- ' mong all ' nations.

2 Let the people ' praise thee
   O ' God : let ' all the ' people '
   praise thee :
O let the nations be glad
   and ' sing for ' joy : for thou
   shalt judge the people
   righteously and ' govern
   the ' nations up · on ' earth.

3 Let the people ' praise thee
   O ' God : let ' all the '
   people ' praise thee :
Then shall the earth ' yield
   her ' increase : and God
   even ' our own ' God shall '
   bless us.

†4 God ' shall ' bless us : and all
   the ' ends of the ' earth
   shall ' fear him.

Glory ' be to the ' Father : and
   to the Son ' and to the '
   Holy ' Ghost
As it ' was in the be- ' ginning:
   is now and ever shall be '
   world without ' end.
         A- ' men.
   † *Second half of Chant*

599

O FATHER, by whose
  sovereign sway
The sun and stars in order
  move,
Yet who hast made us bold to
  say
Thy nature and thy Name is
  love:

2 O royal Son, whose every deed
  Showed love and love's
    divinity,
Yet didst not scorn the hum-
    blest need
  At Cana's feast in Galilee:

3 O Holy Spirit, who dost speak
  In saint and sage since time
    began,
Yet givest courage to the weak
  And teachest love to selfish
    man:

4 Be present in our hearts today,
  All powerful to bless, and give
To these thy children grace
    that they
  May love, and through their
    loving live.

CYRIL ARGENTINE ALINGTON
1872–1955

600

O FATHER, all creating,
  Whose wisdom, love, and
    power
First bound two lives together
  In Eden's primal hour,
The lives of these thy children
  With thy best gifts endue,
A home by thee made happy,
  A love by thee kept true.

2 O Saviour, Guest most boun-
    teous
  Of old in Galilee,
Vouchsafe today thy presence
  With these who call on thee;
Their store of earthly gladness
  Transform to heavenly wine,
And teach them, in the tasting,
  To know the gift is thine.

3 O Spirit of the Father,
  Breathe on them from above,
So mighty in thy pureness,
  So tender in thy love;
That, guarded by thy presence,
  From sin and strife kept free,
Their lives may own thy
    guidance,
  Their hearts be ruled by
    thee.

4 Except thou build it, Father,
  The house is built in vain;
Except thou, Saviour, bless it,
  The joy will turn to pain;
But naught can break the union
  Of hearts in thee made one;
And love thy Spirit hallows
  Is endless love begun.

JOHN ELLERTON, 1826–93, altered

601

O GOD, whose loving hand
  has led
Thy children to this joyful day,
We pray that thou wilt bless
  them now
As, one in thee, they face life's
  way.

2 Grant them the will to follow
  Christ
Who graced the Feast in Galilee,
And through his perfect life of
  love
Fulfilment of their love to see.

3 Give them the power to make
  a home
Where peace and honour shall
  abide,
Where Christ shall be the
  gracious Head,
The trusted Friend, the constant Guide.

4 *To Father, Son, and Holy Ghost,*
  The God whom heaven and earth
    adore,
Be glory, as it was of old,
  Is now, and shall be evermore.
    Amen.

JOHN BOYD MOORE

217

602

O GOD of Love, to thee we
    bow,
And pray for these before thee
    now,
That, closely knit in holy vow,
    They may in thee be one.

2 When days are filled with pure
    delight,
When paths are plain and skies
    are bright,
Walking by faith and not by
    sight,
    May they in thee be one.

3 When stormy winds fulfil thy
    will,
And all their good seems turned
    to ill,

Then, trusting thee completely,
    still
May they in thee be one.

4 Whate'er in life shall be their
    share
Of quickening joy or burdening
    care,
In power to do and grace to
    bear,
May they in thee be one.

5 Eternal Love, with them abide;
In thee for ever may they hide,
For even death cannot divide
    Those whom thou makest
    one.

WILLIAM VAUGHAN JENKINS
1868-1920
The following are also suitable
Nos. 9, 115, 368, 388, 457, 360, 634

FUNERAL SERVICES

603 PSALM 103, verses 13–17

S UCH pity as a father hath
    Unto his children dear;
Like pity shows the Lord to
    such
    As worship him in fear.

2 For he remembers we are dust,
    And he our frame well knows.
Frail man, his days are like the
    grass,
    As flower in field he grows:

3 For over it the wind doth pass,
    And it away is gone;
And of the place where once it
    was
    . It shall no more be known.

4 But unto them that do him fear
    God's mercy never ends;
And to their children's children
    still
    His righteousness extends.

5 *To Father, Son, and Holy Ghost,*
    The God whom we adore,
Be glory, as it was, and is,
    And shall be evermore. Amen.

604

G O, happy soul, thy days are
    ended,
    Thy pilgrimage on earth
    below:
Go, by angelic guard attended,
    To God's own Paradise now
    go.

2 Go; Christ, the Shepherd good,
    befriend thee,
    Who gave his life thy soul to
    win;
'Tis even he that shall defend
    thee,
    Thy going out and coming in.

3 Go forth in peace: farewell to
    sadness:
    May rest in Paradise be
    thine;
In Jesus' presence there is glad-
    ness:
    Light everlasting on the
    shine.

GEORGE RATCLIFFE WOODW
1840
and Com
The BBC H

605 *Jesus lebt, mit ihm auch ich*

JESUS lives! thy terrors now
  Can, O Death, no more
  appal us;
Jesus lives! by this we know
  Thou, O grave, canst not
  enthral us.

Alleluia!

2 Jesus lives! henceforth is death
  But the gate of life immortal;
This shall calm our trembling
    breath
  When we pass its gloomy
    portal.

3 Jesus lives! for us he died;
  Then, alone to Jesus living,
Pure in heart may we abide,
  Glory to our Saviour giving.

4 Jesus lives! our hearts know
    well
  Naught from us his love shall
    sever;
Life, nor death, nor powers of
    hell
  Tear us from his keeping ever.

5 Jesus lives! to him the throne
  Over heaven and earth is
    given;
May we go where he is gone,
  Live and reign with him in
    heaven.

CHRISTIAN FÜRCHTEGOTT GELLERT
1715–69
Tr. FRANCES ELIZABETH COX
1812–97

606

O LORD of life, where'er they
    be,
Safe in thine own eternity,
Our dead are living unto thee.
Alleluia! Alleluia! Alleluia!

All souls are thine, and, here or
    there,
  They rest within thy sheltering
    care,
  A providence alike they
    share.

3 Thy word is true, thy ways are
    just;
  Above the requiem, 'Dust to
    dust',
Shall rise our psalm of grateful
    trust,

4 O happy they in God who rest,
  No more by fear and doubt
    oppressed;
Living or dying, they are blest:

FREDERICK LUCIAN HOSMER
1840–1929

607

GOD of the living, in whose
    eyes
Unveiled thy whole creation
    lies,
All souls are thine; we must not
    say
That those are dead who pass
    away;
From this our world of flesh
    set free,
We know them living unto thee.

2 Released from earthly toil and
    strife,
  With thee is hidden still their
    life;
Thine are their thoughts, their
    works, their powers,
All thine, and yet most truly
    ours;
For well we know, where'er
    they be,
Our dead are living unto thee.

JOHN ELLERTON, 1826–93

608

THERE is a blessèd home
    beyond this land of woe,
Where trials never come,
    nor tears of sorrow flow;
Where faith is lost in sight,
    and patient hope is crowned,
And everlasting light
    its glory throws around.

219

2 O joy all joys beyond!
　　to see the Lamb who died,
For ever there enthroned,
　　for ever glorified;
To give to him the praise
　　of every triumph won,
And sing, through endless days,
　　the great things he hath
　　done.

3 *There is a land of peace;*
　　the angels know it well;
Glad songs that never cease
　　within its portals swell;
Around its glorious throne
　　ten thousand saints adore
Christ, with the Father one
　　and Spirit, evermore. Amen.

HENRY WILLIAMS BAKER
1821–77

DEDICATION OF CHURCH BUILDINGS

609

THIS stone to thee in faith
　　we lay;
　We build the temple, Lord,
　　to thee:
Thine eye be open, night and
　　day,
　To guard this house and
　　sanctuary.

2 Here, when thy people seek thy
　　face,
　And dying sinners pray to
　　live,
Hear thou, in heaven thy
　　dwelling-place,
　And when thou hearest, O
　　forgive!

3 Here, when thy messengers pro-
　　claim
　The blessèd Gospel of thy
　　Son,
Still, by the power of his great
　　Name,
　Be mighty signs and wonders
　　done.

4 'Hosanna!' to their heavenly
　　King
　When children's voices raise
　　that song,
'Hosanna!' let their angels sing,
　And heaven, with earth, the
　　strain prolong.

5 But will the eternal Father
　　deign
　Here to abide, no transient
　　guest?
Will here the world's Re-
　　deemer reign,
　And here the Holy Spirit
　　rest?

6 That glory never hence depart!
　　Yet choose not, Lord, this
　　house alone;
Thy Kingdom come to every
　　heart:
　In all the world be thine the
　　throne.

JAMES MONTGOMERY, 1771–1854
altered

610

ALL things are thine; no gift
　　have we,
Lord of all gifts, to offer thee:
And hence with grateful hearts
　　today,
Thine own before thy feet we lay.

2 Thy will was in the builders'
　　thought;
Thy hand unseen amidst us
　　wrought;
Through mortal motive, scheme
　　and plan,
Thy wise eternal purpose ran.

3 In weakness and in want we call
On thee for whom the heavens
　　are small;
Thy glory is thy children's good,
Thy joy thy tender Father-hood.

4 O Father, deign these walls to
　　bless;
Fill with thy love their empti-
　　ness;
And let their door a gateway be
To lead us from ourselves to
　　thee.

JOHN GREENLEAF WHITTIER
1807–92

The following is also suitable
No.10 Christ is made the sure foundation

VI

TIMES AND SEASONS

NEW YEAR

611

O GOD, our help in ages past,
  Our hope for years to
    come,
Our shelter from the stormy
    blast,
  And our eternal home!

2 Under the shadow of thy throne
  Thy saints have dwelt secure;
Sufficient is thine arm alone,
  And our defence is sure.

3 Before the hills in order stood,
  Or earth received her frame,
From everlasting thou art God,
  To endless years the same.

4 A thousand ages in thy sight
  Are like an evening gone;
Short as the watch that ends the
    night
Before the rising sun.

5 Time, like an ever-rolling
    stream,
  Bears all its sons away;
They fly forgotten, as a dream
  Dies at the opening day.

6 O God, our help in ages past,
  Our hope for years to come,
Be thou our guard while
    troubles last,
  And our eternal home.
           ISAAC WATTS, 1674–1748

612

FOR thy mercy and thy grace,
  Faithful through another
    year,
Hear our song of thankfulness;
  Jesus, our Redeemer, hear.

2 Lo! our sins on thee we cast,
  Thee, our perfect sacrifice,
And, forgetting all the past,
  Press towards our glorious
    prize.

3 Dark the future; let thy light
  Guide us, Bright and Morning
    Star;
Fierce our foes, and hard the
    fight;
  Arm us, Saviour, for the war.

4 In our weakness and distress,
  Rock of strength, be thou our
    stay;
In the pathless wilderness
  Be our true and living way.

5 Keep us faithful, keep us pure,
  Keep us evermore thine own;
Help, O help us to endure;
  Fit us for the promised
    crown.
        HENRY DOWNTON, 1818–85

613

GREAT God, we sing that
  mighty hand
By which supported still we
    stand;
The opening year thy mercy
    shows,
And mercy crowns its lingering
  close.

2 By day, by night, at home,
    abroad,
Still are we guarded by our
    God,
By his incessant bounty fed,
By his unerring counsel led.

3 With grateful hearts the past we
    own;
The future, all to us unknown,
We   to   thy   guardian   care
    commit,
And peaceful leave before thy
    feet.

4 In scenes exalted or depressed
Thou art our joy, and thou our
    rest;
Thy goodness all our hopes shall
    raise,
Adored through all our chang-
    ing days.

5 When death shall interrupt
    these songs,
And seal in silence mortal
    tongues,
Our helper God, in whom we
    trust,
Shall keep our souls and guard
    our dust.

PHILIP DODDRIDGE, 1702–51

614

MARCH on, my soul, with
    strength,
    March forward, void of fear;
He who hath led will lead,
    While year succeedeth year;
And as thou goest on thy way,
* His hand shall hold thee day by
    day.

2 March on, my soul, with
    strength,
    In ease thou dar'st not dwell;
High duty calls thee forth;
    Then up, and quit thee well!
Take up thy cross, take up thy
    sword,
And fight the battles of thy
    Lord!

3 March on, my soul, with
    strength,
    With strength, but not thine
    own;
The conquest thou shalt gain,
    Through Christ thy Lord
    alone;
His grace shall nerve thy feeble
    arm,
His love preserve thee safe from
    harm.

4 March   on,   my   soul,   with
    strength,
    From strength to strength
    march on;
Warfare shall end at length,
    All foes be overthrown.
Then, O my soul, if faithful
    now,
The crown of life awaits thy
    brow.

WILLIAM WRIGHT, 1859–1924

* The last line of each verse is repeated

615

HEAVENLY Father, thou
    hast brought us
    Safely to the present day,
Gently leading on our foot-
    steps,
    Watching o'er us all the way.
Friend and Guide through life's
    long journey,
    Grateful hearts to thee we
    bring;
But for love so true and change-
    less
    How shall we fit praises sing?

2 Mercies new and never-failing
    Brightly shine through all
    the past,
Watchful   care   and   loving-
    kindness,
    Always near from first to
    last,
Tender love, divine protection
    Ever with us day and night;
Blessings more than we can
    number
    Strew the path with golden
    light.

3 Shadows deep have crossed our
    pathway;
    We have trembled in the
    storm;
Clouds have gathered round so
    darkly
    That we could not see thy
    form;
Yet thy love hath never left us
    In our griefs alone to be,
And the help each gave the
    other
    Was the strength that came
    from thee.

4 Many that we loved have left
    us,
  Reaching first their journey's
    end;
Now they wait to give us wel-
    come—
  Brother, sister, child, and
    friend.
When at last our journey's
    over,
  And we pass away from
    sight,
Father, take us through the
    darkness
  Into everlasting light.

HESTER PERIAM HAWKINS
1846-1928

616

AT thy feet, our God and
   Father,
  Who hast blessed us all our
    days,
We with grateful hearts would
   gather,
  To begin the year with
    praise,—

Praise for light so brightly
   shining
  On our steps from heaven
    above,
Praise for mercies daily twining
  Round us golden cords of love.

2 Jesus, for thy love most tender,
  On the cross for sinners
    shown,
We would praise thee, and sur-
   render
  All our hearts to be thine own.
With so blest a Friend provided,
  We upon our way would go,
Sure of being safely guided,
  Guarded well from every foe.

3 Every day will be the brighter
  When thy gracious face we see;
Every burden will be lighter
  When we know it comes from
    thee.
Spread thy love's broad banner
   o'er us;
  Give us strength to serve and
    wait,
Till the glory breaks before us,
  Through the city's open gate.

JAMES DRUMMOND BURNS
1823-64

SPRING

617 PSALM 145 (ii), verses 9,
          10, 15, 16

GOOD unto all men is the
   Lord:
O'er all his works his mercy is.
Thy works all praise to thee
   afford:
Thy saints, O Lord, thy Name
   shall bless.

2 The eyes of all things, Lord,
   attend,
And on thee wait that here do
   live,
And thou, in season due, dost
   send
Sufficient food them to relieve.

3 Yea, thou thine hand dost open
   wide,
And every thing dost satisfy
That lives, and doth on earth
   abide,
Of thy great liberality.

4 *To Father, Son, and Holy Ghost,*
  The God whom earth and heaven
   adore,
Be glory, as it was of old,
  Is now, and shall be evermore.
            Amen.

618

THE glory of the spring how
   sweet!
  The new-born life how glad!
What joy the happy earth to
   greet,
  In new, bright raiment clad!

2 Divine Renewer, thee I bless;
  I greet thy going forth;
I love thee in the lovelinesss
  Of thy renewèd earth.

3 But O these wonders of thy grace,
These nobler works of thine,
These marvels sweeter far to trace,
These new births more divine,

4 This new-born glow of faith so strong,
This bloom of love so fair,
This new-born ecstasy of song,
And fragrancy of prayer!

5 Creator Spirit, work in me
These wonders sweet of thine;
Divine Renewer, graciously
Renew this heart of mine.

THOMAS HORNBLOWER GILL
1819–1906

619

BY the rutted roads we follow,
Fallow fields are rested now;
All along the waking country
Soil is waiting for the plough.

2 In the yard the plough is ready,
Ready to the ploughman's hand,
Ready for the crow-straight furrow,
Farmer's sign across God's land.

3 God, in this good land you lend us,
Bless the service of the share;
Light our thinking with your wisdom,
Plant your patience in our care.

4 This is first of all man's labours,
Man must always plough the earth;
God, be with us at the ploughing,
Touch our harvest at its birth.

JOHN ARLOTT

620

Wir pflügen und wir streuen

WE plough the fields, and scatter
The good seed on the land,
But it is fed and watered
By God's almighty hand;

He sends the snow in winter,
The warmth to swell the grain,
The breezes and the sunshine
And soft refreshing rain.
All good gifts around us
Are sent from heaven above;
Then thank the Lord, O thank the Lord,
For all his love.

2 He only is the Maker
Of all things near and far;
He paints the wayside flower,
He lights the evening star;
The winds and waves obey him,
By him the birds are fed;
Much more to us, his children,
He gives our daily bread.

3 We thank thee then, O Father,
For all things bright and good,
The seed-time and the harvest,
Our life, our health, our food.
Accept the gifts we offer
For all thy love imparts,
And, what thou most desirest,
Our humble, thankful hearts.

MATTHIAS CLAUDIUS, 1740–1815
Tr. JANE MONTGOMERY CAMPBELL
1817–78

621

For younger children

SEE the farmer sow the seed
While the field is brown;
See the furrows deep and straight
Up the field and down:
Farmer, farmer, sow your seed
Up the field and down;
God will make the golden corn
Grow where all is brown.

2 Wait awhile and look again
Where the field was bare;
See how God has sent the corn
Growing golden there:

FREDERICK ARTHUR JACKSON
1867–1942

622 *For younger children*

IN the lanes and in the parks
Little flowers are showing;
God, who made and loves the
flowers,
Watches o'er their growing.

2 In the bushes and the trees,
Birdsong is beginning;
God, who made and loves the
birds,
Listens to their singing.

M. TEMPLE FRERE

623

THE summer days are come
again;
Once more the glad earth
yields
Her golden wealth of ripening
grain,
And breath of clover fields,
And deepening shade of summer
woods,
And glow of summer air,
And winging thoughts, and
happy moods
Of love and joy and prayer.

2 The summer days are come
again;
The birds are on the wing;
God's praises, in their loving
strain,
Unconsciously they sing.
We know who giveth all the
good
That doth our cup o'erbrim;
For summer joy in field and
wood,
We lift our song to him.

SAMUEL LONGFELLOW, 1819–92

624

SUMMER suns are glowing
Over land and sea;
Happy light is flowing,
Bountiful and free.
Everything rejoices
In the mellow rays;
All earth's thousand voices
Swell the psalm of praise.

2 God's free mercy streameth
Over all the world,
And his banner gleameth,
Everywhere unfurled.
Broad and deep and glorious
As the heaven shines,
Shines in might victorious
His eternal love.

3 Lord, upon our blindness
Thy pure radiance pour;
For thy loving-kindness
Make us love thee more.
And, when clouds are drifting
Dark across our sky,
Then, the veil uplifting,
Father, be thou nigh.

4 We will never doubt thee,
Though thou veil thy light;
Life is dark without thee;
Death with thee is bright.
Light of light, shine o'er us
On our pilgrim way;
Go thou still before us,
To the endless day.

WILLIAM WALSHAM HOW, 1823–97

625 *For younger children*

LET us sing our song of praise;
Thank you, God! Thank
you, God!
For the happy summer days,
Thank you, God! Thank you,
God!

2 For the sunshine and the
showers,
Thank you, God! Thank you,
God!
Bringing us the lovely flowers,
Thank you, God! Thank you,
God!

For the green and shady trees,
    Thank you, God! Thank you,
        God!

For the gentle cooling breeze,
    Thank you, God! Thank you,
        God!

WINIFRED EVA BARNARD

SEEDTIME AND HARVEST

626 PSALM 65, verses 9, 11–13

EARTH thou dost visit,
        watering it,
    Making it rich to grow
With thy full flood, providing
        corn;
    Thou hast prepared it so.

2 So thou the year most liberally
        Dost with thy goodness
        crown;
    And all thy paths abundantly
        On us drop fatness down.

3 They drop upon the pastures
        wide,
    That do in deserts lie;
The little hills on every side
    Rejoice right pleasantly.

4 With flocks the pastures clothèd
        be,
    The vales with corn are clad;
And now they shout and sing to
        thee,
    For thou hast made them
        glad.

5 *To Father, Son, and Holy Ghost,*
    The God whom we adore,
Be glory, as it was, and is,
    And shall be evermore. Amen.

627

COME, ye thankful people,
        come,
    Raise the song of harvest-home:
All is safely gathered in,
    Ere the winter storms begin;
God, our Maker, doth provide
For our wants to be supplied:
    Come to God's own temple,
        come,
    Raise the song of harvest-
        home.

2 All this world is God's own
        field,
    Fruit unto his praise to yield;
Wheat and tares together sown,
Unto joy or sorrow grown;
First the blade, and then the ear,
Then the full corn shall appear:
Lord of harvest, grant that we
Wholesome grain and pure
        may be.

3 For the Lord our God shall
        come,
    And shall take his harvest
        home;
From his field shall in that day
All offences purge away;
Give his angels charge at last
In the fire the tares to cast;
But the fruitful ears to store
In his garner evermore.

4 Even so, Lord, quickly come;
Bring thy final harvest home:
Gather thou thy people in,
Free from sorrow, free from sin;
There, for ever purified,
In thy garner to abide:
Come, with all thine angels,
        come,
Raise the glorious harvest-
        home!

HENRY ALFORD, 1810–71

628

FOUNTAIN of mercy, God of
        love,
    How rich thy bounties are!
The rolling seasons, as they
        move,
    Proclaim thy constant care.

2 When in the bosom of the earth
    The sower hid the grain,
Thy goodness marked its secret
        birth,
    And sent the early rain.

The spring's sweet influence was thine;
The plants in beauty grew;
Thou gavest summer suns to shine,
And mild refreshing dew.

4 These various mercies from above
Matured the swelling grain;
A yellow harvest crowns thy love,
And plenty fills the plain.

5 Seed-time and harvest, Lord, alone
Thou dost on man bestow;
Let him not then forget to own
From whom his blessings flow.

6 Fountain of love, our praise is thine;
To thee our songs we'll raise,
And all created nature join
In glad exultant praise.

ALICE FLOWERDEW, 1759–1830
altered
Also suitable are hymns in Section 11

629

FAIR waved the golden corn
In Canaan's pleasant land,
When full of joy, some shining morn,
Went forth the reaper band.

2 To God, so good and great,
Their cheerful thanks they pour,
Then carry to his temple gate
The choicest of their store.

3 For thus the holy word,
Spoken by Moses, ran:
'The first ripe ears are for the Lord,
The rest he gives to man.'

4 Like Israel, Lord, we give
Our earliest fruits to thee,
And pray that, long as we shall live,
We may thy children be.

5 Thine is our youthful prime,
And life and all its powers;
Be with us in our morning time,
And bless our evening hours.

6 In wisdom let us grow,
As years and strength are given,
That we may serve thy Church below,
And join thy saints in heaven.

JOHN HAMPDEN GURNEY, 1802–62

630
For children

THE fields and vales are thick with corn,
The reapers now are there,
They gather in the sheaves where once
The earth was brown and bare.

2 The empty barns will soon be filled
With ripe and golden grain,
For God has given the harvest fruit,
Who gave the sun and rain.

FREDERICK ARTHUR JACKSON
1867–1942

631
For younger children

WE thank thee, Lord, for all thy gifts
Of sunshine warm, and showers of rain
That ripened all the lovely fruits
And fields of golden grain.

2 We thank thee for the joy that comes
To us, when harvest gifts we bring—
That others, too, may know thy love,
Which speaks through everything.

3 O give us loving, thankful hearts,
For all thy goodness, love, and care;
And help us always to be glad
To give away and share.

JESSIE MARGARET MACDOUGALL
FERGUSON, 1895–1964
altered

WINTER

632

'TIS winter now; the fallen
    snow
Has left the heavens all
    coldly clear;
Through leafless boughs the
    sharp winds blow,
    And all the earth lies dead
      and drear.

2 And yet God's love is not with-
    drawn;
    His life within the keen air
      breathes;
His beauty paints the crimson
    dawn,
    And clothes the boughs with
      glittering wreaths.

3 And though abroad the sharp
    winds blow,
    And skies are chill, and frosts
      are keen,
Home closer draws her circle
    now,
    And warmer glows her light
      within.

4 O God! who giv'st the winter's
    cold,
    As well as summer's joyous
      rays,
Us warmly in thy love enfold,
    And keep us through life's
      wintry days.
      SAMUEL LONGFELLOW, 1819–92

633   *For younger children*

LITTLE birds in winter time
    Hungry are and poor;
Feed them, for the Father's
    sake,
Till the winter's o'er.

2 Throw them crumbs that you
    can spare
Round about your door;
Feed them, for the Father's
    sake,
Till the winter's o'er.
      FREDERICK ARTHUR JACKSON
      1867–1942

VII

CLOSE OF SERVICE

CLOSE OF SERVICE

634

MAY the grace of Christ our Saviour,
And the Father's boundless love,
With the Holy Spirit's favour,
Rest upon us from above.

2 Thus may we abide in union
With each other and the Lord,
And possess in sweet communion
Joys which earth cannot afford.

JOHN NEWTON, 1725–1807
Based on 2 Corinthians 13:14

635

ALMIGHTY God, thy word is cast
Like seed into the ground;
Now let the dew of heaven descend,
And righteous fruits abound.

2 Let not the foe of Christ and man
This holy seed remove,
But give it root in every heart
To bring forth fruits of love.

3 Let not the world's deceitful cares
The rising plant destroy,
But let it yield a hundredfold
The fruits of peace and joy.

4 Oft as the precious seed is sown,
Thy quickening grace bestow,
That all whose souls the truth receive
Its saving power may know.

JOHN CAWOOD, 1775–1852

636

AND now the wants are told that brought
Thy children to thy knee;
Here lingering still, we ask for naught,
But simply worship thee.

2 For thou art God, the One, the Same,
O'er all things high and bright;
And round us, when we speak thy Name,
There spreads a heaven of light.

3 O thou, above all blessing blest,
O'er thanks exalted far,
Thy very greatness is a rest
To weaklings as we are;

4 For when we feel the praise of thee
A task beyond our powers,
We say, 'A perfect God is he,
And he is fully ours'.

5 *All glory to the Father be,*
All glory to the Son,
All glory, Holy Ghost, to thee,
While endless ages run. Amen.

WILLIAM BRIGHT, 1824–1901

637

COME, dearest Lord, descend and dwell
By faith and love in every breast;
Then shall we know, and taste, and feel
The joys that cannot be expressed.

2 Come, fill our hearts with inward strength,
  Make our enlargèd souls
   possess
And learn the height and
  breadth and length
  Of thine unmeasurable grace.

3 *Now to the God whose power can*
  do
  More than our thoughts or
  wishes know,
Be everlasting honours done
  By all the Church, through
  Christ his Son. Amen.
     ISAAC WATTS, 1674–1748

638

L ORD, dismiss us with thy
  blessing;
Fill our hearts with joy and
 peace;
Let us each, thy love possessing,
 Triumph in redeeming grace;
O refresh us, O refresh us,
 Travelling through this
  wilderness.

2 Thanks we give and adoration
 For thy Gospel's joyful
  sound;
May the fruits of thy salvation
 In our hearts and lives
  abound,
 May thy presence, may thy
  presence
With us evermore be found.
    JOHN FAWCETT, 1740–1817

639

N OW may he who from the
  dead
 Brought the Shepherd of the
  sheep,

Jesus Christ, our King and
 Head,
 All our souls in safety keep.

2 May he teach us to fulfil
 What is pleasing in his sight,
Perfect us in all his will,
 And preserve us day and
  night.

3 To that dear Redeemer's praise,
 Who the covenant sealed with
  blood,
Let our hearts and voices raise
 Loud thanksgivings to our
  God.
    JOHN NEWTON, 1725–1807

640

    Αἰνεῖτε, παῖδες, Κύριον

P RAISE ye the Lord, ye
  servants of the Lord:
Praise ye his name; his lordly
 honour sing:
 Thee we adore; to thee glad
  homage bring;
Thee we acknowledge; God to
 be adored
 For thy great glory,
  Sovereign, Lord, and King.

2 *Father of Christ—of him whose*
  work was done,
 When by his death he took our
  sins away—
  To thee belongeth worship, day
   by day,
Yea, Holy Father, everlasting
  Son,
 And Holy Ghost, all praise be
  thine for aye! Amen.
  Apostolic Constitutions, 3rd century
    Tr. GEORGE RATCLIFFE
    WOODWARD, 1849–1934
    and Compilers of
    The BBC Hymn Book
  The following are also suitable
    Nos. 204, 463

EVENING

641

A LL praise to thee, my God,
  this night,
For all the blessings of the
 light!

Keep me, O keep me, King of
 kings,
Beneath thy own almighty
 wings.

2 Forgive me, Lord, for thy dear
  Son,
The ill that I this day have done,
That with the world, myself,
  and thee,
I, ere I sleep, at peace may be.

3 Teach me to live, that I may
  dread
The grave as little as my bed;
Teach me to die, that so I may
Rise glorious at the awesome
  day.

4 O may my soul on thee repose,
And may sweet sleep mine eye-
  lids close,—
Sleep that may me more
  vigorous make
To serve my God when I awake.

5 When in the night I sleepless lie,
My soul with heavenly thoughts
  supply;
Let no ill dreams disturb my
  rest,
No powers of darkness me
  molest.

6 *Praise God, from whom all*
  blessings flow;
Praise him, all creatures here
  below;
Praise him above, ye heavenly
  host;
Praise Father, Son, and Holy
  Ghost. Amen.

THOMAS KEN, 1637–1711

642   *Ach bleib bei uns, Herr*
         Jesu Christ

NOW cheer our hearts this
  eventide,
Lord Jesus Christ, and with us
  bide;
Thou that canst never set in
  night,
Our heavenly Sun, our glorious
  Light.

2 May we and all who bear thy
  Name
By gentle love thy cross pro-
  claim,

Thy gift of peace on earth
  secure,
And for thy truth the world
  endure.

ROBERT BRIDGES, 1844–1930
Yattendon Hymnal, 1899
Based on NICOLAUS SELNECKER
1532–92

643   *Die Nacht ist kommen, drin*
         wir ruhen sollen

NOW God be with us, for the
  night is closing;
The light and darkness are of
  his disposing,
And 'neath his shadow here to
  rest we yield us,
For he will shield us.

2 Let evil thoughts and spirits
  flee before us;
Till morning cometh, watch,
  Protector, o'er us;
In soul and body thou from
  harm defend us;
Thine angels send us.

3 Let holy thoughts be ours when
  sleep o'ertakes us;
Our earliest thoughts be thine
  when morning wakes
  us;
All day serve thee, in all that
  we are doing
Thy praise pursuing.

4 We have no refuge, none on
  earth to aid us,
Save thee, O Father, who thine
  own hast made us;
But thy dear Presence will not
  leave them lonely
Who seek thee only.

5 Father, thy Name be praised,
  thy Kingdom given,
Thy will be done on earth as 'tis
  in heaven;
Keep us in life, forgive our sins,
  deliver
Us now and ever.

PETRUS HERBERT, ?–1571
Tr. CATHERINE WINKWORTH
1827–78

231

644

Holy Father, cheer our way
With thy love's perpetual ray;
Grant us, every closing day,
Light at evening time.

2 Holy Saviour, calm our fears
When earth's brightness disappears;
Grant us in our latter years
Light at evening time.

3 Holy Spirit, be thou nigh
When in mortal pains we lie;
Grant us, as we come to die,
Light at evening time.

4 Holy, blessèd Trinity,
Darkness is not dark to thee;
Those thou keepest always see
Light at evening time.

RICHARD HAYES ROBINSON
1842–92

645

Τὴν ἡμέραν διελθών

The day is past and over:
All thanks, O Lord, to thee;
I pray thee now that sinless
The hours of dark may be.
O Jesus, keep me in thy sight,
And guard me through the coming night.

2 The joys of day are over:
I lift my heart to thee,
And pray thee that offenceless
The hours of dark may be.
O Jesus, keep me in thy sight,
And guard me through the coming night.

3 The toils of day are over:
I raise the hymn to thee,
And pray that free from peril
The hours of dark may be.
O Jesus, keep me in thy sight,
And guard me through the coming night.

4 Be thou my soul's Preserver,
O God, for thou dost know
How many are the perils
Through which I have to go.
Lover of men, O hear my call,
And guard and save me from them all.

6th century
Tr. JOHN MASON NEALE, 1818–66

646

The day thou gavest, Lord, is ended;
The darkness falls at thy behest;
To thee our morning hymns ascended,
Thy praise shall sanctify our rest.

2 We thank thee that thy Church unsleeping,
While earth rolls onward into light,
Through all the world her watch is keeping,
And rests not now by day or night.

3 As o'er each continent and island
The dawn leads on another day,
The voice of prayer is never silent,
Nor dies the strain of praise away.

4 The sun that bids us rest is waking
Our brethren 'neath the western sky,
And hour by hour fresh lips are making
Thy wondrous doings heard on high.

5 So be it, Lord! thy throne shall never,
Like earth's proud empires, pass away;
Thy Kingdom stands and grows for ever,
Till all thy creatures own thy sway.

JOHN ELLERTON, 1826–93

647

SUN of my soul, thou Saviour
dear,
It is not night if thou be near:
O may no earth-born cloud arise
To hide thee from thy servant's
eyes.

2 Abide with me from morn till
eve,
For without thee I cannot live;
Abide with me when night is
nigh,
For without thee I dare not die.

3 Watch by the sick; enrich the
poor
With blessings from thy boundless store;
Be every mourner's sleep tonight,
Like infant's slumbers, pure
and light.

4 Come near and bless us when
we wake,
Ere through the world our way
we take,
Till in the ocean of thy love
We lose ourselves in heaven
above.

JOHN KEBLE, 1792–1866

648

ERE I sleep, for every favour
This day showed
By my God,
I will bless my Saviour.

2 O my Lord, what shall I render
To thy Name,
Still the same,
Gracious, good, and tender?

3 Visit me with thy salvation;
Let thy care
Now be near,
Round my habitation.

4 Thou my Rock, my Guard, my
Tower,
Safely keep,
While I sleep,
Me, with all thy power.

5 So, whene'er in death I slumber,
Let me rise
With the wise,
Counted in their number.

JOHN CENNICK, 1718–55

649

SAVIOUR, again to thy dear
Name we raise
With one accord our parting
hymn of praise.
Guard thou the lips from sin,
the hearts from shame,
That in this house have called
upon thy Name.

2 Grant us thy peace, Lord,
through the coming night;
Turn thou for us its darkness
into light;
From harm and danger keep
thy servants free;
For dark and light are both
alike to thee.

3 Grant us thy peace throughout
our earthly life;
Peace to thy Church from error
and from strife;
Peace to our land, the fruit of
truth and love;
Peace in each heart, thy Spirit
from above:

4 Thy peace in sorrow, balm of
every pain;
Thy peace in death, the hope
to rise again;
Then, when thy voice shall bid
our conflict cease,
Call us, O Lord, to thine eternal
peace.

JOHN ELLERTON, 1826–93

650

ROUND me falls the night;
Saviour, be my light:
Through the hours in darkness
shrouded
Let me see thy face unclouded;
Let thy glory shine
In this heart of mine.

2   Earthly work is done,
      Earthly sounds are none;
   Rest in sleep and silence seeking,
   Let me hear thee softly speaking;
      In my spirit's ear
      Whisper, 'I am near'.

3   Blessèd, heavenly Light,
      Shining through **earth's**
        night;
   Voice that oft of love hast **told**
      me;
   Arms so strong to clasp and
      hold me;
      Thou thy watch wilt keep,
      Saviour, o'er my sleep.

WILLIAM ROMANIS, 1824–99

651

A SOVEREIGN Protector I
  have,
   Unseen, yet for ever at hand,
Unchangeably faithful to save,
   Almighty to rule and com-
    mand.
He smiles, and my comforts
   abound;
   His grace as the dew shall
    descend,
And walls of salvation surround
   The soul he delights to defend.

2 Inspirer and Hearer of prayer,
   Thou Shepherd and Guardian
    of thine,
  My all to thy covenant care
   I sleeping and waking resign.
  If thou art my Shield and my
    Sun,
   The night is no darkness to
    me;
  And, fast as my moments roll on,
   They bring me but nearer to
    thee.

AUGUSTUS MONTAGUE TOPLADY
1740–78

652

Christe, qui lux es et dies

O CHRIST who art the Light
  and Day,
Thou drivest darksome night
  away,
We know thee as the Light of
  light,
Illuminating mortal sight.

2 All holy Lord, we pray to thee,
  Keep us tonight from danger
    free,
  Grant us, dear Lord, in thee to
    rest,
  So be our sleep in quiet blest.

3 And while the eyes soft slumber
    take,
  Still be the heart to thee awake,
  Be thy right hand upheld above
  Thy servants resting in thy
    love.

4 Yes, our Defender, be thou
    nigh
  To bid the powers of darkness
    fly,
  Keep us from sin, and guide for
    good
  Thy servants purchased by thy
    blood.

5 *All praise to God the Father be,*
  All praise, eternal Son, to thee,
  Whom with the Spirit we adore,
  For ever and for evermore. Amen.

6th century
Verses 1–4 tr. RICHARD RUNCIMAN
TERRY, 1865–1938
Verse 5 tr. WILLIAM JOHN COPELAND
1804–85

653

For younger children

NOW the day is over,
  Night is drawing nigh,
Shadows of the evening
  Steal across the sky.

2 Now the darkness gathers,
   Stars begin to peep,
  Birds, and beasts, and flowers
   Soon will be asleep.

3 Jesus, give the weary
   Calm and sweet repose;
  With thy tender blessing
   May mine eyelids close.

4 Grant to little children
   Visions bright of thee;
  Guard the sailors tossing
   On the deep blue sea.

5 Comfort every sufferer
   Watching late in pain;
  Those who plan some evil
   From their sin restrain.

6 Through the long night-watches,
  May thine angels spread
Their white wings above me,
  Watching round my bed.

7 When the morning wakens,
  Then may I arise
Pure, and fresh, and sinless
  In thy holy eyes.

8 *Glory to the Father,*
    Glory to the Son,
  And to thee, blest Spirit,
    Whilst all ages run. Amen.
          SABINE BARING-GOULD
                  1834–1924

654   *For younger children*

GENTLE Jesus, hear our
  prayer,
Keep us in thy loving care;
And when evening shadows
  fall,
Casting darkness over all,
Loving Jesus, be thou near,
For with thee we have no
  fear.
      JESSIE MARGARET MACDOUGALL
            FERGUSON, 1895–1964

655   *For younger children*

INTO thy loving care,
  Into thy keeping,
Lord, who art everywhere,
Take us, we pray.
                  Author unknown

656   *For younger children*

JESUS, tender Shepherd, hear
    me;
  Bless thy little lamb tonight;
Through the darkness be thou
    near me;
  Watch my sleep till morning
    light.

2 All this day thy hand has led me,
    And I thank thee for thy care;
  Thou hast clothed me, warmed
      and fed me;
    Listen to my evening prayer.

3 Let my sins be all forgiven;
    Bless the friends I love so
      well;
  Take me, when I die, to heaven,
    Happy there with thee to
      dwell.
        MARY LUNDIE DUNCAN, 1814–40

DOXOLOGIES

657

NOW to him who loved us,
    gave us
Every pledge that love could
    give,
Freely shed his blood to save us,
Gave his life that we might
    live,
  Be the Kingdom
  And dominion
And the glory evermore.
                      Amen.
          SAMUEL MILLER WARING
                  1792–1827

658

PRAISE God, from whom all
    blessings flow;
Praise him, all creatures here
    below;
Praise him above, ye heavenly
    host;
Praise Father, Son, and Holy
    Ghost. Amen.
          THOMAS KEN, 1637–1711

659   *Lob, Ehr' und Preis sei Gott*

ALL praise and thanks to God
    The Father now be given,
The Son, and him who reigns
With them in highest
      heaven,—
  The one, eternal God,
    Whom earth and heaven
      adore;
  For thus it was, is now,
    And shall be evermore.
                      Amen.
        MARTIN RINKART, 1586–1649
        Tr. CATHERINE WINKWORTH
                  1827–78

660

Gloria et honor Deo

UNTO God be praise and
honour:
To the Father, to the Son,
To the mighty Spirit, glory—
Ever Three and ever One:
Power and glory in the highest
While eternal ages run. Amen.

Tr. WILLIAM MAIR, 1830–1920
and ARTHUR WELLESLEY
WOTHERSPOON, 1853–1936

661

Gloria et honor Deo

LAUD and honour to the
Father,
Laud and honour to the Son,
Laud and honour to the Spirit,
Ever Three and ever One,
One in might, and One in glory,
While unending ages run.
Amen.

7th or 8th century
Tr. JOHN MASON NEALE, 1818–66

*The following Doxologies are included
elsewhere in the book*

No.

1, v. 5 (*and elsewhere*) To Father, Son, and
Holy Ghost (L.M.)
5, v. 6 (*and elsewhere*) To Father, Son, and
Holy Ghost (C.M.)
30, v. 7 Let all things their Creator bless
70, v. 3 (*ll.* 5–8) Now glory be to God
74, v. 6 To thee be glory, Lord
135, v. 6 To God the Father, Son
198, v. 5 Christ to thee, with God the
Father
301, v. 4 Glory to God the Father, the
unbegotten One
392, v. 5 Glory to God the Father, God
the Son

*The following hymns also end in Doxo-
logies*

31, 37, 43, 56, 75, 118, 182, 189, 199,
208, 209, 223, 257, 264, 305, 329, 330,
348, 352, 358, 366, 400, 402, 414, 429,
455, 493, 532, 535, 539, 568, 575, 576,
581, 582, 636, 637, 640, 652, 653.
Gloria Patri appears at No. 344

662

AMENS.

VIII

PERSONAL FAITH AND DEVOTION

663

O FOR a closer walk with
    God,
  A calm and heavenly frame,
A light to shine upon the road
  That leads me to the Lamb!

2 Where is the blessedness I knew
    When first I saw the Lord?
  Where is the soul-refreshing
    view
    Of Jesus and his word?

3 What peaceful hours I once
    enjoyed!
    How sweet their memory still!
  But they have left an aching
    void
    The world can never fill.

4 Return, O Holy Dove! return,
    Sweet messenger of rest!
  I hate the sins that made thee
    mourn,
    And drove thee from my
    breast.

5 The dearest idol I have known,
    Whate'er that idol be,
  Help me to tear it from thy
    throne,
    And worship only thee.

6 So shall my walk be close with
    God,
    Calm and serene my frame;
  So purer light shall mark the road
    That leads me to the Lamb.

WILLIAM COWPER, 1731–1800

664

O FOR a faith that will not
    shrink,
    Though pressed by many a
    foe,

That will not tremble on the
    brink
    Of poverty or woe,

2 That will not murmur nor com-
    plain
    Beneath the chastening rod,
  But, in the hour of grief or
    pain,
    Can lean upon its God;

3 A faith that shines more bright
    and clear
    When tempests rage without,
  That when in danger knows no
    fear,
    In darkness feels no doubt;

4 A faith that keeps the narrow
    way
    Till life's last spark is fled,
  And with a pure and heavenly
    ray
    Lights up a dying bed!

5 Lord, give me such a faith as
    this,
    And then, whate'er may
    come,
  I taste even now the hallowed
    bliss
    Of an eternal home.

WILLIAM HILEY BATHURST
1796–1877

665

O GOD, thou art my God
    alone,
    Early to thee my soul shall
    cry,
A pilgrim in a land unknown,
    A thirsty land whose springs
    are dry.

2 O that it were as it hath been
When, praying in the holy
place,
Thy power and glory I have
seen,
And marked the footsteps of
thy grace!

3 Yet through this rough and
thorny maze
I follow hard on thee, my
God;
Thine hand unseen upholds my
ways;
I safely tread where thou hast
trod.

4 Thee, in the watches of the
night,
When I remember on my bed,
Thy presence makes the darkness light;
Thy guardian wings are
round my head.

5 Better than life itself thy love,
Dearer than all beside to me;
For whom have I in heaven
above,
Or what on earth, compared
with thee?

6 Praise, with my heart, my
mind, my voice,
For all thy mercy I will give;
My soul shall still in God rejoice;
My tongue shall bless thee
while I live.

JAMES MONTGOMERY, 1771–1854

666

O THOU, my Judge and
King—
My broken heart, my voice-
less prayer,
My poverty, and blind des-
pair,
To thee, O Christ, I bring.

2 O thou, my Judge and King—
My treason to thy love most
sweet,
My pride that pierced thy
weary feet,
To thee, O Christ, I bring.

3 O thou, my Judge and King—
My tearful hope, my faith's
distress,
For thee to pardon and to
bless,
To thee, O Christ, I bring.

4 O thou, my Judge and King—
With no excuse, for thou art
just,
My sins, that set me in the
dust,
To thee, O Christ, I bring.

5 O thou, my Judge and King—
My soul, from depths of my
disgrace,
To seek for mercy at thy face,
To thee, O Christ, I bring.

LAUCHLAN MacLEAN WATT
1867–1957

667

APPROACH, my soul, the
mercy-seat,
Where Jesus answers prayer;
There humbly fall before his
feet,
For none can perish there.

2 Thy promise is my only plea;
With this I venture nigh:
Thou callest burdened souls to
thee,
And such, O Lord, am I.

3 Bowed down beneath a load of
sin,
By Satan sorely pressed,
By war without and fears with-
in,
I come to thee for rest.

4 Be thou my Shield and Hiding-
place,
That, sheltered near thy side,
I may my fierce accuser face,
And tell him thou hast died.

5 O wondrous love! to bleed and
die,
To bear the cross and shame,
That guilty sinners, such as I,
Might plead thy gracious
Name!

JOHN NEWTON, 1725–1807

668 *Wer nur den lieben Gott*
lässt walten

IF thou but suffer God to guide
  thee,
  And hope in him through all
  thy ways,
He'll give thee strength,
  whate'er betide thee,
  And bear thee through the
  evil days;
Who trusts in God's unchanging
  love
Builds on the rock that naught
  can move.

2 What can these anxious cares
  avail thee,
    These never-ceasing moans
    and sighs?
  What can it help if thou bewail
  thee
    O'er each dark moment as it
    flies?
  Our cross and trials do but press
  The heavier for our bitterness.

3 Only be still, and wait his leisure
    In cheerful hope, with heart
    content
  To take whate'er thy Father's
  pleasure
    And all-discerning love have
    sent;
  Nor doubt our inmost wants are
  known
  To him who chose us for his own.

4 Sing, pray, and keep his ways
  unswerving;
    So do thine own part faith-
    fully,
  And trust his word,—though
  undeserving,
    Thou yet shalt find it true for
    thee;
  God never yet forsook at need
  The soul that trusted him indeed.

  GEORG NEUMARK, 1621–81
  Tr. CATHERINE WINKWORTH
  1827–78

669 *Befiehl du deine Wege*

PUT thou thy trust in God,
  In duty's path go on;
Walk in his strength with faith
  and hope,
  So shall thy work be done.

Give to the winds thy fears;
Hope, and be undismayed;
God hears thy sighs and counts
  thy tears,
  God shall lift up thy head.

2 Through waves, and clouds,
  and storms
  He gently clears thy way;
Wait thou his time; so shall this
  night
  Soon end in joyous day.
  Leave to his sovereign sway
  To choose and to command;
So shalt thou, wondering, own
  his way
  How wise, how strong his
  hand.

3 Thou seest our weakness,
  Lord;
  Our hearts are known to thee:
O lift thou up the sinking hand,
  Confirm the feeble knee.
  Let us, in life, in death,
  Thy steadfast truth declare,
And publish, with our latest
  breath,
  Thy love and guardian care.

  PAUL GERHARDT, 1607–76
  Par. JOHN WESLEY, 1703–91
  and others

670

WORKMAN of God! O lose
  not heart,
  But learn what God is like,
And, in the darkest battle-field,
  Thou shalt know where to
  strike.

2 Thrice blest is he to whom is
  given
  The instinct that can tell
That God is on the field when he
  Is most invisible.

3 He hides himself so won-
  drously,
  As though there were no God;
He is least seen when all the
  powers
  Of ill are most abroad.

4 Ah! God is other than we think;
  His ways are far above,
Far beyond reason's height, and
  reached
  Only by childlike love.

5 Then learn to scorn the praise
     of men,
   And learn to lose with God;
For Jesus won the world
     through shame,
   And beckons thee his road.

6 For right is right, since God is
     God,
   And right the day must win;
To doubt would be disloyalty,
To falter would be sin.

FREDERICK WILLIAM FABER
1814–63

671 *Wem in Leidenstagen*

O LET him whose sorrow
   No relief can find,
Trust in God, and borrow
Ease for heart and mind.

2 Where the mourner, weeping,
   Sheds the secret tear,
God his watch is keeping,
   Though none else be near.

3 God will never leave thee;
   All thy wants he knows,
Feels the pains that grieve thee,
Sees thy cares and woes.

4 If in grief thou languish,
   He will dry the tear,
Who his children's anguish
Soothes with succour near.

5 All thy woe and sadness,
   In this world below,
Balance not the gladness
Thou in heaven shalt know,

6 When thy gracious Saviour,
   In the realms above,
Crowns thee with his favour,
Fills thee with his love.

HEINRICH SIEGMUND OSWALD
1751–1834
Tr. FRANCES ELIZABETH COX
1812–97

672

CHRIST who knows all his
     sheep
Will all in safety keep,
   He will not lose one soul,
     Nor ever fail us;
Nor we the promised goal,
   Though hell assail us.

2 I know my God is just;
   To him I wholly trust
     All that I have and am,
       All that I hope for:
All's sure and seen to him,
   Which here I grope for.

3 Lord Jesus, take this spirit:
   We trust thy love and merit.
     Take home the wandering
       sheep,
     For thou hast sought it;
This soul in safety keep,
   For thou hast bought it.

RICHARD BAXTER, 1615–91
altered

673 *Stille, mein Wille; dein*
     Jesus hilft siegen

BE still, my soul: the Lord is
   on thy side;
     Bear patiently the cross of
       grief or pain;
Leave to thy God to order and
   provide;
     In every change he faithful
       will remain.
Be still, my soul: thy best, thy
   heavenly Friend
Through thorny ways leads to
   a joyful end.

2 Be still, my soul: thy God doth
     undertake
       To guide the future as he has
         the past.
   Thy hope, thy confidence let
     nothing shake;
       All now mysterious shall be
         bright at last.
   Be still, my soul: the waves
     and winds still know
   His voice who ruled them while
     he dwelt below.

3 Be still, my soul: when dearest
     friends depart,
       And all is darkened in the
         vale of tears,
   Then shalt thou better know
     his love, his heart,
       Who comes to soothe thy
         sorrow and thy fears.
   Be still, my soul: thy Jesus can
     repay,
   From his own fullness, all he
     takes away.

4 Be still, my soul: the hour is
    hastening on
  When we shall be forever
    with the Lord,
  When disappointment, grief,
    and fear are gone,
    Sorrow forgot, love's purest
    joys restored.
  Be still, my soul: when change
    and tears are past,
  All safe and blessèd we shall
    meet at last.

KATHARINA VON SCHLEGEL
1697–?
Tr. JANE LAURIE BORTHWICK
1813–97

674

JESUS, these eyes have never
    seen
  That radiant form of thine;
  The veil of sense hangs dark
    between
  Thy blessèd face and mine.

2 I see thee not, I hear thee not,
  Yet art thou oft with me;
  And earth hath ne'er so dear a
    spot
  As where I meet with thee.

3 Like some bright dream that
    comes unsought,
  When slumbers o'er me roll,
  Thine image ever fills my
    thought,
  And charms my ravished
    soul.

4 Yet, though I have not seen,
    and still
  Must rest in faith alone,
  I love thee, dearest Lord, and
    will,
  Unseen but not unknown.

5 When death these mortal eyes
    shall seal,
  And still this throbbing heart,
  The rending veil shall thee re-
    veal
  All glorious as thou art.

RAY PALMER, 1808–87

675

'TWIXT gleams of joy and
    clouds of doubt
  Our feelings come and go;
  Our best estate is tossed about
    In ceaseless ebb and flow.
  No mood of feeling, form of
    thought,
    Is constant for a day;
  But thou, O Lord, thou changest
    not:
    The same thou art alway.

2 I grasp thy strength, make it
    mine own,
  My heart with peace is blest;
  I lose my hold, and then comes
    down
    Darkness, and cold unrest.
  Let me no more my comfort
    draw
    From my frail hold of thee,
  In this alone rejoice with awe—
    Thy mighty grasp of me.

3 Out of that weak, unquiet drift
    That comes but to depart,
  To that pure heaven my spirit lift
    Where thou unchanging art.
  Lay hold of me with thy strong
    grasp,
    Let thy almighty arm
  In its embrace my weakness
    clasp,
    And I shall fear no harm.

4 Thy purpose of eternal good
    Let me but surely know;
  On this I'll lean—let changing
    mood
    And feeling come or go—
  Glad when thy sunshine fills my
    soul,
    Not lorn when clouds o'ercast,
  Since thou within thy sure con-
    trol
    Of love dost hold me fast.

JOHN CAMPBELL SHAIRP, 1819–85

676

HARK, my soul! it is the
    Lord;
  'Tis thy Saviour, hear his word;
  Jesus speaks, and speaks to thee:
  'Say, poor sinner, lov'st thou me?

2 'I delivered thee when bound,
　　And, when bleeding, healed thy
　　　　wound ;
　Sought thee wandering, set thee
　　right ;
　Turned thy darkness into light.

3 'Can a woman's tender care
　Cease towards the child she bare?
　Yes, she may forgetful be,
　Yet will I remember thee.

4 'Mine is an unchanging love,
　Higher than the heights above,
　Deeper than the depths be-
　　neath,
　Free and faithful, strong as
　　death.

5 'Thou shalt see my glory soon,
　When the work of grace is done ;
　Partner of my throne shalt be ;
　Say, poor sinner, lov'st thou
　　me ?'

6 Lord, it is my chief complaint
　That my love is weak and faint ;
　Yet I love thee, and adore ;
　O for grace to love thee more !
　　　　　WILLIAM COWPER, 1731–1800

677

O LOVE that wilt not let me
　　go,
I rest my weary soul in thee :
I give thee back the life I owe,
That in thine ocean depths its
　　flow
　　May richer, fuller be.

2 O Light that followest all my
　　way,
　I yield my flickering torch
　　to thee :
My heart restores its borrowed
　　ray,
That in thy sunshine's blaze its
　　day
　May brighter, fairer be.

3 O Joy that seekest me through
　　pain,
　I cannot close my heart to
　　thee :
I trace the rainbow through the
　　rain,
And feel the promise is not vain,
　That morn shall tearless be.

4 O Cross that liftest up my head,
　I dare not ask to fly from thee :
I lay in dust life's glory dead,
And from the ground there
　　blossoms red
　Life that shall endless be.
　　　　　GEORGE MATHESON, 1842–1906

678　　　*Ich will Dich lieben,
　　　　　meine Stärke*

THEE will I love, my
　　Strength, my Tower ;
　Thee will I love, my Joy, my
　　Crown ;
Thee will I love with all my
　　power,
　In all thy works, and thee
　　alone ;
Thee will I love, till sacred fire
Fill my whole soul with pure
　desire.

2 I thank thee, uncreated Sun,
　　That thy bright beams on me
　　have shined ;
　I thank thee, who hast over-
　　thrown
　　My foes, and healed my
　　wounded mind ;
　I thank thee, whose enlivening
　　voice
　Bids my freed heart in thee
　　rejoice.

3 Thee will I love, my Joy, my
　　Crown ;
　　Thee will I love, my Lord
　　my God ;
　Thee will I love, beneath thy
　　frown
　　Or smile, thy sceptre or thy
　　rod ;
　What though my flesh and
　　heart decay,
　Thee shall I love in endless day.
　　　　　JOHANN SCHEFFLER, 1624–77
　　　　　Tr. JOHN WESLEY, 1703–91
　　　　　　　　　　altered

679

LORD, it belongs not to my
　　care
　Whether I die or live ;
To love and serve thee is my
　　share,
　And this thy grace must give.

2 If life be long, I will be glad,
  That I may long obey;
If short, yet why should I be sad
  To welcome endless day?

3 Christ leads me through no
  darker rooms
  Than he went through before;
He that into God's Kingdom
  comes
  Must enter by this door.

4 Come, Lord, when grace hath
  made me meet
  Thy blessèd face to see;
For, if thy work on earth be
  sweet,
  What will thy glory be?

5 My knowledge of that life is small,
  The eye of faith is dim;
But 'tis enough that Christ
  knows all,
  And I shall be with him.

  RICHARD BAXTER, 1615–91

680

M Y times are in thy hand:
  My God, I wish them
  there;
My life, my friends, my soul
  I leave
Entirely to thy care.

2 My times are in thy hand,
  Whatever they may be,
Pleasing or painful, dark or
  bright,
As best may seem to thee.

3 My times are in thy hand:
  Why should I doubt or fear?
My Father's hand will never
  cause
His child a needless tear.

4 My times are in thy hand,
  Jesus, the Crucified;
Those hands my cruel sins had
  pierced
Are now my guard and guide.

5 My times are in thy hand:
  I'll always trust in thee;
And, after death, at thy right
  hand
I shall for ever be.

  WILLIAM FREEMAN LLOYD
  1791–1853

681

I N heavenly love abiding,
  No change my heart shall
  fear;
And safe is such confiding,
  For nothing changes here:
The storm may roar without me,
  My heart may low be laid;
But God is round about me,
  And can I be dismayed?

2 Wherever he may guide me,
  No want shall turn me back;
My Shepherd is beside me,
  And nothing can I lack.
His wisdom ever waketh,
  His sight is never dim:
He knows the way he taketh,
  And I will walk with him.

3 Green pastures are before me,
  Which yet I have not seen;
Bright skies will soon be o'er me,
  Where the dark clouds have
  been.
My hope I cannot measure:
  My path to life is free:
My Saviour has my treasure,
  And he will walk with me.

  ANNA LAETITIA WARING
  1820–1910

682

L EAD, kindly Light, amid
  the encircling gloom,
  Lead thou me on;
The night is dark, and I am far
  from home;
  Lead thou me on.
Keep thou my feet; I do not ask
  to see
The distant scene,—one step
  enough for me.

2 I was not ever thus, nor prayed
  that thou
  Shouldst lead me on;
I loved to choose and see my
  path, but now
  Lead thou me on;
I loved the garish day, and,
  spite of fears,
Pride ruled my will: remember
  not past years.

3 So long thy power hath blest
    me, sure it still
  Will lead me on,
O'er moor and fen, o'er crag
    and torrent, till
  The night is gone,
And with the morn those angel
    faces smile,
Which I have loved long since,
    and lost awhile.

JOHN HENRY NEWMAN, 1801–90

683

I HEAR thy welcome voice
  That calls me, Lord, to thee,
For cleansing in thy precious
    blood
  That flowed on Calvary.
  I am coming, Lord,
    Coming now to thee;
  Wash me, cleanse me in the
    blood
    That flowed on Calvary.

2 'Tis Jesus calls me on
  To perfect faith and love,
To perfect hope and peace and
    trust,
  For earth and heaven above.

3 'Tis Jesus who confirms
  The blessèd work within,
By adding grace to welcomed
    grace,
  Where reigned the power of sin.

4 All hail, atoning blood!
  All hail, redeeming grace!
All hail, the gift of Christ our
    Lord,
  Our Strength and Righteous-
    ness!

LEWIS HARTSOUGH, 1828–72

684

BENEATH the cross of Jesus
  I fain would take my
    stand—
The shadow of a mighty rock
  Within a weary land;
A home within a wilderness,
  A rest upon the way,
From the burning of the noon-
    tide heat
  And the burden of the day.

2 O safe and happy shelter,
  O refuge tried and sweet,
O trysting-place where heaven's
    love
  And heaven's justice meet!
As to the exiled patriarch
  That wondrous dream was
    given,
So seems my Saviour's cross
    to me—
  A ladder up to heaven.

3 Upon that cross of Jesus,
  Mine eye at times can see
The very dying form of One
  Who suffered there for me;
And from my smitten heart,
    with tears,
  Two wonders I confess—
The wonder of his glorious love,
  And my own worthlessness.

4 I take, O cross, thy shadow
  For my abiding-place;
I ask no other sunshine than
  The sunshine of his face:
Content to let the world go by,
  To know no gain nor loss—
My sinful self my only shame,
  My glory all, the cross.

ELIZABETH CECILIA CLEPHANE
1830–69

685

I AM trusting thee, Lord Jesus,
  Trusting only thee,
Trusting thee for full salvation,
  Great and free.

2 I am trusting thee for pardon:
  At thy feet I bow,
For thy grace and tender mercy
  Trusting now.

3 I am trusting thee to guide me;
  Thou alone shalt lead,
Every day and hour supplying
  All my need.

4 I am trusting thee for power:
  Thine can never fail;
Words which thou thyself shalt
    give me
  Must prevail.

5 I am trusting thee, Lord Jesus;
   Never let me fall;
I am trusting thee for ever,
   And for all.
          FRANCES RIDLEY HAVERGAL
                  1836–79

686

JESUS, I will trust thee,—
   Trust thee with my soul;
Guilty, lost, and helpless,
   Thou canst make me whole.
There is none in heaven
   Or on earth like thee;
Thou hast died for sinners—
   Therefore, Lord, for me.

2 Jesus, I will trust thee;
   Name of matchless worth,
Spoken by the angel
   At thy wondrous birth,
Written, and for ever,
   On thy cross of shame:
Sinners read and worship,
   Trusting in that Name.

3 Jesus, I will trust thee,
   Pondering thy ways
Full of love and mercy
   All thine earthly days.
Sinners gathered round thee,
   Lepers sought thy face,
None too vile or loathsome
   For a Saviour's grace.

4 Jesus, I will trust thee,
   Trust without a doubt;
Whosoever cometh
   Thou wilt not cast out.
Faithful is thy promise;
   Precious is thy blood;
These my soul's salvation,
   Thou my Saviour God!

         MARY JANE WALKER, 1816–78

687

I AM not skilled to understand
   What God hath willed,
     what God hath planned;
I only know at his right hand
   Stands One who is my
    Saviour.

2 I take God at his word and
   deed:
   'Christ died to save me', this
    I read;
And in my heart I find a need
   Of him to be my Saviour.

3 And was there then no other
   way
   For God to take?—I cannot say;
I only bless him, day by day,
   Who saved me through my
    Saviour.

4 That he should leave his place
   on high
And come for sinful man to die,
You count it strange?—so do
   not I,
   Since I have known my
    Saviour.

5 And O that he fulfilled may see
The travail of his soul in me,
And with his work contented
   be,
   As I with my dear Saviour!

6 Yea, living, dying, let me bring
My strength, my solace, from
   this spring,
That he who lives to be my King
   Once died to be my Saviour.
        DORA GREENWELL, 1821–82

688

I NEED thee every hour,
   Most gracious Lord;
No tender voice but thine
   Can peace afford.

2 I need thee every hour;
   Stay thou near by;
Temptations lose their power
   When thou art nigh.

3 I need thee every hour,
   In joy or pain;
Come quickly and abide,
   Or life is vain.

4 I need thee every hour;
   Teach me thy will;
And thy rich promises
   In me fulfil.
     ANNIE SHERWOOD HAWKS
              1835–1918

689

NEARER, my God, to thee,
  Nearer to thee!
Ev'n though it be a cross
  That raiseth me,
Still all my song would be,
'Nearer, my God, to thee,
  *Nearer to thee!'

2 Though, like the wanderer,
    The sun gone down,
  Darkness be over me,
    My rest a stone,
  Yet in my dreams I'd be
  Nearer, my God, to thee,
    Nearer to thee!

3 There let the way appear
    Steps unto heaven,
  All that thou send'st to me
    In mercy given,
  Angels to beckon me
  Nearer, my God, to thee,
    Nearer to thee!

4 Then, with my waking thoughts
    Bright with thy praise,
  Out of my stony griefs
    Bethel I'll raise,
  So by my woes to be
  Nearer, my God, to thee,
    Nearer to thee!

5 Or if on joyful wing
    Cleaving the sky,
  Sun, moon, and stars forgot,
    Upwards I fly,
  Still all my song shall be,
  'Nearer, my God, to thee,
    Nearer to thee!'
      SARAH FLOWER ADAMS, 1805–48

* When Tune (ii) PROPIOR DEO is used
the last line of each verse is repeated.

690

TEACH me to serve thee,
  Lord,
I humbly pray.
Help me the path to tread
In thine own way.
As thou hast promised, Lord,
O let thy living Word
New strength to me afford
For every day.

2 Teach me, O Lord, to give,
  Nor count the cost,
  For what is given for thee
  Is never lost.
  Whate'er I lend to thee
  Thou first didst give to me,
  Thy debtor I must be
  Till Jordan's crossed.

3 Teach me, O Lord, to fight,
  Nor heed the pain:
  Since he who fights for thee
  Ne'er fights in vain.
  Help me to stand for right,
  Be thou my guiding light,
  And daily by thy might
  I shall attain.

4 Teach me to labour on,
  Nor ask reward,
  To toil, nor seek for rest
  While sin's abroad.
  And should I faithful be,
  Grant I may dwell with thee,
  Through all eternity,
  My King, my Lord.
      EDNA MARTHA PHILLIPS

691

DEAR Master, in whose life
  I see
All that I would but fail to be,
Let thy clear light for ever shine,
To shame and guide this life
  of mine.

2 Though what I dream and what
    I do
  In my weak days are always
    two,
  Help me, oppressed by things
    undone,
  O thou, whose deeds and dreams
    were one!
      JOHN HUNTER, 1848–1917

692

TEACH me, my God and
  King,
In all things thee to see;
And what I do in anything,
  To do it as for thee!

2   A man that looks on glass,
     On it may stay his eye;
Or if he pleaseth, through it
     pass,
     And then the heaven espy.

3   All may of thee partake;
     Nothing can be so mean,
Which with this tincture, 'for
     thy sake',
     Will not grow bright and
     clean.

4   A servant with this clause
     Makes drudgery divine:
Who sweeps a room, as for thy
     laws,
     Makes that and the action
     fine.

5   This is the famous stone
     That turneth all to gold;
For that which God doth touch
     and own
     Cannot for less be told.
          GEORGE HERBERT, 1593–1633

693

MY soul, there is a country
   Afar beyond the stars,
Where stands a wingèd sentry
All skilful in the wars.

2 There, above noise, and danger,
   Sweet peace sits, crowned
     with smiles,
And One born in a manger
   Commands the beauteous
     files.

3 He is thy gracious friend,
   And—O my soul, awake!—
Did in pure love descend,
   To die here for thy sake.

4 If thou canst get but thither,
   There grows the flower of
     peace,
The rose that cannot wither,
   Thy fortress, and thy ease.

5 Leave then thy foolish ranges;
   For none can thee secure,
But One, who never changes,
   Thy God, thy Life, thy Cure.
        HENRY VAUGHAN, 1621–95

694

THE sands of time are
   sinking;
   The dawn of heaven breaks;
The summer morn I've sighed
   for,
   The fair, sweet morn, awakes.
Dark, dark hath been the mid-
   night,
   But dayspring is at hand,
And glory, glory dwelleth
   In Immanuel's land.

2 O Christ! He is the fountain,
   The deep, sweet well of love;
The streams on earth I've tasted
   More deep I'll drink above:
There to an ocean fullness
   His mercy doth expand,
And glory, glory dwelleth
   In Immanuel's land.

3 With mercy and with judgment
   My web of time he wove,
And aye the dews of sorrow
   Were lustred by his love;
I'll bless the hand that guided,
   I'll bless the heart that
     planned,
When throned where glory
     dwelleth
   In Immanuel's land.

4 I've wrestled on towards
     heaven,
   'Gainst storm and wind and
     tide;
Now, like a weary traveller
   That leaneth on his guide,
Amid the shades of evening,
   While sinks life's lingering
     sand,
I hail the glory dawning
   In Immanuel's land.
      ANNE ROSS COUSIN, 1824–1906

695

ABIDE with me: fast falls the
   eventide;
The darkness deepens; Lord,
   with me abide:
When other helpers fail, and
   comforts flee,
Help of the helpless, O abide
   with me.

2 Swift to its close ebbs out life's
　　little day;
Earth's joys grow dim, its
　　glories pass away;
Change and decay in all around
　　I see:
O thou who changest not,
　　abide with me.

3 I need thy presence every
　　passing hour;
What but thy grace can foil the
　　tempter's power?
Who like thyself my guide and
　　stay can be?
Through cloud and sunshine,
　　O abide with me.

4 I fear no foe with thee at hand
　　to bless;
Ills have no weight, and tears
　　no bitterness;
Where is death's sting? where,
　　grave, thy victory?
I triumph still if thou abide
　　with me.

5 Hold thou thy cross before my
　　closing eyes,
Shine through the gloom, and
　　point me to the skies;
Heaven's morning breaks, and
　　earth's vain shadows flee:
In life and death, O Lord, abide
　　with me.

HENRY FRANCIS LYTE, 1793–1847

INDEX OF PSALMS

The metrical psalms have been taken from the *Scottish Metrical Psalter* of 1650 and the *Irish Metrical Psalter* of 1880.

Psalms taken from other sources are printed in *italic* and the sources are given. AV = Authorized Version; NEB = New English Bible.

INDEX OF PSALMS

TABLE OF LITURGICAL ITEMS

INDEX OF FIRST LINES

Hymns for Children are marked with an asterisk

INDEX OF FIRST LINES

253

INDEX OF FIRST LINES

254

INDEX OF FIRST LINES

INDEX OF FIRST LINES

INDEX OF FIRST LINES

INDEX OF FIRST LINES

INDEX OF FIRST LINES

INDEX OF FIRST LINES

INDEX OF FIRST LINES

INDEX OF FIRST LINES

263

INDEX OF FIRST LINES